T0323825

Media Theory for A Level

Media Theory for A Level provides a comprehensive introduction to the 19 academic theories required for A Level Media study.

From Roland Barthes to Clay Shirky, from structuralism to civilisationism, this revision book explains all the core academic concepts students need to master to succeed in their exams. Each chapter contains comprehensive explanations of the academic ideas and theories specified for GCE Media study as well as practical tasks, higher level 'challenge activities', glossaries, reference tables and revision summaries.

The second edition of this best-selling guide features:

- Updated and revised chapters and exemplars, reflecting the new A Level Media specification (AQA, Eduqas, OCR and WJEC).
- Overviews of core areas and potential approaches that could be taken in exam responses.
- Overviews of secondary theory that can be used in responses.

This book is key reading for teachers and students of A Level Media Studies and is also a useful resource for GCSE students.

Media Theory for A Level is accompanied by the www.essentialmediatheory.com website that contains a wide range of supporting resources including revision flashcards, worksheets and more exemplar applications of theory to current set texts.

Mark Dixon is an Eduqas A Level examiner and Head of Media and Film at Durham Sixth Form Centre. He is also a freelance author, and has written for *The Guardian, TES, Media Magazine* and *Teach Secondary* as well as authoring a range of digital resources for Eduqas Media.

Media Theory for A Level
The Essential Revision Guide
Second Edition

Mark Dixon

Routledge
Taylor & Francis Group

LONDON AND NEW YORK

Designed cover image: LANDMARK MEDIA / Alamy Stock Photo

Second edition published 2025
by Routledge
4 Park Square, Milton Park, Abingdon, Oxon, OX14 4RN

and by Routledge
605 Third Avenue, New York, NY 10158

Routledge is an imprint of the Taylor & Francis Group, an informa business

First edition published by Routledge 2020

British Library Cataloguing-in-Publication Data
A catalogue record for this book is available from the British Library

Library of Congress Cataloging-in-Publication Data
Names: Dixon, Mark (Teacher), author.
Title: Media theory for A-level : the essential revision guide / Mark Dixon.
Description: Second edition. | Abingdon, Oxon ; New York, NY : Routledge, 2024. | Includes bibliographical references and index.
Identifiers: LCCN 2023059100 (print) | LCCN 2023059101 (ebook) | ISBN 9781032421032 (hardback) | ISBN 9781032421025 (paperback) | ISBN 9781003361220 (ebook)
Subjects: LCSH: Mass media—Examinations—Study guides. | A-level examinations—Study guides.
Classification: LCC P91.3 .D59 2024 (print) | LCC P91.3 (ebook) | DDC 302.2076—dc23/eng/20240325
LC record available at https://lccn.loc.gov/2023059100
LC ebook record available at https://lccn.loc.gov/2023059101

ISBN: 9781032421032 (hbk)
ISBN: 9781032421025 (pbk)
ISBN: 9781003361220 (ebk)

DOI: 10.4324/9781003361220

Typeset in Galliard
by codeMantra

Access the Instructor and Student Resources: www. essentialmediatheory.com

For Steph, Maisie and Preston

Contents

Media language

1 **Semiotics: Roland Barthes**   1
Concept 1: denotation and connotation 1
Concept 2: the media's ideological effect 12

2 **Structuralism: Claude Lévi-Strauss**   17
Concept 1: binary oppositions 17
*Concept 2: binary oppositions and ideological
   significance 24*

3 **Narratology: Tzvetan Todorov**   31
Concept 1: the three-act ideal 31
*Concept 2: the ideological effects of story
   structure 41*

4 **Genre theory: Steve Neale**   46
Concept 1: repetition and difference 46
*Concept 2: industry effects on genre-driven
   content 54*

5 **Postmodernism: Jean Baudrillard**   61
Key concept: the real and the hyperreal 61

Media representation

6   **Representation: Stuart Hall**   75
    Concept 1: media representation processes 75
    Concept 2: stereotypes and power 82

7   **Postcolonial theory: Paul Gilroy**   93
    *Concept 1: racial binaries, otherness and
        civilisationism 93*
    *Concept 2: the legacy of Empire and British
        identity 99*

8   **Feminist theory: Liesbet van Zoonen**   106
    Concept 1: the female body as spectacle 106
    Concept 2: masculinity in the media 115

9   **Intersectionality: bell hooks**   119
    Concept 1: interconnected oppression 119
    Concept 2: hooks' call to action 124

10 **Gender as performance: Judith Butler**   130
    *Concept 1: gendered identities are constructed
        through repetition and ritual 130*
    *Concept 2: gender subversion and gendered
        hierarchies 134*

11 **Media and identity: David Gauntlett**   143
    *Concept 1: traditional and post-traditional
        media consumption 143*
    Concept 2: reflexive identity construction 145

Media industries

12 **Ownership effects: James Curran and
    Jean Seaton**   156
    Concept 1: media concentration 157

Concept 2: effects of concentration on media content 164

Concept 3: diverse ownership creates diverse products 170

13 Regulation: Sonia Livingstone and Peter Lunt　　**178**
Concept 1: citizen and consumer models of media regulation 179
Concept 2: regulation in the globalised media age 188

14 The culture industry: David Hesmondhalgh　　**193**
Concept 1: maximising profits and minimising risks 194
Concept 2: the effects of the internet revolution are difficult to diagnose 200

Media audiences

15 Media modelling effects: Albert Bandura　　**207**
Concept 1: violent behaviours are learned through modelling 208
Concept 2: audiences copy media modelling 208

16 Cultivation theory: George Gerbner　　**219**
Concept 1: fear cultivation 219
Concept 2: media consumption leads audiences to accept mainstream ideologies 224

17 Reception theory: Stuart Hall　　**233**
Concept 1: encoding and decoding 233
Concept 2: dominant, negotiated and oppositional decoding 238

18 Fandom: Henry Jenkins　　**245**
Concept 1: fan appropriation 245

Concept 2: audience–producer convergence in the digital age 248
Concept 3: fans use participatory culture to effect wider social change 254

19 The end of audience: Clay Shirky   **261**
Concept 1: everybody makes the media 261
Concept 2: everyday communities of practice 270

Bibliography   275
Index   279

1   Semiotics
Roland Barthes

Up until the 1950s, the study of cultural products – music, television, advertising and the news – was largely limited, with most academics and academia promoting an exploration of high culture instead. Only literature, art, architecture and non-popular music were deemed worthy of study because, supposedly, they articulated sophisticated and nuanced modes of thinking. Popular culture, conversely, was rejected as unworthy of analysis because the stories told by advertising, cinema and the then emerging media form of television were thought to be constructed with so little precision, and their effects so simple, that any academic attention was undeserving.

In contrast, Barthes argued that the products of popular culture ought to be subject to academic criticism, and his 1957 essay collection, *Mythologies*, stands as one of the first serious attempts to evaluate the impact of the mass media. Indeed, Barthes' *Mythologies* revels in popular culture, analysing everything from wrestling to horoscopes, car adverts and political news stories. In contrast to his academic contemporaries, Barthes' argued that mass media forms had a profound social effect – an ideological presence, that, ironically, outstripped the reach of high culture.

Concept 1: denotation and connotation

Denotation/connotation

Barthes tells us that media products are initially decoded by readers using what he calls a *denotative reading*. Denotative readings, he argues, occur when audiences recognise the literal or physical content of media imagery. For example, a denotative reading of the *Daily Mirror* front page in Figure 1.1 would simply acknowledge

DOI: 10.4324/9781003361220-1

Figure 1.1 Daily Mirror, 16 June 2023 © Mirror newspaper, UrbanImages/Alamy Stock Photo.

that the photograph depicts a dishevelled middle-aged man with a hand placed on his forehead.

Barthes, however, goes on to tell us that audiences quickly move beyond the simple recognition of image content to produce what he called connotative readings. Connotative readings, Barthes argues, subtly and subconsciously push readers to think or feel in a particular way. Connotative readings, he argues, invest media products with emotional, symbolic or even ideological significance.

The *Daily Mirror* front page in Figure 1.1, for example, signifies various meanings through a range of subtle cues: the man's body language and gesture codes suggest anguish, his dishevelled appearance, perhaps, signifies tiredness or an unprofessional demeanour, while the dark vignette surrounding the man connotes a sense of doom and finality. Audiences, Barthes explains, subconsciously recognise the subtle connotative cues produced by imagery, using their cultural knowledge and experience of similar material to help them understand their significance.

Table 1.1 Connotative effects of photographic imagery

Image makers use a range of strategies to infer meaning within imagery – look out for the following when analysing the meaning making effects of your set texts.

Image features	*Look out for*
Pose Subject positioning, stance or body language	**Fourth wall breaks:** where the photographic subject meets the gaze of the audience. This can create a confrontational, aggressive or invitational feel.
	Off-screen gaze: upward gazes can suggest spirituality; right-frame gazes can suggest adventure or optimism; left-frame gazes can suggest regret or nostalgia.
	Body language control: might be open or closed, passive or active, strong or weak.
	Subject positioning: the way that group shots are arranged is usually significant with power conferred on those characters that occupy dominant positions.
	Proxemics: refers to the distance between subjects – the closer the characters are to one another the closer their relationship.
	Left-to-right/right-to-left movement: characters who travel from screen left to screen right create positive connotations – they are adventurers and we might feel hopeful about their prospects; right-to-left movements can suggest failure or an impending confrontation.

(*Continued*)

Table 1.1 (Continued)

Image features	Look out for
Mise en scène Props, costume and setting	**Symbolic props:** props are rarely accidental – their use and placement generally infer symbolic meanings. **Pathetic fallacy:** settings and scenery often serve further symbolic functions – weather, for example, infers the tone of characters' thoughts. **Costume symbolism:** character stereotypes are constructed through costuming, helping us to decipher a character's narrative function.
Lighting connotations	**High-key lighting:** removes shadows from a scene, often producing a much lighter, more upbeat feel. **Low-key lighting:** emphasises shadows and constructs a much more serious set of connotations. **Chiaroscuro lighting:** high contrast lighting usually created through the use of light beams penetrating pitch darkness and connotes hopelessness or mystery. **Ambient lighting:** infers realism.
Compositional effects Shot distance, positioning of subjects within the frame	**Long shots:** imply that a subject is dominated by their environment. **Close ups:** intensify character emotion or suggest impending drama. **Left/right compositions:** traditionally the left side of the screen is reserved for characters with whom the audience is meant to empathise and vice versa. **Open/closed frames:** open framing suggests freedom, while enclosing a character within a closed frame can suggest entrapment. **Tilt and eyeline:** tilt-ups and high eyelines convey power, while tilt-downs and low eyelines connote powerlessness and vulnerability.
Post-production effects	**Colour control:** colours are often exaggerated for specific connotative effect – red: anger; white: innocence; blue: sadness and so on. **High saturation:** colour levels are increased creating a cheerier, upbeat feel. **Desaturation:** taking colour out of an image generates a serious or sombre tone.

The combination of media elements

Barthes also draws attention to the way that media elements combine to shape meaning. Media imagery, he argues, is prone to producing what he calls polysemy (*poly*=multiple/*semy*=meanings) – or, put more simply, that readers are likely to read the same photographic content in highly different ways. If a producer wants to engineer a more concrete and universally understood set of connotations, they must add additional elements to provide what Barthes calls anchorage. Anchorage, Barthes tells us, constructs, 'a vice which holds connoted meanings from proliferating' (Barthes, 2007, 39).

In print media, for example, the impact of photographic content is often shaped by text elements that surround imagery. Headers, captions and taglines, in particular, tie down the meanings of photographic components, directing us to think about imagery in a highly specific way. In Figure 1.1, for example, the prominence of the word 'Liar' below Boris Johnson distances the ex-PM from the reader – without that text-based element, we might just as easily feel sympathy for the anguished figure presented to us.

Barthes further explains that the exact meanings produced when combining text and image-based components is determined by the positioning and the size of each element. Elements that are positioned near one another are more likely to work together to produce meaning, while components that dominate layouts in terms of their size are likely to play a more crucial role in shaping audience thinking. Again, if we look at Figure 1.1, the dominance of the headline plays an overriding or determining effect in positioning us to agree with the *Mirror*'s left-wing news bias.

Barthes anchorage argument can also be observed in audio-visual media. In television, for example, musical scores and ambient sound play an invisible role in guiding viewers towards predetermined emotional responses: discordant drones might be used to underline moments of horror or mystery, increasing volume adds energy to action sequences, while reducing sound reverb on dialogue tracks can suggests that a character is positioned close to us.

Indeed, audio-visual material that lacks sound elements can often be hard for audiences to pin down in terms of meaning. The lack of dialogue and non-diegetic sound components means music videos need to rely on visual components alone to produce meaning. As such, colour palettes, acting styles, costuming and sets are pushed to the fore in music videos to help audiences make sense of the underlying themes that producers might want to communicate.

Box 1.1   Apply it: diagnose the connotations constructed by media set texts

Use the following questions to help you construct a detailed analysis of the media language effects of relevant set texts:

Pose connotations

- Who is pictured within key imagery? And with whom? What kind of relationship do the characters have with each other?
- What is significant about their pose? Where is the character looking and in what ways is that significant?
- What does their body language reveal?

Mise en scène

- What is the significance of props, setting and costuming?
- Do costumes tell us who the character is or what role they play in the overarching narrative?

Lighting

- What kind of lighting is used and with what emotional or connotative effect?
- Who is placed in shadow? Who is given light?

Composition

- What shot distance is used to depict the subject?
- Is the shot composed with the subject on the left or right side of the frame? What connotations does this positioning create for the audience?
- Is the shot constructed as an open or closed frame shot?
- Is tilt applied to the composition and with what effect?

Post-production

- What colours are foregrounded and with what connotative effect? Is colour taken out of the shot?

Anchorage

- What elements, if any, anchor the meanings constructed by your set texts?

Exemplar: River Island's 'Labels are for Clothes' campaign (OCR). The imagery used for River Island's much lauded campaign is carefully crafted to challenge traditional stereotypes surrounding disability. The high eyeline and super smiler pose of the model combined with his extradiegetic gaze creates an authoritative and powerful set of connotations that defy traditional representations of disability as something to be pitied. The golden jacket of the character further implies a sense of positivity, presenting us with a winning character whose strong grip on his wheelchair suggests that he is in full control of the limitations posed by his disability. Strength gesture codes are enhanced further by the advert's high-key lighting with the emotive adjective 'smooth' deployed in the header to anchor the notion that fashion can and should be inclusive.

Further set text help is available for a range of products for all exam boards at www.essentialmediatheory.com

Barthes five code symphony

Barthes' denotation/connotation model is less effective when we have to analyse time-related effects. Television dramas, for instance, often set up meanings at the start of stories that are only fully understood as the plot unfolds: scripts, for example, routinely tease audiences with mysteries that are only resolved at the end of an episode or a season – using enigmas to capture and maintain audience interest.

Similarly, some connotations are used throughout a media product in ways that generate a cumulative connotative effect. The repeated references to horses, for example, in *Peaky Blinders* – the Shelby's betting business, Tommy's episode one entrance, the repeated motif of a white horse – are used as a metaphor to explain Tommy's relationship with the wider world.

In recognition of the limitations of his denotation/connotation model, Barthes produced a more nuanced communications analysis tool in which he proposes the existence of five different types of coding effects. These code types, he argues, operate like voices or instruments – at moments of peak interest all five codes might play together producing moments that are rich with multiple meanings. At other moments, a lone single code might be used to deliver a concentrated emotional, symbolic or ideological effect. Barthes details his five code symphony as follows:

- **Hermeneutic codes (enigmas):** construct moments of mystery that are engineered to engage audience interest. Enigma codes hook readers, compelling further reading or viewing to locate answers to the questions posed. The header of the 'Tide' advert in Figure 1.2, for instance, invites readers to ponder what exactly it is that 'women want,' the enigma only resolved once we've read the rest of the advert and are led to the conclusion that women want, perhaps, romance, clean clothes or social acceptance. Some products, Barthes argues, use hermeneutics more than others – crime dramas, for instance, usually convey and reinforce teasing enigmas throughout their narratives.
- **Proairetic codes (actions):** are moments of suspense constructed via an action of some kind. In crime dramas, for example, a gangster reaching for their gun tells audiences to expect a shootout, prompting readers to question who is going to be shot and whether they might die of not. Proairetic suspense tends to be resolved by further actions quite quickly. The finger pointing woman, for example, in the bottom left of the Tide advert (Figure 1.2) works as an action code, her pointing gesture creating a moment of reader excitement that is only resolved when we read her 'remember' advice in the adjacent copy. Again, Barthes tells us that some literary forms deploy proairetic codes more than others. In media narratives we are more likely to see proairetics in science fiction, thrillers and crime dramas – genres which rely on moments of concentrated action to generate viewer excitement.
- **Semantic codes (connotative elements):** refers to any element within a media text that produces a single connotative effect. Semantic codes might include lighting, *mise en scène* and colour usage. They also refer to the use of compositional effects, pose or even to typographic decisions and the significations that text size or font selection convey. Semantic codes are evidenced, for example, in the 'Tide' advert (Figure 1.2) via the wavelike arrangement of the 'What Women Want' header, connoting

Figure 1.2 Tide washing powder advert (1950). Source: Retro AdArchives/Alamy Stock Photo.

an upbeat jaunty tone, while the repeated use of exclamation marks suggests energy and volume.

- **Symbolic codes:** semantic and symbolic codes are closely related, and, possibly, are the most difficult to locate in a media text. One of the easiest ways to seek out symbolic codes is to search for repeated motifs or similar instances of a connotative code that are somehow connected. The repetition of such elements is often used to infer a deeper meaning of some sort. In television, symbolic codes, as discussed earlier, often surface as repeated themes or visual motifs, referenced throughout a narrative to generate subtextual or hidden meaning.

- **Cultural codes (referential codes):** refer to the inclusion of material that generates meaning from outside the product being read. Cultural codes, for example, might include the use of proverbs, sayings or idioms – language use that depends upon the cultural knowledge of readers to be accurately decoded. Cultural codes might also include references to scientific or historical knowledge – in short, anything that invokes audience knowledge from outside the text being consumed. Intertextual moments – deliberate references to other media – can be considered as cultural codes in that they import external meanings from media sources beyond the text being consumed. Intertextuality is often used to reward audiences or to provoke nostalgia. Tide, for example, offers cultural coding through the intertextual reference made to the 'We can do it' Second World War propaganda poster (Figure 1.3). The allusion here constructs the suggestion that Tide is a patriotic product, providing too a sense of familiarity and relatability for the advert's post Second World War audience.

Box 1.2 Apply it: apply Barthes' five code symphony to set texts

Work through set texts that require an understanding of the effects of media language. Identify how each text crafts hermeneutic, proairetic, semantic, cultural and symbolic codes to create meaning.

Further set text help is available for a range of products for all exam boards at www.essentialmediatheory.com

Figure 1.3 'We Can Do It!' American Second World War propaganda poster (1943). Source: incamerastock/Alamy Stock Photo.

Concept 2: the media's ideological effect

Media as myth

Myths, Barthes tells us, are important narrative forms that unwittingly communicate concentrated ideological messages. Myths, he tells us, appear to convey a collective or agreed view of the world, transmitting morals that are important enough to be passed down from one generation to the next. Their existence as products whose authorship is unknown works to dial up their ideological thrust, suggesting a collective view rather than that of a singular author. Myths, too, are allegorical – they present moral outlooks and tell us how we ought to behave. When Narcissus, for example, falls in love with his own reflection in the famous Greek myth, we too are being warned about the dangers of vanity and self-absorption.

Importantly, Barthes suggests that the media has replaced, or at least replicates, the functions of traditional myth making. Newspapers, television, advertising and radio, he argues, convey meaning with the same sort of authority as myths and, more, importantly, have the ability to construct similarly powerful ideological effects.

Barthes' hugely influential essay collection *Mythologies* sought to identify the mythic effects of 1950s French media, suggesting that advertising invests cars with a godlike spirituality, that politicians manufacture imagery to convince us of their ordinariness and that soap detergents effect a 'euphoria' of cleanliness through their marketing appeals (Barthes, 2009, 32). Advertising, Barthes tells us, invests products with magical properties, while magazines manufacture dream worlds that charm their readers with 'fairy-land' imagery (Barthes, 2009, 90).

Barthes identifies the following features of media authorship as potential sources of ideological influence:

- **Naturalisation:** because the media looks and feels realistic, Barthes tells us, media texts present ideas as natural, matter of fact or common sense. The news, for example, trades in imagery that reflects the everyday – audiences, as such, can identify with those worlds without realising that they are mediated versions of reality.
- **Repetition effects:** if media texts repeat the same idea enough times, Barthes asserts, audiences can believe that those ideas

are not a matter of perspective but are, in fact, immutable social norms. Advertising, for example, that repeatedly associates women with motherhood or domestic chores might lead audiences to infer that women are naturally predisposed to cleaning or looking after children.

- **Reductive presentations:** Barthes tells us that the media, by and large, simplifies, reduces or purifies ideas, turning complexity into easily digestible information. The use of simplistic messaging creates audience appeal, Barthes argues, but also has the effect of de-intellectualising and depoliticising ideas. Message reduction, in short, discourages audiences from questioning or analysing media content too closely.

- **Media myths reinforce existing social power structures:** 'The oppressed is nothing, he has only one language, that of his emancipation,' Barthes writes, while 'the oppressor is everything, his language is rich, multiform, supple' (Barthes, 2009, 176). Here Barthes argues that those who have power tend to control the myth-making process, either owning or indirectly channelling media content through privileged access arrangements. The powerful, in this sense, hold all the cards, and can harness the creative allure of the media industry to maintain the illusion that the system we live in, the system that benefits the powerful the most, is naturally ordered and unchangeable.

Box 1.3 Discuss it: what effect do media products have on society?

- Can you think of a media product that consistently turns complexity into a simplified or reductive message?
- Do any of your set texts deploy message reduction? Why?
- Can you think of an idea, behaviour or norm that the media naturalises?
- Are modern audiences more suspicious of the media than Barthes suggests?
- Do media products reinforce existing power structures? Can you think of any media products that challenge those who have power?

Box 1.4   Apply it: diagnose the ideological subtexts of your set texts

Use the following questions to help you identify the ideological subtexts of set text products:

- **Naturalisation effects:** in what ways does the set text present key ideas, values or behaviours as common sense or the norm?
- **Simplification effects:** in what ways does the text create appeal for those ideas through a simplistic presentation? How does that simplicity discourage audience questioning?
- **Reinforcement of existing power structures:** who has power within the set text? How does that power mirror real world power?

Exemplar: *Woman's Realm* (Eduqas). In *Women's Realm*, domesticated femininity is repeatedly offered to readers as an aspirational norm – in, for example, the content gesture codes of the mother figure in the Sunday Cook illustration and also in the 'presentable' female ideal of the Atrixo advert – both of which present the mundane activities associated with homemaking as a magical agent that can transform the female experience into a self-fulfilling utopia. Barthes might argue that here *Woman's Realm* exemplifies the mythologising strategies that enable media texts to be effective tools for communicating ideology. He tells us that the media's use of repetition, message reduction and anonymised authorship work to present ideological messaging as a common-sense perspective – presenting and representing ideals in ways that audiences consume with little resistance. Barthes might also argue that the simplicity of the Atrixo message – reducing the role of women to the reductive list of keeping everything 'clean and spotless and shining and bright' – means that readers are less likely to challenge the advert's ideological inference and that the repetition of similar messaging across the magazine infers that female domesticity is a natural or given state that women must accept.

Exemplar analysis and further set text help is available for a range of products at www.essentialmediatheory.com

Table 1.2 Speak Roland Barthes

Anchorage	The process of fixing meaning, usually the meaning of an image, through the use of another component – usually a text-based feature such as a header or caption.
Denotation/ connotation	Denotation refers to the literal meaning of a media element, whilst connotation refers to the emotions, ideas or symbolic meanings produced by that element.
Hermeneutic codes	Hermeneutic elements construct mystery or enigma, encouraging the reader to engage further with a product in order to discover the answer to the puzzle posed.
Naturalisation	The process of making ideas or viewpoints feel like they are common sense or articulate shared viewpoints. In reality, all media output is authored via selection and mediation processes by media authors.
Message reduction	Barthes argues that the media tends to simplify or purify complex ideas. This reductive impulse discourages audiences from questioning the ideas presented.
Proairetic codes	Refers to moments of action within a media text. Proairetic moments create excitement or suspense for audiences.
Semiotics	The study of signs and symbols. Semiotic theory seeks to understand how signs communicate meaning.
Signification	The process of meaning creation. Media elements signify or produce meanings when consumed by audiences.

Table 1.3 Barthes: ten-minute revision

Concept 1: *the media constructs meaning through a process of denotation and connotation*

- We read the media imagery in the same way that we read written or spoken language.
- We decode media imagery in two distinctly different ways: first, producing a denotative reading that recognises the literal content of an image, and, second, producing a connotative reading that diagnoses deeper symbolic or emotional meanings.
- Image-based connotations are created through props, post-production effects, pose, costuming, composition and lighting.
- Media imagery is polysemic – likely, in other words, to produce a number of connotative effects.
- The meaning of polysemic elements can be anchored, where, for example, captions, headers or taglines tie down the meaning of an image for the reader.
- Barthes suggests that meaning is produced via the use of hermeneutic, proairetic, semantic, cultural and symbolic features.

Concept 2: *the media has an ideological effect on audiences*

- The media has a myth-like capacity to guide and influence our behaviours and actions.
- The media naturalises ideas through repetition.
- The media reduces or simplifies ideas, discouraging audiences from questioning its specific presentation of the world.
- The media tends to reinforce the worldview of those who affect social power.

Challenging Barthes' thinking

Barthes can be critiqued for the lack of emphasis he places on audience agency. Barthes' works cited in this chapter suggest that audiences respond in a similar way to media texts, and, more importantly, that they aren't savvy enough to resist the ideological messaging produced by the media. Much like Strauss and Todorov, Barthes' ideas are superseded by the post-structuralist revolution of the 1970s and its emphasis on how audiences might engage with media texts during consumption. Stuart Hall's reception theory exemplifies much of that approach, arguing that audiences use their experiences, beliefs and knowledge to decode media products.

Two named theorists who might challenge Barthes' thinking

- **Claude Lévi-Strauss:** would be more interested in the way that media products arrange elements to articulate oppositions rather than in the effect that single ingredients might produce.
- **Tzvetan Todorov:** would argue that media products produce meaning via narrative progression and that isolated instances of connotation are less significant. Todorov, for example, might argue that the transformation of characters in media narratives provide audiences with moral messages regarding their own behaviours and outlooks.

---

2 Structuralism

Claude Lévi-Strauss

Lévi-Strauss painstakingly analysed the narrative content of hundreds of mythic tales he collected from around the globe. From the tribal stories of the Amazonian rainforest to the ancient myths of Greece, he sought to uncover the invisible rule book of storytelling in order to diagnose what it means to be human. Strauss is best described as a structuralist theorist in that he adhered to the notion that all of humankind have always shared essential traits, and if he located any common themes or motifs in the myths he collected, they would reveal essential truths about the way the human mind structures the world.

The stories that he collected, Lévi-Strauss concluded, worked through oppositional arrangements – through the construction of characters or narrative incidents that clashed or jarred. These binary arrangements, Strauss further suggested, were the result of a universally shared thought process – that humankind naturally divided the world into binary units. Stories and storytelling, Strauss also concluded, perform a vital social function in that they outline societal taboos and socially acceptable behaviours.

Concept 1: binary oppositions

Lévi-Strauss outlines the key academic ideas used to explore media products in his 1962 book, *The Savage Mind*, in which he suggests that a subliminal set of structural rules inform myth production. Individual cultures might speak different languages, Lévi-Strauss argues, but all stories told across the globe and throughout history employ a remarkably simple but stable formula. Myths, Lévi-Strauss infers, universally explore human experience using

DOI: 10.4324/9781003361220-2

polarised themes: births mirror deaths, success juxtaposes against failure, wisdom trades blows with innocence. The Old Testament, for instance, suggests that the Earth was formed from a series of oppositional constructs – God separated light from darkness, the sky from the sea, the land from the water. We see similar narrative patterns forming in fairy tales too – the innocence and youth of Little Red Riding Hood, for example, takes on the greed and cunning of the Big Bad Wolf.

Lévi-Strauss infers that the universal use of oppositions to organise stories is prompted by humankind's innate bias for organising the world using binary thinking. The need for hunter-gatherers to distinguish poisonous from edible foodstuffs, Lévi-Strauss argues, embedded a cognitive blueprint that directs human beings to read the world using oppositional descriptors.

Humans do not do ambiguity, Lévi-Strauss tells us. We simplify the world around us using an age-old bias towards binary thinking. Certainly, binary labels and binary thinking are evidenced aplenty in today's complex world. We continue to label ourselves as female or male, masculine or feminine, despite the multiplicity of gender choices at play in Western society. Similarly, our political governance is polarised as left or right wing, while human morality is packaged up in deeds that are reductively categorised as good or evil, saintly or sinful.

Media-based binary oppositions

Lévi-Strauss did not allude to the structure of contemporary media products directly, but if we buy into the idea that binary thinking is a universal feature of storytelling, then it stands to reason that media narratives are organised using the same structural blueprints as those offered in myths. Oppositions in media products might be inferred through the following:

- **Character oppositions:** audiences expect villains to battle heroes in fictional narratives. Oppositions, too, might centre on secondary characters, with contrasts constructed in terms of youth or maturity, strength or intelligence, masculinity or femininity. Character oppositions can also be found in non-fiction products – in news crime reportage, for example, criminals exploit innocent victims, while in the gladiatorial world of political news, right- and left-wing politicians battle against one another to secure public support for their policies.

- **Narrative oppositions:** media stories, too, are organised to construct moments of opposition. In print and television advertising, for instance, simplistic before and after transformations demonstrate how products can deliver us guaranteed success. Television narratives, too, routinely use juxtaposition and contrast in montage sequences, shifting from moments of loss to gain, from poverty to affluence in sweeping cross cuts.
- **Stylistic oppositions:** media producers encode products using juxtaposed stylistic presentations. Camera work might change from quiet stasis in one scene to a series of frenzied whip pans in another. Transitions of this kind can reinforce wider character-oriented oppositions or are deployed to maintain audience interest via the use of contrast. Table 2.1 identifies some of the common stylistic oppositions used by contemporary media texts.
- **Genre-driven binary oppositions:** some binary oppositions are so deeply entrenched within genres that they become a convention or expectation of that genre. Science-fiction products, for example, regularly offer audiences 'technology versus humanity'-driven narratives; crime dramas routinely deploy 'law enforcer/law breaker' character stereotypes; romances resolve in romantic couplings.

Box 2.1 Think about it: do humans organise the world using binary thinking?

Can you think of any further evidence that would reinforce the idea that humans naturally organise the world using simplified binaries?

- What kinds of media products are particularly prone to using binary oppositions?
- In what ways do your set texts use oppositions?
- Do any of your set texts resist the use of simple binary oppositions?

Box 2.2 Apply it: diagnose genre-driven oppositions in your set texts

Use Table 2.3 at the end of this chapter to identify the genre-driven oppositions present within the set texts you are studying. Think about the following questions to help you add further detail:

- Which thematic oppositions are presented by your set texts?
- How do the characters in your set texts reflect those oppositions?
- How do stylistic/design decisions used within those set texts reflect the character oppositions presented? Think in terms of camera work, *mise en scène*, sound, editing, language or imagery usage, typography and layout.

Exemplar: *Peaky Blinders* (Eduqas). The arrival of Inspector Campbell in episode 1 provides audiences of *Peaky Blinders* with a conventional crime drama character-driven opposition – pitting the clean-cut puritanical bent of Campbell against the lawlessness of the Shelby clan. The gangster genre revels in the use of such oppositions, placing likable anti-heroes in conflict with law-abiding fanatics like Campbell whose pursuit of justice always comes at a human cost. Thomas Shelby, of course, is framed as the named antithesis to Campbell – his lawlessness coloured by a Robin Hood likability. Shelby's criminal activity, importantly, is framed as a necessary evil that seeks to nurture the needs of his community. Campbell, in contrast, is a Sheriff of Nottingham outsider to that community – his brutal policing methods imported from his experience in Ireland. And where Thomas Shelby is acknowledged as a First World War hero, Campbell's lack of military service is quickly foregrounded in juxtaposition. What forms is a classic lawbreaker versus lawmaker narrative that enables the show to explore archetypal thematic binaries of the gangster genre, setting

state-sponsored power in conflict with a heroic but tragi-
cally flawed individual.

Exemplar analysis and further set text help is available for a range of
products at www.essentialmediatheory.com

The function of oppositions in media products

Media producers use binary oppositions to create a range of
audience-oriented functions. Those functions include the following:

- **Using reductive storytelling to assist audience comprehen-
sion.** Binary oppositions can be used to simplify viewpoints or to
make complicated ideas understandable for viewers and readers.
Television news stories, for instance, often explain complex topics
by using two interviewees who have opposing views: a narrative
strategy that reduces fast-moving news stories into easily digestible polemics. Binaries can also speed up audience understanding,
crucial to producers when they have to capture and maintain audience attention in the highly competitive media landscape of today.
- **Creating compelling narratives.** The inclusion of binary characters inevitably creates conflict. Audiences are more likely to
engage with a media product if they are presented with the
promise of a narrative clash. Foregrounding oppositional characters early in narratives will capture and retain audience interest.
- **Creating identifiable character archetypes.** Audiences can
quickly gain a sense of the direction of a story once oppositional characters are introduced. We implicitly understand that
heroes must defeat villains or that protagonists are compelled to
unmask their false hero adversary. The use of clashing characters can also produce a range of other narrative gratifications –
comedy, fear and so on. The banana/straight man character duo,
for example, is a staple ingredient of the comedy genre, producing visual and physical comedy through character archetypes.
- **Creating audience identification.** Binary oppositions prompt
audiences to identify with one central character or viewpoint.
An advert, for instance, that contrasts humdrum reality with the
sparkle of an advertised product clearly positions the audience
to align with the brand ideals of the promoted product.

Box 2.3   Revise it: prepare your own stylistics analysis paragraphs

This exercise will take lots of time to execute, but ought to help produce detailed responses that can be adapted for a huge variety of exam questions. Use Table 2.1 and the following prompts to help you develop your responses:

Relating stylistic oppositions to wider themes

- In what ways do stylistic oppositions reinforce genre-oriented expectations?
- In what ways do stylistic oppositions narrate the wider themes of the set text?
- What messages and emotions do stylistic oppositions convey?

Stylistic analysis prompts

- Are there moments where locations, props or costuming contrast? Why have they been styled this way?
- Are colour contrasts offered in your set texts and to what effect?
- How do editing, camera or lighting styles change across the timelines of your set texts? How do these stylistic oppositions support wider narrative themes?
- Do sound elements offer significant moments of contrast in terms of volume, tone, key signatures or instrumentation? What effect do these aural contrasts have on audiences?

Exemplar: *Killing Eve* **(Eduqas/OCR).** The essential narrative dynamic of *Killing Eve* is driven by its presentation of Eve and Villanelle as binary characters, with episode 1 using cross-cutting to introduce us to the parallel worlds of both characters. The implicit suggestion of that narrative strategy – and a key driver of audience engagement – is that the two worlds of those characters will inevitably meet, and, in so doing, will produce a must-see television drama character clash. Of course, that clash must be held back from the viewer to increase the show's narrative tension. The series must also concentrate the oppositional energies of the two characters before they finally collide, using a wide range of binary stylistics to reinforce Eve and Villanelle's diametrically opposed natures. Eve's screaming intro in episode 1, for example, uses low-key lighting and a desaturated colour palette to construct a downbeat and chaotic character. Villanelle's high-key lit introduction, in contrast, is sophisticated and opulent, with stretched editing used to connotate the poise and self-agency of Eve's adversary. Sound too underlines Villanelle's demure presence using the Xpectations' song 'Unloved' to lend the scene a celestial calm and more than a hint of European panache. Eve's prolonged high-volume scream suggests an entirely different interiority – a character who neither controls her external nor internal existence.

Exemplar: *Deutschland 83* **(AQA/Eduqas).** The historical East Germany of the 1980s is depicted in a highly stylised way in *Deutschland 83*. Gaunt actors are rendered powerless in claustrophobic closed-frame compositions, canted angles deployed freely to suggest instability, with tilt-ups applied to the greying soldiers who interrogate the innocent civilians of the opening sequence. Sets too have been carefully choreographed to enhance the dystopian tone of East Germany, yellowing net curtains and wallpaper connote decay and disease, with backlighting and low-key shadows used to conjure up a sense of authoritarian fear from the outset. The gloom and depression of the East is subsequently contrasted with the opulence and freedom found when Martin finds himself in West Germany: closed-frame compositions give way to open landscapes, grey cloud to summer sunshine, while Martin's starched over-sized soldier's uniform is replaced by the high-energy red of his Puma branded t-shirt. In terms of editing, too, the slow sedate tempo of the East is replaced by high tempo jump cuts that add energy and vitality to the show's depiction of the Capitalist West.

Further exemplar paragraphs for set texts from all exam boards are available at www.essentialmediatheory.com

Concept 2: binary oppositions and ideological significance

Myths, according to Lévi-Strauss, articulate a version of the world around us, generating culturally specific cues that define acceptable or unacceptable social norms. Those cues, Lévi-Strauss infers, are created as a result of the way that story oppositions resolve – in the way that select oppositions are disregarded in favour of their counterparts. Narratives, in this sense, provide audiences with a set of privileged behaviours or ideals that they are encouraged to copy or adopt.

Lévi-Strauss proposed, for example, that a principal function of primitive myth was to describe incest taboos and the rules of marriage. For example, Sophocles' famous Oedipus myth, Lévi-Strauss explains, illustrates the dangers of unnatural sexual relationships. The binary oppositions constructed in the story, he suggests, centre on the masculine energy of Oedipus and the femininity of Oedipus' mother. Famously, Oedipus blinds himself when he discovers he has accidentally married his own mother – Oedipus' shame in transgressing natural incest taboos is so deeply felt that he can longer bear to look upon the world. The resolution of the male/female oppositions presented, Lévi-Strauss explains, convey a clear warning to the myth's readers and listeners – don't have sex with your own mother.

Likewise, cultural products – art, literature and the media – present more than just conflict in their narratives, they offer resolutions to those oppositions. In film, for example, protagonists invariably win their battles. In spy movies, James Bond always crushes the terrorist plot that threatens to destroy world peace. Superheroes inevitably destroy their seemingly undefeatable enemies, while the supernatural presence that terrorises us in horror films is terminally exorcised in time for the end credits to roll.

Narratives resolve oppositions, and that resolution process allows media products to play a significant role in promoting an explicit set of values and ideologies. James Bond's triumph over the forces of evil, for example, privileges a quintessential sense of Britishness. He not only fights bad guys, but also reinstates democracy, moral decency and English tradition at the expense of totalitarianism, capitalist greed or religious fanaticism.

Oppositional resolutions in news products

The news, too, resolves stories in a manner that privileges one set of oppositions. Newspapers teach us that criminals are caught, that corrupt politicians lose elections, or that wayward celebrities must endure rehab hell. The news does not just represent the chaos of the world, nor does it merely order that chaos into neat binaries – news stories are crafted in ways that reinforce cultural or editorial biases.

A news product reporting a terrorist attack, for example, might outline the suffering and death inflicted, yet the individual tragedies of the event are often offset by coverage that emphasises the everyday acts of heroism also observed. Police officers and fire crews step into the fray when bombers attack, innocent members of the public sacrifice themselves to save others, and, when the terrorist dust has settled, the news cycle inevitably concludes with follow-ups that articulate the ongoing solidarity and defiance of the communities affected by the bombing. Yes, the news articulates oppositions and conflict to engage audience interest, yet, much like fictional media, news narratives privilege one set of binaries in ways that foreground editorial biases or that reinforce cultural norms.

Table 2.2 further outlines the uses and purposes of binary oppositions by print news and a range of other media forms. Use Table 2.3 to help you uncover the narrative oppositions presented by your set texts.

Box 2.4 Revise it: prepare your own set text resolution analysis paragraphs

Lévi-Strauss' ideas concerning narrative resolution can be used to determine the underlying ideological significance of a media product. Most media products give an uneven presentation of oppositional conflicts, positioning their audiences to agree with one set of ideas at the expense of their oppositional counterparts. Use the following questions to construct power paragraphs that define the character, genre and stylistic oppositions constructed by set texts and to reach conclusions as to how the product's binary presentation construct ideological messaging.

Genre/narrative resolutions

- Use Table 2.3 to help you identify the genre-based op-positions created. Which of the oppositions triumph in the set text? Where and how?
- How do narratives end? Do the resolutions offered at the end of stories tell us anything about the ideological subtexts of your set products?

Character resolutions

- How does characterisation produce conflict?
- Have the product's authors crafted oppositional characters?
- How are audiences positioned to empathise or align with one specific set of characters?
- Which characters triumph in the product and with what ideological effect?

Exemplar paragraph: *Atypical* (OCR). *Atypical*'s success as a family comedy lies in its ability to nurture relatability for a diverse range of viewers, providing parent and child audiences with characters of their own age that they can align with. Sam, however, is clearly established as the lead voice of the show, allowing audiences of all persuasions to gain an insight into the world of an everyday American teen who also happens to have autism. Sam's episode 1 dialogue clearly shows his troubled relationship with the wider world. 'I'm a weirdo, that's what everyone says,' he tells us, delineating a conventional disability versus society binary that *Atypical* pursues for the rest of its four-season run. What clearly differentiates *Atypical* from more traditional representations of autism is the way that Sam is clearly privileged within that binary presentation. The use of voiceover coupled with point of view (POV) gives us access to the lead character's perspective, suturing us into the experience of Sam in ways that radically reshape viewer preconceptions regarding autism.

Further set text help is available for a range of products for all exam boards at www.essentialmediatheory.com

Table 2.1 Common stylistic oppositions used within media texts

Cinema-tography	Open/closed framing Left/right frame composition Left/right tracking Up/down tilt Thin/thick depth of field Static/handheld movement Extreme close up/long shot	**Sound**	Loud/soft volume High/low pitched instrumentation Minor key/major key score String/brass timbre Agitated/calm room tone Ascending/descending tones
Editing	Slow/fast editing rhythm Stretched/elliptical edits Continuity/montage editing Straight cut/dissolve transitions Long takes/jump cutting Saturated/desaturated edit	*Mise en scène*	Low/high-key lighting Warm/cold lighting Realistic/escapist *mise en scène* Lifeless/animated body language Real/ideal costuming Sunny/stormy weather

Table 2.2 Binary oppositions in different media: uses and applications revision overview

Form	*Where to look for oppositions*	*Reasons for use*
News, magazines	• **Opposing viewpoints** of different commentators and interviewees. • Within **imagery** that depicts oppositional characteristics. • **Language** might use oppositional descriptors, semantic fields or contrasting lexical styles. • **Profile pieces** are likely to present conflict outlining the barriers and binary choices that interviewees have had to overcome.	• To explain and simplify complex issues. • To position audiences so that they identify with the editorial stance of the paper. • To construct an emotional response from the audience. • To construct crisis-driven stories that offer conflict and enigma.
Film marketing, gaming, television, music video	• **Character construction:** look beyond simple antagonist and protagonist oppositions. Think about age, gender and class-based oppositions offered via secondary characters. • *Mise en scène:* costumes, locations, body language and colour palettes are likely to offer juxtapositions to support the wider themes of narratives or to identify character conflict.	• To create compelling narratives that offer conflict. • To outline overarching narrative themes. • To produce oppositions that enable the product to be recognisable as genre driven.

(*Continued*)

Table 2.2 (Continued)

Form	Where to look for oppositions	Reasons for use
	• **Narrative events:** identify story points that can be ordered as oppositional – repeated sequences or moments that use cross-cutting are likely to offer visible oppositions.	
Advertising	• **Narrative construction:** classic binary story structures in adverts include before and after product use, non-ideal/ideal lifestyle positioning, problem/solution product positioning. • ***Mise en scène:*** costumes, locations, body language and colour palettes are likely to be juxtaposed to support the wider themes of a product.	• To enable speedy character identification. • To create simplified narratives that justify product needs. • To enable audiences to understand the advantages of using a product in terms of the lifestyle advantages it could bring.

Table 2.3 Common oppositions found with genres and forms that are popular within the contemporary media landscape

Music video	News	Magazines
Desire/rejection	Chaos/order	Freedom/control
Loss/belonging	Green issues/economics	Happiness/responsibility
Love/loneliness	Justice/injustice	Health/illness
Masculinity/femininity	Left wing/right wing	Loss/belonging
Nostalgia/reality	Poverty/greed	Love/loss
Oppression/freedom	Power/powerlessness	Masculinity/femininity
Rebellion/authority	Society/the individual	Romance/lust
Youth/authority	Victims/perpetrators	Work/leisure

Science fiction	Crime/politics	Horror
Aliens/humans	Chaos/order	Chaos/order
Corporate power/individualism	Choice/necessity	Darkness/light
	Corruption/innocence	Death/life
Exploitation/freedom	Freedom/duty	Good/evil
Knowledge/ignorance	Guilt/innocence	Known/unknown
Machine/man	Law/justice	Past/present
Man/nature	Lawfulness/lawlessness	Reality/supernatural
Reality/deception	Morality/greed	Reason/madness
Technology/humanity	Power/weakness	Religion/disbelief
	Self-interest/society	Repression/acceptance

(*Continued*)

Table 2.3 (Continued)

Romance	War	Spy/thriller
Experience/youth	Allies/enemies	Democracy/tyranny
Family ties/romance	Duty/morality	Heroism/greed
Friendship/betrayal	Experience/innocence	Hunter/hunted
Loneliness/belonging	Family/duty	Intellect/action
Masculinity/femininity	Home front/the front line	Order/chaos
Relationships/freedom	Honour/self-interest	Patriotism/treachery
Romance/money	Sacrifice/self-interest	State/individual
	Survival/patriotism	Surveillance/subterfuge

Table 2.4 Speak Claude Lévi-Strauss

Binary oppositions	The use of paired elements within a narrative that provide contrast.
Character oppositions	The construction of characters that are juxtaposed – oppositions might be based on age, ability, moral outlook or social position.
Genre-based oppositions	Paired elements that are commonly found in specific genres – these might be character, narrative or theme-based oppositions.
Opposition resolution	Refers to the way that binary opposites resolve within a narrative – the dominant partner in an oppositional arrangement will often dictate the ideological bias of a media product.
Structuralism	An analytical model that suggests that human behaviour is directed by a universally applicable set of rules. Lévi-Strauss, for example, suggests that humans naturally explain the world in terms of oppositions and contrast.
Stylistic oppositions	The use of contrasting design elements. Stylistic oppositions often reinforce the narrative themes of a text or help encode character oppositions.

Table 2.5 Lévi-Strauss: ten-minute revision

Concept 1: *media narratives use binary oppositions*

- Lévi-Strauss offers a structuralist approach to media analysis, suggesting that humans encode and decode the world using universally shared principles.
- The media uses binary oppositions to explain and categorise the complexities of the world around us.
- Oppositions can be found in the way that characters or narrative themes are presented to audiences.

(*Continued*)

Table 2.5 (Continued)

- Media makers also apply stylistic oppositions to *mise en scène*, camera work, editing applications and image construction.
- Thematic oppositions in media products can be genre driven.

Concept 2: *the way binary oppositions are resolved creates ideological significance*

- Media products construct ideologies by positioning their audiences to favour one side of an opposition.
- Narrative resolutions – the endings of media products – often help us to diagnose which oppositions a product favours.

Challenging Lévi-Strauss' thinking

Much like Barthes, Strauss provides us with an excellent model to explore the authorial intentions of media producers but falls short when we start to consider how audiences might engage with binary presentations. It is entirely possible that audiences might read against the grain of a text's intentions, aligning themselves with non-privileged binaries, for example.

We might also argue that Strauss' binary model is stretched by the complexities of contemporary media texts, where, for example, long-form dramas increasingly muddy the black and white certainties of traditional protagonist/antagonist pairings. Where contemporary character complexity often means that characters present as nuanced and interchangeable presences.

Three named theorists who might challenge Strauss' thinking

- **Stuart Hall:** would argue that media products can be encoded using binary oppositions, but he would add that audiences do not necessarily decode the products in the way that media makers intend.
- **Paul Gilroy:** argues that Western binary thinking has traditionally classified ethnicity in terms of simplified white/non-white and civilised/uncivilised categories. He calls for the media to move beyond these simplistic and hugely damaging binary classifications.
- **Judith Butler:** similarly argues that conventional Western gender binaries mask the complex nature of sexuality. She also argues that individuals have resisted the gender binary by using 'gender trouble'.

---

3   Narratology

Tzvetan Todorov

Todorov, like Lévi-Strauss, was interested in the possibility that stories share similar narrative features, and that if we can understand and detect those features, we can better comprehend the subtextual meanings that stories might communicate. However, a crucial factor differentiates the two theorists' ideas, with Todorov arguing that the importance of narratives lies not in their use of oppositional moments or characterisation, but in the way that characters are transformed by the conflicts they undergo during their narrative journeys. More importantly, the recognition of those character transformations by audiences creates moments of ideological instruction, prompting readers and viewers to reshape their own real-world behaviours.

Concept 1: the three-act ideal

The influence of Vladimir Propp

Russian literary theorist Vladimir Propp's 1929 book, *Morphology of the Folktale*, played a pivotal role in shaping Todorov's ideas. Propp famously analysed hundreds of Russian folk stories in an attempt to uncover their underlying narrative structures. Importantly, Propp arrived at the conclusion that folk tales drew from a highly stable list of characters whose roles and narrative functions he defined as follows (Propp, 2009):

- **The hero:** Propp identifies two significant types of hero-protagonist – first, the seeker-hero, who rights wrongs that are done to others, and second, the victim-hero, who must overcome a personal weakness to complete their quest.
- **The villain:** who fights or pursues the hero and must be defeated if the hero is to accomplish their quest.

DOI: 10.4324/9781003361220-3

- **The princess and the princess's father:** the princess usually represents a reward that the hero pursues and achieves at the end of their quest. The princess's father often sets the hero difficult tasks during the course of a narrative that tests the hero or that prevents them from marrying the princess.
- **The donor:** provides the hero with a magical agent that allows them to defeat the villain.
- **The helper:** usually accompanies the hero on their quest, often saving them during the struggles encountered on their journey or helping the hero overcome narrative barriers.
- **The dispatcher:** sends the hero on his or her quest, usually at the start of the story.
- **The false hero:** performs a largely villainous role, usurping the true hero's position in the story. The false hero is usually unmasked in the last act of a narrative by the central protagonist.

Propp suggested that stories do not necessarily have to use all the characters listed, though most are organised around the interplay of the hero, villain and princess archetypes. Propp also discovered that the fairy stories he analysed followed a remarkably similar narrative structure, organised using a combination of just 31 closely defined plot moments that he called 'narratemes'. Propp tells us that the starting points of most stories (narratemes 1–7) usually introduce the hero and other key characters. The villain, Propp tells us, conventionally appears at narrateme 4, prompting the hero to embark on a quest and culminates in one last final struggle with the villain at narrateme 26. Propp suggests that stories do not necessarily have to be composed of all 31 narratemes, but those that are used are relayed in strict linear fashion. See Table 3.1 for a further outline of the narrative progression Propp identified in *Morphology of the Folktale*.

Todorov's refinement of Propp's narrative theory

Todorov refined Propp's narrative theory in the 1970s, arguing that media narratives are created using moments of action, or as Todorov called them 'propositions', and that those moments combine to form narrative sequences. Broadly speaking, Todorov argued that narratives tend to follow similar patterns: that the start of any story is largely concerned with the narration of characters who exist in stable or harmonious worlds with later sequences offering challenges to that stability. Like Propp, Todorov also highlighted

Table 3.1 Key narrative moments – as described in Propp's *Morphology of the Folktale*

Movement	Narrative stage	Potential plot points
First movement	**The initial situation**	• The hero's home life is described.
	The preparatory section	• The false hero is introduced. • The hero faces a significant barrier that disrupts their home life. • The hero is deceived by the villain. • The hero uncovers the deception.
	The complication	• The villain's influence increases and/or the princess is captured. • The hero's quest is defined, and they are dispatched on a journey to complete that quest.
	The donor	• Appearance of the donor character who provides a magic agent so that the hero can complete their quest.
	The helper	• The hero faces struggles that they overcome with the assistance of the helper. • The hero does battle with the villain for the first time. • The false hero wins favour with the father of the princess. • The hero pursues the villain.
Second movement	**Repetition**	• The hero continues to battle the villain using both the donor and helper's assistance. • The hero continues to face barriers that prevent the completion of their quest.
	The difficult task	• The hero engages in a final struggle with the villain. • The false hero is unmasked. • The hero is recognised as the true hero. • The world is transfigured. • The false hero is punished. • The hero marries the princess.

the importance of character transformation within a story. Characters do not just experience adversity, they are transformed by those experiences.

Box 3.1 Think about it: the use of Proppian character/narrative archetypes in contemporary media products

Many would argue that Propp's analysis is equally applicable to contemporary media products. Think about the following questions:

- Can you think of any media products that use Propp's character archetypes?
- Can you think of any media products that use a similar structure to that defined in Table 3.1?
- Do you enjoy watching media products that follow this structure? Why or why not?

Todorov suggests, as a result, that an 'ideal' narrative is organised using the following story structure (Todorov, 1977, 111):

- **Equilibrium:** the story constructs a stable world at the outset of the narrative. Key characters are presented as part of that stability.
- **Disruption:** Oppositional forces – the actions of a villain, perhaps, or some kind of calamity – destabilise the story's equilibrium. Lead protagonists attempt to repair the disruption caused.
- **New equilibrium:** disruption is repaired, and stability restored. Importantly, the equilibrium achieved at the end of the story is different from that outlined at the start. The hero's world is transformed.

The three-act narrative structure described above can be seen as a storytelling template that has been used to build stories across a range of media. From Hollywood films to television drama, the equilibrium/disequilibrium/transformation formula provides the narrative backbone for a great deal of the screen-based fiction we

Table 3.2 Examples of Todorov's ideal narrative formula in popular TV drama genres

Genre	Equilibrium	Disruption	New Equilibrium
Science fiction	The world is at peace. A dysfunctional family recovers from a messy divorce.	Aliens land. The family have to survive and are drawn into a battle to save the planet.	The aliens are defeated. The family is healed – the separated parents are reunited.
Horror	An ordinary family home – teenagers fight with their parents.	A supernatural force takes over the home.	The supernatural entity is banished. The teenagers and parents learn to respect one another.
Romance	Single girl yearns for romance. The girl is also stuck in a dead-end job that she hates.	The girl falls in love with a bad guy who leads her astray.	The bad guy is ditched and the girl finds her true love. She also sets up a successful business.

consume (see Table 3.2 for further examples). Three-act narratives can also be seen in print media forms where celebrity interviews, for example, use traditional victim-hero progressions that outline revelations of personal crisis and a subsequent search for repair – where alcoholism, the difficulties of producing a film or marriage break-ups are used to construct moments of narrative disequilibrium. Todorov's three-act formula is also universally present in factual programming, where, for example, reality television shows are edited to narrate contestant journeys, celebrating the way that participants have been transformed via the ordeals encountered during the making of the show. True-crime documentaries, too, plot truth-finding missions on the part of victims or police operatives, delineating a journey to establish a new equilibrium harmony where perpetrators are caught, and justice is served.

Overarching features of Todorov's three-act narrative formula

In their purest form, traditional three-act narratives are typically delivered to audiences using the following features:

- **Linear storytelling:** conventionally, three-act narratives move forward in time, progressing through Todorov's equilibrium, disequilibrium and new equilibrium formula using successive narrative events.
- **Proppian character stereotypes are used:** in their purest form, Todorovian narratives tend to use conventional Proppian archetypes, clustering around heroes, princesses and villains.
- **Single character transformations are pursued:** traditional Todorovian story arcs habitually place one lead hero at the centre of the story. Secondary characters, Proppian helpers, false heroes and so on are deployed to assist that single central hero in their narrative quest.

A more sophisticated application of Todorov

Todorov, importantly, recognises that stories are constructed in ways that test and subvert the three-act narrative structure outlined above. Stories, he acknowledges, can reverse equilibrium and disruption stages. They can condense stages or start with moments of crisis. A more sophisticated application of Todorov might also consider:

- **Plot and subplot(s):** contemporary film and television drama is traditionally constructed using an overarching master plot accompanied by a series of subplots. Often master plots and subplots use different lead characters with each narrative layer articulating its own equilibrium, disequilibrium and transformation story arc.
- **Multiple equilibrium/disruption sequences:** contemporary media products often try to produce a roller-coaster effect for their audiences by deploying several equilibrium/disequilibrium sequences before resolving in a final transformation. The alternating repose/action effect of such narratives offers audiences multiple moments of narrative calm and excitement.
- **Flexi-narratives:** long-format television products deploy multiple three-act structures in a similar pattern to that used by master plot/subplot sequences, with some narratives resolved in a single episode and others concluded over the course of a whole season or even longer in some instances. These flexible narratives offer audiences quick-fix single episode resolutions, while also nurturing long-term viewing engagement by building season-long three-act arcs.
- **Condensed equilibriums:** contemporary audiences, arguably, have a much lower boredom threshold, expecting products to deliver action or disruption quickly. Producers therefore propel narratives towards moments of immediate disruption to hook audience engagement from the outset.

Alternative story ordering devices

Audience demand for story novelty has encouraged writers and directors to test the three-act narrative formula in ever more ingenious ways. Indeed, today's media-saturated landscape means that consumers skim across products at the tap of their remote controls or the swipe of a tablet screen, compelling contemporary storytellers to create ever faster product engagement. The accelerated, multifaceted nature of media consumption is reflected in the construction of ever more complex narratives that are not afraid to test the linear rules of storytelling.

Contemporary media stories move backwards and forwards. They skip or recap, they start at the end and end at the start.

Contemporary viewers, moreover, shift their attention continuously: from TV screens to tablets, from tablets to smartphones, watching and listening to two or more products simultaneously. And audiences do not wait for their media to appear in fixed-schedule broadcasting slots. Consumption is slaked in binge-watching gulps or, conversely, is nibbled upon in YouTube-friendly shorts. Briefly, contemporary audiences expect more of the narratives they engage with. The complex consumption habits of those audiences, moreover, equip them to decode products that bend or refashion Todorov's ideal formula.

In this sense we might link the changing nature of narrative construction to wider changes across the industry in terms of distribution practice. The domination of global streaming services that, by and large, allow audiences to binge watch content has reshaped the storytelling strategies of television. End of episode disequilibriums, for example, produce cliffhangers that propel audiences to keep hitting play on their remotes, while the extension of television drama in terms of season length and total season delivery means that scriptwriters have more space to fill. As such, whole episodes can be given over to flashback standalones and other diversionary narrative tactics.

The sheer volume of storytelling space also drives output to nurture ensemble casts where it is difficult to differentiate primary and secondary characters. It might be argued, as such, that we live in a golden age of television drama – that the global revenues of companies like Netflix and Amazon Prime have been ploughed into expensive epic storytelling as evidenced by series like *The Crown* (Netflix) or *The Rings of Power* (Amazon Prime).

Perhaps we are seeing the first signs that that golden age is drawing to a close as ever more entrants – Apple TV+, Disney Plus, Hayu – join the global television market, providing increased competition for viewers and diluting subscription revenues. Television distributors, as a result, are concentrating spends and are less likely to fund experimental drama formats. Apple TV and Sky have also spearheaded a return to episodic consumption, releasing new episodes for big releases on a week-by-week basis. Netflix too have reintroduced ad breaks to boost income, with a potential further reshaping of content needed to sustain audience interest across advertising interludes. There are signs too that audiences are wearying of the current trend for complex television storytelling with shorter season runs and standalone dramas making a comeback.

No matter the direction of contemporary television formats, it is true that the shift to global television streaming has significantly stretched the rules of Todorov's three-act ideal. Here are some of the contemporary narrative strategies used that test or break that traditional storytelling formula:

- **Anachronic devices (flash forward/flashback):** these subvert traditional linear storytelling techniques through time bending. Flash forwards provide moments of disequilibrium before equilibrium – reversing Todorov's ideal flow by telling us the end of the story before it has begun. Flashbacks, too, are injected to disrupt the highly predictable nature of the three-act structure.
- *In media res:* contemporary stories often start mid-action, delivering immediate crisis, inverting Todorov's ideal narrative progression through the presentation of disequilibrium before equilibrium.
- **Multi-perspective narratives:** contemporary stories are often told from different character perspectives, repurposing equilibriums as disequilibrium when the story shifts from one character viewpoint to another.
- **Metanarratives:** provide audiences with moments that draw attention to the idea that they are watching a story. Metanarration might knowingly refer to the product as a media construct or speak directly to audiences through fourth wall breaks.
- **Unreliable narration:** deliberately deceives audiences, providing plots that deliver unexpected moments by revealing that a character is not who they claim to be.
- **Frame stories:** are stories told inside of bigger stories, testing Todorov's ideal narrative structure through the presentation of nested moments of equilibrium and disequilibrium.

Box 3.2   Apply it: in what ways can the Todorov formula be applied to your set texts?

Use the following questions to help you explore the use of equilibrium/disequilibrium sequences in your set texts.

- Do the set texts use Proppian character types?
- Do products use Todorov's equilibrium, disequilibrium and transformation formula?

- Do products revolve around one lead character?
- Do set text products provide plot/subplot sequences? Flexi-narratives?
- Do the set texts condense or shorten equilibriums?
- Do stories resolve narrative strands at different points across the text?
- In what ways are lead characters transformed in new equilibrium stages?
- In what ways are the ideas by Propp and Todorov tested by your set texts?
- In what ways does the broadcast format of the text shape narrative?
- Is the product distributed via streaming service, using a flexi-narrative structure to nurture binge watching?
- Does the set text target a media-savvy audience who are able to decode complex plotting techniques?

Exemplar: *No Offence* **(AQA).** *No Offence* simultaneously applies and adapts Todorov's ideal narrative formula. The opening sequence of season 2 offers us a compressed sense of equilibrium – reintroducing the audience to the main characters of the narrative and their character quirks. The lead hero, Viv, is identified immediately with secondary team members (Dinah and Joy) positioned as her Proppian helpers. The opening scene presents a moment of compressed equilibrium – outlining the dysfunctional nature of the team via Joy's indiscretion in the surveillance van, while Viv's exposed fashion label reinforces the hero's lack of traditional femininity. Equilibrium, however, quickly gives way to *in media res* – the terrorist explosion producing a quick narrative hook for the audience while also engaging viewers in a narrative arc that unfolds across the whole of season 2. *No Offence*, in this sense, is best defined as a contemporary flexi-narrative, as opposed to offering its audience a traditional Todorovian three-act structure.

Exemplar: *The Returned* **(Eduqas).** The single character titles of each episode of *The Returned* suggest the use of a traditional Todorovian narrative structure, the kind of self-contained narrative format that satisfied audience needs when consuming single episodes in fixed-schedule distribution systems. The focus on Camille in episode 1, season 1 does indeed deliver a self-contained story, outlining the resurrection of the French teen and the resulting impact on her family, as well as detailing the nature of Camille's death. To suggest, however, that the episode uses Todorov's three-act narrative ideal would be wrong. The episode's bus crash flashback at the start delivers an *in media res* hook for the audience instead of establishing narrative equilibrium, with the return to the details of the crash at the end of the episode providing narrative circularity rather than the establishment of new equilibrium harmony. Indeed, we are left with more questions than answers at the end of the episode, partly because the narrative delivers a heavy dose of character-based narrative enigmas that the rest of the season is expected to deliver. In this sense, we might describe *The Returned* as a flexi-narrative; a prime example of the kinds of global television series that were made in the mid-2010s to satisfy the needs of audiences who consumed television series in concentrated bursts of binge watching via streaming services.

Further set text help is available for a range of products at www.essentialmediatheory.com

Concept 2: the ideological effects of story structure

Stories, Todorov suggests, invite audiences to interpret meanings – to decode the presentation of characters and narrative action as substitutes for ideas that exist beyond immediate plot presentations. 'An adventure,' he writes, 'is *at the same time* a real adventure and the symbol of another adventure' (Todorov, 1977, 127). Stories, Todorov tells us, are metaphors – places where contradictory forces do battle, where human desires can be articulated and curtailed. Stories, too, provide collisions, delineating harmony and disruption, and, in this sense, their effect upon the reader is both persuasive and ideological.

Todorov draws attention to the following ways in which narratives construct symbolic meaning:

- **Narratives are significations.** Even when narratives are set within relatable settings, the construction of that reality is symbolic –

offering us a version of the world that is ordered by the ethical, moral or ideological viewpoints of a text's author.

- **Stories articulate desire.** Todorov's 'ideal' narrative structure is often underlined by the desire of lead characters to return to the stable world presented during the initial equilibrium stage. Moments of initial equilibrium, therefore, represent ideals for the audience watching the text.
- **Stories invoke desire.** Story quests, the journeys taken by lead characters, are also motivated by the desire to change – to move beyond the initial circumstances in which a character is placed. That journey, Todorov suggests, prompts the reader to change too.
- **Disequilibrium and transgression.** Todorov identifies the use of transgressive action as a mechanism that enables ideological meanings to form. Characters break rules or violate social norms, and to repair those transgressions they must be punished or effect a transformation. The ideological effect of these moments is to outline social ideals or modes of behaviour that audiences might also use to guide their own behaviours.
- **Disequilibrium and ideological villainy.** Narrative disequilibrium is constructed through the presence and actions of symbolic villains. Here, the hero must battle an external foe, who, Todorov argues, symbolises qualities that audiences are guided to avoid.

Box 3.3   Think about it: the power of narrative transformation

Todorov argues that narrative transformation is a defining feature of fiction, differentiating stories from other modes of discourse such as factual or historical narration. Todorov suggests that stories can construct the following types of transformation:

1 **Transformation in attitude:** media products construct characters who must develop new outlooks to overcome the challenges posed at the outset of their story arc.
2 **Transformations of belief:** narratives outline both the ideas and the ideals that we must believe in if we are to succeed, while also outlining destructive beliefs.

3 **Transformations of knowledge:** character quests provoke heroes to uncover new forms of knowledge and to
dispense with knowledge that is no longer useful.

- Can you think of any media products that construct the
different types of transformation outlined above?
- What life lessons do the products identified above pass
on to their audiences?
- What are the ideological effects of these products –
what attitudes, beliefs and knowledge do they suggest
the readers of these texts ought to foster?

**Box 3.4   Apply it: diagnose the ideological effects
of narrative transformation in your set texts**

Questions to ask about equilibrium stages

- In what ways does initial narrative stability provide an
ideal state?
- In what ways does the narrative attempt to restore that
initial harmony?

Disequilibrium effects

- Do characters produce disequilibrium by breaking social
norms or rules?
- How are characters punished for those transgressions?
- What negative traits or behaviours are embodied by narrative villains?

New equilibrium effects

- Do characters affect attitude, behaviour or knowledge-
based transformations?
- What do these transformations suggest?

Exemplar: *Killing Eve* **(Eduqas/OCR).** Todorov tells us
that the ideological driver of any text lies in the depiction of

characters who audiences are positioned to identify with and who later undergo what he tells us is a transformation of attitude. Certainly, the *Nice Face* episode delivers a conventional Todorovian act one equilibrium, delineating Eve as a seeker-hero who exists within a satisfying relationship with husband Niko. Eve's apparent domestic harmony is complemented by her work as an MI5 security officer, a role that she is accomplished at, but one that Eve is unfulfilled by. By the end of the first episode, Eve's unsanctioned investigation into Villanelle results in her dismissal and subsequent recruitment as an MI6 spy. Arguably, this end of series crisis instigates an equally conventional moment of Todorovian disruption that ultimately propels Eve to abandon her humdrum existence, and, more interestingly, her relationship with Niko. During the narrative arc that follows, Eve's heteronormative equilibrium gives way to a gender fluid outlook and to a same-sex relationship with Villanelle. It could be argued that Eve's transformation – her acquisition of new gender norms – provides audiences with a gender-based blueprint that positions them to question their own heteronormative values.

Exemplars that explore narrative transformation effects in set texts for all exam boards are available at www.essentialmediatheory.com

Table 3.3 Speak Tzvetan Todorov

Ideological effect	An ideology is a set of ideas or beliefs. Media products have an ideological effect in that they channel their audiences to believe those ideas or beliefs. Villains, for instance, might represent outlooks that are undesirable. Hero quests might also identify ideals in terms of beliefs, knowledge or behaviours.
Narrative transformation	Todorov suggests that one of the major effects of narrative lies in the way that characters or the worlds that characters inhabit are transformed at the end of a story.
Quest narrative	A narrative in which the central hero goes on a journey – usually in an attempt to repair the narrative equilibrium constructed at the start of the story.
Ideal narrative arc	Todorov suggests that the 'ideal' narrative structure follows an equilibrium, disequilibrium and new equilibrium formula. This formula is used extensively across a number of media products and forms.

Table 3.4 Todorov: ten-minute revision

Concept 1: *narrative patterns – equilibrium, disequilibrium and new equilibrium*

- Todorov suggests that meaning in media products is constructed through narrative sequences and transitions rather than through any individual effect or single moment within a product.
- Todorov suggests that an ideal narrative structure follows a pattern of equilibrium, disequilibrium and new equilibrium.
- The new equilibrium stage transforms characters and the world they inhabit.

Concept 2: *the ideological effects of story structure*

- The power of stories lies in their deeper symbolic meanings.
- Narratives construct ideals for the audience through the use of equilibrium.
- Disequilibrium sequences represent ideas, values or behaviours that are deemed problematic – often these negative ideologies are embodied through the villain character.
- Narrative transformation produces further ideals or positive models of behaviour for a media audience.

Challenging Todorov's thinking

Todorov's narrative theory is hugely useful when considering both the structure of story-driven media and their ideological effects, less so when we are presented with print adverts or extracts from stories. Indeed, Todorov's ideas regarding character transformation require viewers to patiently reach the conclusion of any given narrative strand before the full ideological impact of a narrative is realised.

Todorov's ideas were forged in the literary world, and, as such, lack the scope to consider how editing, cinematography or sound elements contribute to the ideological impact of media texts. Todorov's arguments, moreover, were conceived when, arguably, storytelling offered far less narrative complexity than that found within the contemporary media landscape. Much like Strauss and Barthes, Todorov's ideas also fail to take account of how audiences engage with products – specifically audiences who read against the grain of a narrative's intended meaning.

Two named theorists who might challenge Todorov' thinking

- **Steve Neale:** would argue that story structures are continuously adapting and changing. The idea that there exists an 'ideal' story structure, as such, is problematic for Neale.
- **Lévi-Strauss:** is concerned with the way that narratives present oppositions rather than the way those oppositions are transformed or synthesised.

---

4 Genre theory

Steve Neale

Traditionally, genre-based labelling classifies media and film output into categories or families that share common ingredients. In cinema, for instance, we usually determine whether films are best identified as westerns, horrors, melodramas, comedies and so on. Neale argues, however, that genre-based categories are not fixed commodities. Genres change and subdivide; they fuse and die. Neale also suggests that the kinds of tests that can be used to determine genre are hard to pinpoint. Is narrative structure or characterisation the principal determinant of a genre? Is a product's genre best identified by length or the audience-based pleasures generated?

Neale concludes that listing fixed ingredients to determine genre will always throw up exceptions – grey products that use some ingredients some of the time. Genre-driven output, he further argues, creates audience appeal through the repetition of some ingredients, some of the time, and, as a result of economic necessity, that producers have to adapt genre-based formulas to maintain their commercial viability and maximise audience engagement.

Concept 1: repetition and difference

The number of genre-based categories used to label contemporary media products has mushroomed exponentially. The growth of subgenres and the recognition of defined genre hybrids have made the process of classification far more complicated than it has ever been. Indeed, what aspects of a media product might we use to even begin diagnosing the genre of a product? Neale draws attention to the following key factors:

DOI: 10.4324/9781003361220-4

- **Levels of verisimilitude.** The degree to which a media product references the real world can be an incredibly useful indicator of genre. Genres that offer high levels of verisimilitude – that reference the real world with a high degree of accuracy – include news-based products, documentaries, biopics and historical drama. Conversely, genres that offer limited verisimilitude (science fiction and fantasy) transport their audiences to worlds that are escapist or fantastical.
- **Narrative similarities.** Genre-based classification can be determined via the identification of defined story structures or formulaic narrative devices. Murder mysteries, for instance, offer audiences the twin pleasures of suspense and surprise within their narratives. Spy thrillers usually follow a narrative journey to uncover a hidden secret that's crucial to the safety of a wider community of some kind or other. Products might also employ specific presentation techniques: print news stories, for instance, conventionally start with introductory paragraphs that summarise the who, when and where of news events. The style and pace of narrative delivery might be genre specific: voiceover narration, for example, is a staple feature of the gangster genre, while the pace and length of magazine features tends to be much slower than conventional newsprint. Genres, too, deal in specific narrative themes or subject matter: science fiction plots, for instance, often invoke 'man versus machine' plotlines – crime dramas, conversely, have justice-oriented narrative themes.
- **Character-driven motifs.** Audiences might expect some genres to deliver character-driven motifs. Lead characters might have defined conventional attributes or follow genre-driven narrative arcs. Crime dramas, for instance, often use anti-heroes as leads, propelling those characters on tragic narrative journeys that involve loss or redemption. Secondary character inclusion, too, might be heavily defined by genres – romances invariably contain best friend confidents while science fiction output regularly invokes mad scientist character archetypes.
- **Iconography.** Iconography refers to *mise en scène* expectations (setting, costume, makeup expectations) as well as camera and editing styles. In print products, genre-driven iconography is deployed through layouts, header styles or page construction motifs. Tabloid front pages, for example, deliver high image to

text ratio layouts with red top mastheads used. In film, westerns will be readily identifiable through fixed *mise en scène* expectations where guns, desert settings, horses, saloon bars and so on will dominate the visual encodings presented to audiences.

- **Audience targeting.** Neale highlights the way that genres are crafted to create appeal for specific audience segments. Romantic comedies are traditionally constructed to appeal to female audiences through the application of relationship-based narratives. Science fiction, conversely, has traditionally been crafted to create appeal for male audiences through action-based male leads.

- **Representational effects.** Neale also suggests that genres might be recognisable through their application of gender-specific representations. Horror films, for instance, have traditionally constructed women as passive victims while crime dramas are conventionally led by emotionless male detectives.

Box 4.1   Apply it: what conventions define the genres to which your moving image set texts belong?

Use the following questions to help you locate and determine the conventions of the genres that your moving image set texts belong to.

Verisimilitude

- Does the genre attempt to replicate or explain the real world?
- Does the genre present audiences with fantastical or otherworldly settings?

Narrative considerations

- **Structure:** What kinds of narrative structures are readily found in the genre?
- **Themes:** What binary oppositions does the genre usually deploy?

- **Narrative devices:** Does the genre use montage, flash-backs or smashed time frames? Are their narratives linear, multi-strand, tragic or resolved?

Character conventions

- What genre-based stock character types occupy lead roles?
- What secondary characters do audiences expect in the genre?

Iconography

- What genre-based conventions do audiences expect to see in terms of: *mise en scène* decisions (costume, setting, makeup), cinematography, editing styles and sound usage?

Audience appeal and representation

- For which audience is the genre traditionally constructed?
- What sorts of gender-based stereotypes does the genre deploy?

Exemplar: *Tehran* **(Eduqas).** *Tehran* clearly draws inspiration from the success of globally successful output like *Homeland* and *24*, delivering a relentlessly paced spy thriller that places its central protagonist within a narrative of ever-present danger. The success and ubiquitous presence of the spy thriller on streaming services, perhaps, is driven by audience fears of terrorism in the wake of 9/11. The spy thriller genre also translates well as a global commodity with heavy use of action sequences minimising the need for distracting dialogue, and, more importantly, providing global audiences with easily decodable plotting. Steve Neale also suggests that iconography provides producers with opportunities to deliver genre-driven familiarity: global settings, guns, interrogation rooms, tech support bases and airports all providing *Tehran*'s audience with a familiar range of iconography from the spy genre. Character use too is conventional in the show, with the Tamar/Zhila mistaken identity narrative strand providing readers with a familiar secret agent trope in episode 1, while Faraz's quietly spoken willingness to abandon his romantic getaway so that he might interrogate passengers provides us with the kind of classic cold-hearted villain that we expect from such output.

Visit www.essentialmediatheory.com to see more exemplars

Repetition and audience pleasure

The use of repeated motifs, themes or stylistic devices allows audiences to recognise and access media products that create the kinds of appeal they are engaged by. Genre-driven products provide familiar narrative structures and character types that create audience engagement quickly. Genres, of course, create their own specific sets of pleasures or gratifications. The appeal of science fiction lies in the construction of off-world settings. News-based products enable political engagement. Musicals provide audiences with performative pleasures through the inclusion of song and dance routines, while crime dramas traditionally provide narrative satisfaction using enigma and surprise. In this sense, the labelling of products by media makers using genre-based categories allows audiences to identify products that generate specific pleasures or benefits.

Genre subversion

Neale, however, resists the suggestion that genres deliver stable products for any length of time. All genres, he argues, are subject to a continuous process of evolution and/or subversion. He identifies the following drivers of genre difference:

- **Audience needs.** Audiences, of course, gain enjoyment from recognising the use of genre-driven tropes, but they also gain pleasure in identifying moments that depart from those expectations. These differences, Neale argues, provide moments of audience pleasure, delivering output with a unique selling point.

- **Contextual influences.** Media makers adapt genre-driven content because of historical, political or social influences. The #Metoo movement and fourth wave feminism, for example, have presented contemporary script writers and producers with an opportunity to repurpose the traditional male lead convention familiar to so many television drama genres.
- **Economic influences.** Falling sales or poor audience engagement can create commercial imperatives to change or adapt genre-driven content. Similarly, budgetary constraints, or indeed budgetary freedoms, can curtail or free up media makers in ways that subvert genre-based expectations. The box office success of Marvel, for instance, has led to a rapid expansion of the super-hero genre.

Box 4.2   Apply it: identify set text genre subversion

Think about the following questions to help you identify the presence of genre subversion in your set texts:

- **Cultural effects:** in what ways does the set text react to its cultural context? What cultural trends affect the style and content of the product?
- **Social context:** how are characters shaped to create representations that are relevant to the historical context of the product?
- **Historical effects:** what big historical events have shaped the product or are reflected within the narratives offered? To what extent is the product reacting to the political landscape in which it is situated?
- **Economic context:** how have economic factors shaped the product? How has the budget of the product shaped

its ability to deliver genre-based expectation? How have commercial imperatives shaped the product?

- **Audience saturation effects:** in what ways have audience needs shaped the product? Where do moments of genre subversion create novelty or surprise?

Exemplar: *Huck* (Eduqas). *Huck*'s minimalist front cover design and candid photography signal the magazine's highly unconventional approach to the lifestyle magazine genre. Importantly, Steve Neale tells us that genre differences like these form because of contextual influences, audience needs and economic effects. We might argue that Huck's historically dynamic interpretation of the lifestyle genre is affected by all three of those forces, offering audiences a stripped back slow-journalism antidote to the publish-first mantra of the newsprint industry. The choice of a non-white female soldier as the cover model reflects the contextual influences of intertextual feminism, purposefully offering Huck's readership an active female ideal instead of the more conventional use of objectified white-centric femininity. The stripped back sell-lines of the front cover also reflect the economic context of Huck's digital distribution model. Where traditional sales of magazines rely on retail impulse buys, *Huck* uses online marketing and social media to sell subscriptions direct to its customer base. That direct engagement means that the front cover doesn't have to oversell the magazine with dense sell-lines to help differentiate it from competitors in retail outlets.

More exemplar analysis and set text help is available for a range of products at www.essentialmediatheory.com

Genre hybridity: contemporary media products

Neale suggests that contemporary media products are marked by their use of genre hybridity – the deliberate inclusion or intertwining of conventions from across several genres. Contemporary dramas like *Stranger Things*, for instance, pastiche several genre-driven tropes. The otherworldliness of Eleven's experimentation is culled from science fiction, while the creature-based antagonist in *Stranger Things* is a horror borrowing. The potential appeal of genre hybridity to contemporary media makers can be described as follows:

- **Hybridity enables quick tonal shifts:** products can quickly invoke the various emotional intensities of different genres through hybridity. Switching from an otherworldly science fiction setting to the isolation of a conventional horror, for example, can move an audience from awe to fear within the time frame of two scenes.
- **Genre piggybacking:** products can cash in on the relative popularity of a genre-driven product by incorporating elements or motifs of that genre. The enormous popularity of *24* and *Homeland*, for example, have prompted a rush of shows in the spy thriller genre.
- **Creates individual product character:** hybridisation allows products to construct originality by mixing ingredients from pre-existing media products.
- **High and low culture remixing:** hybrid products allow producers to shape products that have serious subtexts while also deploying narrative content that is accessible and popular.
- **Expands audience appeal:** combining romance with comedy, for example, expands the target audience of a product to include males and females.
- **Nostalgia:** hybrid products often revive genres, applying nostalgia to satisfy audience sentimentality.
- **Knowing audiences:** contemporary audiences are far more knowledgeable than audiences in the past. Hybrid products acknowledge and reward that media knowledge by using intertextuality and allusion.
- **Mirrors contemporary audience consumption experiences:** hybridity replicates the multi-channel, media-meshing consumption experiences of contemporary audiences through the simultaneous presentation of disparate genres.

**Box 4.3   Think about it: genre hybridity
in the contemporary media landscape**

- Do contemporary audiences expect their media to be
  hybridised?
- Which of your set text products provide examples of
  genre hybridity and for what reasons are those products
  hybridised?

Concept 2: industry effects on genre-driven content

Auteur-based effects

In creative terms, the writers, stars and directors of products often deflect and subvert genre-driven themes to accommodate the
stories they want to tell. The *Star Wars* reboot serves as a classic example of this process: it is, first and foremost, a science fiction product, yet the directorship of J.J. Abrams significantly
shaped the story to accommodate his own auteur-driven concerns.
Abrams' obsession, for instance, with lens flares and moments
of poetic stillness are clearly laid on top of the film's sci-fi driven
aesthetic.

Genre planning and institutional mediation

The broader effect of media institutions on genre output is also
enormous – in terms of both scheduling effects and the impact
that a parent media company's values have in shaping genre-driven
output. Media schedules, Neale says, are dominated by several
genre-specific openings. In film marketing, horror films are scheduled for Halloween releases, while family-oriented blockbusters
are premiered during school holidays. In television, big budget
dramas are usually premiered in autumn to take advantage of
the boost to viewership that dark evenings bring. Historical dramas are constructed for Sunday evening broadcasts, while diet
shows are commissioned annually to cash in on New Year health
resolutions. In short, media organisations, Neale tells us, effect

calendared production routines using genre-driven content as a key planning tool.

Genre-driven content, Neale tells us, is also shaped by the specific ethos of producer-oriented practices. The approaches taken by individual television production companies or by the editorial teams of single news titles, for example, will invariably subvert genre-based conventions using their own house styles and templates. *The Guardian*, *The Times* and *The Telegraph*, for instance, are all broadsheet newspapers which, broadly speaking, publish the same sorts of content – politics, sports, hard news and so on. Yet the teams of journalists who construct each title are wholly different from one another in terms of their writing styles and political leanings. In this sense the styling and application of genre-driven ingredients work alongside the wider institutional needs and skill bases of the individuals working within those institutions.

The same process is evident in the television industry, the output of which is dominated by a fixed number of genres and subgenres. Crime drama, for example, is a staple ingredient in most UK broadcasters' schedules, with most products deploying victim/perpetrator-driven characters within a police procedural narrative, but the values of the commissioning broadcaster provide a fundamental steer to the final product. BBC crime dramas will be guided by their public service broadcasting ethos, for example – foregrounding diversity and new talent as key ingredients. Conversely, commercial broadcasters might try to garner mass audience appeal by using star power and a more mainstream take on genre codes.

Box 4.4   Apply it: diagnose the auteur and institutional effects on genre-driven set texts

Auteur effects

- Who are the key personnel who shaped the set text? Identify writers, directors and performers.
- In what ways have auteurs placed their own personal stamp on the product? What is that stamp?

Institutional effects

- What kind of media organisation commissioned and made the set text?
- How has the organisation type (public service broadcaster, commercial, conglomerate, etc.) shaped the narrative or styling of the product?
- How have budgetary factors influenced the product?
- How has scheduling and distribution shaped the product?

Exemplar: *Killing Eve* (Eduqas/OCR). In many senses, *Killing Eve* provides audiences with a familiar range of genre-driven expectations. Carolyn's MI6 spymaster characterisation, for example, feels and looks like M from James Bond. Konstantin, Villanelle's Russian handler, presents as the kind of aloof foreign villain we might expect to stumble across in the *Mission Impossible* franchise, with Villanelle's Paris life providing the exotic escapist allure we expect to see in the spy thriller genre. Yet, *Killing Eve* is substantially different from other spy products, most especially in terms of its representation of gender, delivering Villanelle as an ironic and dissatisfied female ideal alongside the unconventional use of Eve as the drama's washed-out female protagonist. This foregrounding of the female experience and the show's concern to depict female desire is driven by *Killing Eve*'s auteur writer, Phoebe Waller-Bridge, whose television debut, *Fleabag*, places transgressive femininity centre stage. We might also point to the BBC's involvement in terms of delivering genre difference, producing what Neale calls an institutional mediation effect – their public service broadcasting ethos providing a good fit with Waller-Bridge's experimental approach.

The marketing functions of genre

Neale also alerts us to the use of genre as a marketing tool, outlining the importance of genre within the 'intertextual-relay' (Neale, 2001, 39) of a product (trailers, posters, reviews, etc.). Genre labelling, Neale tells us, is an important feature of marketing – used predominantly to give an indication to audiences of the specific satisfactions that a product will generate. This material, Neale says, inadvertently plays a crucial role in defining the genre of a product for the following two reasons:

- **Intertextual relay builds a product image.** Marketing materials determine what Neale calls the 'narrative image' (Neale, 2001, 39) of a product. The genre-based labels used by publicity material and those applied by reviewers and critics fix the genre of a text before it is released. These genre-based stamps can be very hard to shift afterwards.
- **Intertextual relay guides audience readings.** Publicity builds audience expectation, which, Neale argues, play a huge role in framing audience readings. Audiences, he suggests, adapt their viewing conclusions as a direct result of these labels.

Box 4.5　Apply it: diagnose the use and effect of intertextual relay on set texts

Locate genre labelling in promotional material

- How is genre foregrounded within publicity material?
- How does imagery, *mise en scène*, costume, colour, setting, etc. construct genre-driven expectations for the target audience?
- In what ways is genre foregrounded within language components of intertextual relay?
- Is genre labelling visible within reviews, credits, headers or taglines?
- In what ways is genre inferred through star power?

Explain why genre labelling is used

- What narrative pleasures does genre labelling suggest to the audience?

- In what ways does genre labelling help create a recognisable identity for the product?
- Does genre labelling take advantage of cultural trends through piggybacking effects?

Exemplar: *Money Heist* **(OCR).** Originally broadcast by the Spanish television network Antena 3, *Casa de Papel* (translated as 'The House of Paper') was later picked up and redistributed by streaming giant Netflix, who retitled the series *Money Heist*. The retitling, perhaps, was a conscious decision to emphasise the show's global credentials as a crime drama, alongside a carefully orchestrated marketing campaign that consistently drew attention to the series – in the UK at least – as a 'thriller' via named endorsements from the *Daily Telegraph*. Certainly, *Money Heist*'s high-octane plot provides viewers with a new form of European television – a radical departure from the slow brooding darkness of Nordic Noir. Yet *Money Heist* also raises important political subtexts, pointing to the vast social and financial inequalities that exist around the world – a subtext that's quietly hidden from view in Netflix's marketing. Steve Neale argues that genre labelling in marketing often packages products using similar tactics, using what he would call intertextual relay to create commercially driven appeals for audiences that overplay genre-driven components. He further asserts that intertextual relay can frame and direct audience experiences, positioning viewers to pick up on the genre-driven ingredients that have been pre-fixed via marketing appeals. If true, we might argue that global viewers and a domestic Spanish audience might have had subtly different expectations and experiences of *Money Heist* given the different marketing approaches in each territory.

Further set text help is available for a range of products for all exam boards at www.essentialmediatheory.com

Table 4.1 Speak Steve Neale

Auteur effects	Relates to the input that individual producers have on genre-driven products.
High/low culture remixing	A common form of genre hybridisation in which products mix pop culture genre forms with motifs from more serious genres.
Hybridisation	Using the styles, narratives or other motifs from multiple genres in one product.
Iconography	The visual components of a media product. Iconography might refer to *mise en scène* elements (settings, costume and acting style) or to other stylistic devices (camera work, editing treatments, layout or typography).
Institutional mediation	The effect of institutions in shaping genre-driven products. Institutions might take a specialised approach to genre production or might shape genre output as a result of their company type/ethos.
Intertextual relay	Refers to the range of production and marketing materials that are used by products (trailers, posters, reviews, press packs, interviews and so on). Intertextual relay fixes the narrative image of a product through genre labelling.
Narrative image	Refers to the set of expectations and persona built for a media product through marketing and the reception of the product by its audience.

Table 4.2 Neale: ten-minute revision

Concept 1: *the pleasures afforded through repetition and difference*

- The genre of a product is determined by a variety of factors.
- Genres offer specific pleasures to their audience.
- Audiences enjoy genre subversion as well as repetition.
- Genres are not fixed but are subject to constant change because of real-world effects and the needs of audiences.
- Genre hybridisation is a common feature within the contemporary media landscape.

Concept 2: *industry effects on genre-driven media*

- Genre-driven output is shaped by auteurs and is also subject to the effects of institutional mediation.
- Genre labelling is widely practised by media producers to create a narrative image for a media product.
- Promotion and marketing materials (intertextual relay) can fix the genre of a product.

(*Continued*)

Table 4.2 (Continued)

Challenging Neale's thinking

Neale's writing is hugely influential but is largely limited to discussion of the film industry. When applied to other media sectors, it's much harder to observe the dynamic model he proposes, with some genres and subgenres remaining highly stable over long periods. In print media, for example, popular press news titles, arguably, have delivered a stable content formula since the 1980s – providing readers with an unchanging menu of celebrity gossip, sports news and tabloidesque political coverage.

We might argue that Neale's ideas propel us towards simplistic readings of the media, asking us to break down texts into moments or elements that provide familiarity and difference. Some critics have pointed to the limitations of that model: that it omits to consider the ideological or representational effects of media products, and that it does not take account of the way that audiences interact with genre-driven material. Are viewers and readers, for example, engaged and absorbed by some genres more than others? Do some genre-driven products produce concentrated ideological effects while others lead audiences to an apathetic engagement?

Three named theorists who might challenge Steve Neale's thinking

- **Stuart Hall:** would agree that products construct viewing pleasures for audiences but would also emphasise the potential dangers that certain genres have in effecting audience thinking through genre-specific character representations and stereotypes.
- **James Curran and Jean Seaton:** might challenge the notion that genre experimentation is a significant feature of the contemporary landscape, arguing that media concentration has led to fewer experimental forms – that, instead, media companies are overly reliant on tried and tested formulas that are designed to garner mass audience appeal.

5 Postmodernism
Jean Baudrillard

Baudrillard refused to adopt the stiff academic tone used by many of his predecessors and contemporaries in his writing, producing instead an almost prophetic and strident set of texts that feel out of place within wider academia. Yet, the impact of Baudrillard's writing has been enormous, introducing a whole new glossary of media terminology – terms link hyperreality, media implosion and simulacra – to suggest that contemporary mass media messages are inescapable and all-consuming but also empty of meaning. As the academic William Merrin tells us, Baudrillard's books are, 'standard reference points for any understanding of our cultural processes' (Merrin, 2005, 5).

Key concept: the real and the hyperreal

Baudrillard's key argument stems from his observation that society has experienced three distinct stages of cultural evolution that he labels 'the precession of the simulacra' (see Box 5.1). In many ways, Baudrillard's precession relates the story of twentieth-century secularisation and the replacement of religion as society's primary meaning maker by the mass media. The three phases of Baudrillard's precession can loosely be described as follows:

- **Phase 1 – Early modernity.** This covers the period from the Renaissance to the Industrial Revolution. In this stage, cultural products (literature, music and art) map closely to what Baudrillard calls 'a profound reality' (Baudrillard, 2018, 6). Culture, in this sense, creates an authentic experience when consumed. Mass culture, moreover, is dominated by the lone voice of religion and connects the masses to a singular

DOI: 10.4324/9781003361220-5

ideology – to one version of the world. Culture, too, Baudrillard tells us, is 'sacramental' in that it communicates profound spiritual experiences. As a result, early modernity produces authenticity and a collectively agreed set of truths about the world in which we live.

- **Phase 2 – Modernity.** The second phase, modernity, covers the period from the Industrial Revolution to the Second World War. In this stage, religion and religious certainties begin to fragment, eventually giving way to early mass media forms like cinema, radio and photography. During modernity, Baudrillard argues, the authenticity and collective truths of early modernity begin to 'dissimulate' (Baudrillard, 2018, 6), breaking down into competing versions of reality.

- **Phase 3 – Postmodernity.** The final phase in which we now live is labelled 'postmodernity'. In postmodernity, Baudrillard argues, mass media forms dominate culture, replacing the single voice of religion with the multi-channel, multi-media whirlwind of contemporary mass media consumption. This, Baudrillard tells us, is the age of 'hyperreality' in which cultural products no longer reference the deeper unified significations that religion once provided. In the postmodern era, culture is fragmented, its meanings and instructions are temporary, its messages commercialised and inauthentic.

The ecstasy of communication

Significantly for Baudrillard, the technologies of the mass media have helped construct what he calls an 'ecstasy of communication' (Baudrillard, 1987, 11), arguing that the process of meaning making has exponentially expanded in the postmodern era, permeating modern life in ways that lie far beyond the cultural capacities of previous historical periods. Baudrillard identifies the following effects of postmodernity:

- **The media is everywhere.** In today's hyperreal world, every bus hoarding, street corner and shop window is an advertising opportunity – indeed, our public spaces are so saturated with media that it is almost impossible to avoid the tidal wave of cultural messages beamed at us.

- **Our private spaces have been invaded.** Baudrillard also tells us that today's hyperreal media even penetrates the once safe havens of our family homes. There is no escape, Baudrillard says, from the incessant chatter of hyperreality: 'One's private living space,' Baudrillard writes, 'is conceived of as a receiving and operating area, as a monitoring screen endowed with telematic power' (Baudrillard, 1987, 17).
- **Authenticity is impossible to find or keep.** Because the hyperreal world of modern media is so all-encompassing and so incessant, Baudrillard tells us, the deluge of messages offered have limited significance. Cultural products in postmodernity construct throwaway messages, forgotten almost as instantly as they are consumed.
- **Repetition and duplication effects.** The postmodern media, Baudrillard further argues, repeats and repurposes content in a never-ending chain of replication. Commercially successful products are repurposed, remade, serialised or copied to attract and maintain audiences, while genre-oriented storytelling replicates narrative formulas in endless echoes of products that are themselves copies of something that was made a long time ago. In this sense, Baudrillard tells us, we know the end of any news event before it has happened. We know how our streamed box sets will resolve and how our gaming cut scenes will play out, because 'everything is already dead and resurrected in advance' (Baudrillard, 2018, 6).

Box 5.1   Know it: why does Baudrillard describe culture as 'simulacra'?

Baudrillard uses the word 'simulacra' to suggest that culture (mass media, religion, art, etc.) produces versions of reality to help explain our place and function in the universe. Christian religion, for instance, constructed a version of reality in which, crudely speaking, God is said to have created the universe in seven days. We now know that to be untrue, and that the story stands as an early religious attempt to explain the complexities of the universe before science could give us a more accurate picture. Culture, of course, authors numerous other stories that attempt to explain the world we live in. Importantly, Baudrillard argues, those cultural products – or versions of reality – are all simulations of the real world. The 'precession of the simulacra' is Baudrillard's attempt to explain how those simulations have changed since the Renaissance.

Box 5.2 Think about it: what effect does postmodern hyperreality have on audiences?

- To what extent is it true that we live in a world in which it is impossible to escape the reach of media? Is it possible to completely escape the reach of the media?
- In what ways have smartphone ownership and the digital revolution expanded the reach of hyperreality?
- How many media products have you seen today? How many advertisements have you seen? How much time have you spent on social media?
- How many contemporary media messages have a deeper meaning or connect us to authentic or satisfying experiences?
- Is it true that the contemporary media duplicates and replicates the same stories over and over? Can you provide any examples of this?
- Has media proliferation meant that we have lost touch with the natural world?

Box 5.3   Know it: intertextuality as a staple ingredient in contemporary media products

The prevalence of intertextuality as a familiar feature in media design provides substantial evidence to corroborate Baudrillard's assessment that media in the postmodern age is marked by replication and duplication effects. The ubiquitous referencing of external character tropes, dialogue snippets, settings or costume design in media products clearly demonstrates both the power and the presence of media iconography in the lives of mass audiences across the globe. Intextextual moments in today's media landscape might be said to act as an alternative language form – as shorthand signals that communicate complex meanings to those global audiences without the need for exposition or explanation.

Intertextuality might be applied to generate the following effects:

- **Escapism invites:** intertextuality can generate the illusion that the media is a parallel universe that operates alongside the real world. The illusion of product interconnectedness reinforces that alternative reality – that the fictional inhabitants of the media are living out their fictional lives in parallel to those of their audiences. Audiences, in turn, draw comfort from that deceit or experience escapist gratifications when they enter the parallel universes inferred by interconnected media products.
- **To reward audience recognition:** recognising intertextual references places the audience in the same consumption orbit as media producers, and, as such, forges a stronger connection between both parties. Moments of intertextuality might also generate feelings of audience privilege or belonging when readers are able to trace the origins of a reference that might not be universally understood.
- **Borrowing effects:** intertextuality can be used to copy the same tonal, emotional or intellectual effects of the

original reference. Spielberg, for example, famously referenced the horror and fear of Stanley Kubrick's *The Shining* in *Ready Player One*, piggybacking on the iconic hotel setting and soundtrack of the original movie to effect a similar emotional response.

Meaning implosion

The proliferation of media comes at a further cost in that the variety of arguments and opinions presented via television, news and online media makes it difficult for audiences to reach an objective conclusion about the real world. News outlets, for instance, produce a version of the world that we implicitly understand to be biased towards one political viewpoint, and in today's media landscape it does not take too long to locate an opposing source or contradictory analysis.

Indeed, products internally neutralise content using opposing editorials, balanced quote inclusion or objective reportage. The resulting effect is that the news and wider media present a world in which simultaneous truths exist – a presentation, moreover, that lacks certainty and that leaves media audiences to experience what Baudrillard calls hyperreal 'inertia' (Baudrillard, 2018, 68). Hyperreal inertia leaves audiences mesmerised by the constant barrage of media experienced, yet simultaneously paralysed by the contradictory messaging of contemporary media consumption.

The age of advertising

'Promotion,' Baudrillard writes, 'is the most thick-skinned parasite in our culture. It would undoubtedly survive a nuclear conflict … it allows us to turn the world and the violence of the world into a consumable substance' (Baudrillard, 2018, 31). Where the age of modernity was dominated by cinema and photography, advertising, Baudrillard explains, presides over the postmodern age. That ascendancy, Baudrillard further explains, has important repercussions in that audience response mechanisms to adverts influence how we read all other media products.

Advertising, Baudrillard suggests, holds us in a hypnotic state of 'superficial saturation and fascination' (Baudrillard, 2018, 91), teaching us from an early age that the mesmerising ideals of commercial advertising are rarely realised in real life. The ensuing mistrust of commercial media imagery, Baudrillard further argues, is readily applied to other media forms. We are compelled to watch, he says, but we do not quite believe what we see.

Box 5.4   Apply it: locating 'meaning implosion' in newspaper set texts

- Do your magazine, online or newspaper set texts offer oppositional points of view?
- How might those presentations affect audience readings of those stories?
- In what ways are audiences immune to the ever-present nature of news media?
- Are audience reactions to news events minimised because of the ever-changing cycle of news stories?

Exemplar: *Attitude* **(Eduqas).** *Attitude*'s Real Bodies series offers readers a collection of candid autobiographical YouTube videos that explore a range of mental health concerns. Nick Charles' emotive short exploring his experience of body dysmorphia serves as an excellent example, outlining Charles' weight issues, as well as the pressures placed upon men by the narrow beauty standards that are routinely used across the media. The Real Bodies series is a good fit with the overriding ethos of the magazine – serving the gay community in ways that are socially responsible. Yet, arguably, those messages are often undercut by *Attitude*'s own imagery. Notable examples of that contradictory messaging include their Glam Look YouTube series where celebrities like Plastic Boy 'share his top glam tips', outlining a superficial message regarding looks and self-confidence. These contradictory impulses, perhaps, might lead to what Baudrillard would call hyperreal inertia, where audiences readily consume the high-energy saturated imagery of both videos yet fail to meaningfully engage with content because of the contradictory messaging relayed. That inertia might also be dialled-up by Glam Look's partnership with Superdrug – a clear example of what Baudrillard might call 'advertising infection' wherein audiences implicitly realise that content has been tailored to sell beauty products rather than impart meaningful advice.

Further set text help is available for a range of products for all exam boards at www.essentialmediatheory.com

Baudrillard suggests that the language and narrative structures of advertising have infected other media products. News bulletins, for example, are reduced to easily digestible packages, their stories built upon the same strategies of suspense and revelation that we find in short-form advertising. Politicians, too, Baudrillard argues, have sacrificed debate and argument for news-friendly sound bites designed to effect political branding and voter seduction. Drama also pulses in shorter and shorter scenes, while YouTube vloggers have swallowed, wholesale, advertising's commercial mantra by commodifying themselves – branding themselves in the same way that a shampoo advert might affect audience appeal via choreographed representations of impossible ideals.

Box 5.5   Apply it: how might advertising lead audiences to respond with hyperreal inertia?

Advertising set text applications

- Do your set text advertising products nurture mistrust? Are they too ideal to be believed?
- In what ways do the exaggerated worlds of the advertising set texts feel fake or too ideal?

Exemplar: Sephora – *Black Beauty is Beauty* (AQA). Sephora's approach in *Black Beauty is Beauty* has much to celebrate in it, delivering a socially aware message regarding Black-centric beauty ideals. A wide spectrum of body shapes is powerfully packaged within everyday settings that are realistically encoded. The advert, as such, produces a sense of relatability and connection for a Black female demographic – an audience group that, bell hooks tells us, is often marginalised by the mainstream media. Yet, Baudrillard might argue, audiences could intuit that the glamorous showgirl world depicted midway through the advert lies beyond their reach, that its colour-saturated high-key depiction adds a hyperreal gloss that is both inauthentic and fake. Audiences, too, are increasingly inert to social messaging by commercial companies, often dismissing them as virtue signalling packaging that conceals a harder sell. Audiences might be seduced, Baudrillard argues, but they respond with a sense of hyperreal inertia, dismissing, at best, the sincerity of any political subtext as a throwaway gimmick.

Further set text help is available for a range of products for all exam boards at www.essentialmediatheory.com

Fictionalised reality/realised fiction

The blending of media forms is a further symptom of our hyperreal age. Baudrillard tells us that products borrow and steal at will to attract our attention in today's media saturated landscape, fashioning products through bricolage (constructing media using diverse influences) and pastiche (imitating a style of media product). *Peaky Blinders*, for example, blends historical drama, the gangster genre and social realism to produce a patchwork of narrative effects – romance, action, social commentary and so on. It references something of a historical truth in that a street gang of a similar name did terrorise the streets of Birmingham in the early 1900s. Thomas Shelby, however, is a fictional character – a bricolage composite taken from gangster films like *Goodfellas*, *The Godfather* and *Scarface*.

Peaky Blinders isn't alone in its blending of real and imagined elements. Contemporary media texts, Baudrillard tells us, routinely blur fact and fiction to the extent that audiences can no longer tell them apart. Reality television documentaries, for example, cast their participants as if they were actors, deliberately orchestrating moments of narrative crisis to produce entertainment. *Geordie Shore*, *TOWIE* and *Love Island* might cast participants from the real world, but no one is fooled. Contestants knowingly engineer their onscreen selves to maximise the opportunities such shows present, guided, of course, by the careful hand of TV producers so that their cast might satisfy audience expectation. There is little that is 'real' in today's reality TV.

Baudrillard too suggests that the news similarly effects an ever-present discourse of fictionalised crisis, generating daily doses of real-life entertainment that are populated with cameos of TV savvy politicians and business leaders who are media trained so that they can relay camera-friendly news sound bites. News narratives, too, replicate the language and imagery of disaster movies. The news, Baudrillard argues, is a never-ending soap opera, packaged into easily digestible parcels – into three-act narratives that are instantly forgotten once delivered. Any meanings and emotions produced are temporary, Baudrillard argues, replaced by the next news cycle in an 'accelerated circulation of meaning' (Baudrillard, 2018, 80).

The shallowness of contemporary media hyperreality, Baudrillard further argues, produces a deep yearning by media audiences for products that provide authenticity. The endless churn of contemporary culture, he tells us, produces a requisite desire for stability and validity that the media tries to satisfy through nostalgic appeals and an attempt to embed reality in programming.

The real world has thus become a staple ingredient in postmodern fiction. Biopics and historical drama readily reinterpret history without due regard for historical accuracy – repackaging the world of yesterday using stock characters and audience-friendly narrative formulas. Horror films also call upon their audiences to believe that they are genuine via the ubiquitous 'based on real events' tagline. The word 'based', of course, gives due licence to magnify, distort or change any historical truth as of the writer's choosing. And, of course, soap operas, crime dramas, family dramas and work-based dramas all purport to offer us a view of the world using the tropes of realism, convincing us of their actuality via gritty sets and regional accents, yet do so in ways that reflect nothing of reality at all.

Box 5.6   Think about it: does the media produce a fictionalised version of reality?

- To what extent are audiences aware that reality TV is manufactured?
- What TV products do you watch that claim to deal with real life yet depict reality using the strategies of fictional products? Think here about documentaries, historical dramas, biopics and even the news.
- What fiction-based narrative strategies do non-fiction forms use to present real-world events? Think about characterisation, story structure, editing techniques and language devices.
- Can fictionalised realities have an impact on the real world?

Box 5.7   Apply it: diagnose the use and effect of 'realised fiction' in your set texts

- Do any of your set texts use historical settings as their story premise?
- Do shows make appeals to audiences via nostalgia?
- Do shows blend archive footage with drama to convince us of their real-world settings?

Exemplar: *Deutschland 83* **(AQA/OCR).** Baudrillard suggests that the surface values of postmodern hyperreality produce a deep yearning for the authentic or real. Arguably, the use of historical verisimilitude as a narrative ingredient within fictionalised television drama creates products that anchor that need using nostalgia. *Deutschland 83* clearly evidences this approach. The use of authentic footage of 1980s icon Ronald Reagan provides an instant point of nostalgic reference for the product's audience, further reinforced within the title sequence through its archive-driven montage. *Deutschland 83*, however, also references an imagined or fictionalised East Germany – the East Germany of television spy movies. Its canted cinematography, its spy-based characters (the rebel, the double agent, the master spy) are stereotypical expectations of the genre. The resulting blend of fact and fiction leads us to conclude that *Deutschland 83* is most assuredly a postmodern text – a text that Baudrillard might suggest distances us from authentic experience rather than bringing us closer to it.

Further set text help is available for a range of products for all exam boards at www.essentialmediatheory.com

Table 5.1 Know it: Baudrillard's three phases of the simulacra

Phase	Historical time period	Key features
Early modernity	Renaissance to the early Industrial Revolution	• Limited cultural production. • Cultural production is dominated by a few authors (the church and the state). • The masses are held firmly in their positions by cultural messages.
Modernity	The Industrial Revolution to the Second World War	• Cultural representations begin to break down – producing multiple versions of reality. • Cultural production is dominated by the bourgeoisie and legitimises the capitalist system. • Mass media forms dominate.
Postmodernity	Post-Second World War onwards	• The media produces hyperreality – an explosion of meaning. • The media makes everyone a consumer – audiences have a limited relationship with authentic meanings. • Advertising and television ascend as the dominant cultural forces. • Contemporary digital technologies accelerate the effects of postmodernity

Table 5.2 Speak Jean Baudrillard

Hyperreality	Baudrillard suggests that we are unable to separate the real world from that which is manufactured by the media. In this sense we live in a world that is beyond reality or is hyperreal.
Inertia	Baudrillard's argument that suggests the constant stream of media to which we are subject paralyses us or makes us unable to feel or act in a way that creates deep meaning.
Meaning implosion	The sheer volume of media and the multiplicity of voices within the contemporary media landscape produces a cocktail of opinion and counter opinion that audiences cannot disentangle.
Media blending	Media forms in the postmodern age blur – the narrative strategies of news, for example, become absorbed into fiction and vice versa.

Table 5.3 Baudrillard: ten-minute revision

Key concept: *from the real to the hyperreal*

- Baudrillard suggests that there have been three distinct cultural phases: pre-modernity, modernity and postmodernity.
- We now live in the postmodern age which is marked by a massive proliferation in media content and media messaging.
- Media proliferation has resulted in an implosion of meaning through the simultaneous presentation of oppositional truths.
- Media proliferation is enabled through the endless copying of pre-existing media. Media forms 'blend' and hybridise during this copying process. Media producers use pastiche and bricolage when creating new content.
- The postmodern age is marked by the dominance of advertising as a media form. Advertising has also impacted on other media forms creating hyperreal inertia.
- Baudrillard suggests that media blending has resulted in the construction of fictionalised reality.
- Audiences yearn for authenticity in the postmodern age; the media industry tries to satisfy this yearning through realised fiction.

Challenging Baudrillard's thinking

In today's always-on digital media landscape, it's easy to gain a sense of Baudrillard's hyperreal explosion, where media content is copied, recirculated and appropriated at will. Baudrillard's argument that objective truth is the first casualty of that explosion is hard to argue with, in a world where fake news can help elect politicians, where the culture wars dominate our social media feeds, it feels like the media is everywhere but means nothing.

(Continued)

Table 5.3 (Continued)

Some producers, however, are actively engaged in media production that tries to combat the fast media churnalism of contemporary news production. The slow journalism revolution found in magazines like *Attitude* and *Delayed Gratification*, for example, champion investigative writers, embedding journalists in long-term projects so that they can gain a deeper sense of their subject matter, so they can relate more than the surface truth of the issues they are covering.

Audiences, too, know that there are significant problems that society needs to address. Global warming, Russian invasions and the cost-of-living crisis are more than news headlines that readers consume and throwaway. They result in real audience action, in people opening their homes to Ukrainian refugees, in readers taking measures to curb their energy use.

Two named theorists who might challenge Baudrillard's thinking

- **Roland Barthes:** would argue that media products have a clear relationship with reality. Media texts represent and naturalise the worldviews of those who hold power in society.
- **Henry Jenkins:** would contest the idea that postmodernity results in hyperreal inertia. Contemporary digital audiences, he would argue, can make a positive difference in the real world by engaging in what he called participatory culture.

6   Representation

Stuart Hall

Hall's contribution to our understanding of the representational processes used by the media cannot be underestimated. His academic work helped to construct an understanding of how the media industry and the routine production practices employed by media producers shapes our understanding of the world in subtle and not so subtle ways. Hall, too, shone a critical light on the media's ability to manufacture and reinforce social inequalities through stereotyping practices and, more importantly, articulated an understanding of how stereotypical representations might be subverted and resisted.

When we talk about representation issues, we are thinking about the way that the media makes us think about the world at large: the way, for example, that the news reconstructs real-world events or the processes that television and film adopt to tell us about the world beyond our screens.

Concept 1: media representation processes

The 'reflective' school of thought

One view of the media is that television, print and online products faithfully capture the real world without distortion. According to this view, the media acts like a mirror – reproducing and relaying a faithful version of the real world to audiences everywhere. The joy of consuming media, in this sense, is that it can take us to places we have never been to. The media provides a window to the world, a faithful and accurate means of reproducing information that we might ordinarily be unable to access. Accordingly, the job of media professionals – news journalists, documentary filmmakers and so

DOI: 10.4324/9781003361220-6

on – is to observe and record these inaccessible wonders so that audiences at home can similarly bear witness.

Representations are built via codes

Stuart Hall acknowledges the imitative capacity of the media. The camera, he tells us, reflects the real world around us. If we record or photograph a countryside scene, a version of that scene is created in which the trees, grass and land are accurately depicted. But, Hall reminds us, professional media representations offer us more than just imitation. Media products, he tells us, are composed through the selection and ordering of visual, aural and linguistic elements. Media products, in this sense, do not offer us accurate or objective reflections of the world at large, but, rather, produce versions of reality that are shaped by the subjective viewpoints of their creators.

A news story, for example, might tell us about a real-world event, but the way that story is relayed – through the use of linguistic effects or supporting imagery – produces an edited version of the event reported. News stories, for example, are encoded using stylised features – through the deployment of emotive headlines or edited imagery that audiences have learned to decode because of their previous exposure to similar imagery. In this sense, the media not only contributes to our understanding of the world, but also uses a shared symbolic language that audiences have internalised through their media consumption experiences.

A portrait image that is photographically composed, for instance, tells us a great deal about the individual depicted – whether that subject is powerful or powerless or, indeed, whether we are meant to like that person at all. A fourth wall break can connote authority. A subject who directs their gaze to the left of the frame might infer regret or nostalgia, while a high angle composition might suggest vulnerability or helplessness. Importantly, Hall tells us, our ability to decode such imagery is not innate – we are not born with a natural knowledge of photographic composition. Our ability to decode the meanings of media imagery, Hall argues, is produced because of our continued exposure to media products. The media, therefore, both uses and shapes our shared understanding of the real world around us.

Box 6.1   Know it: Galtung and Ruge's news values

One theoretical strand not named in A-Level specifications, but that is hugely useful in explaining the editorial processes that underpin news selection is Galtung and Ruge's news values theory. Developed in 1965, the two researchers sought to diagnose the factors that led reporters and editors to foreground the reporting of some news events over others. Their findings concluded that a range of 12 values underpinned news selection processes. The most important of these include:

- **References to elite nations and people.** Events that take place in, or that affect, those countries that have close relationships with the readers' country of origin are more likely to feature in prominent editorial slots. The close connection, for example, of the USA to the UK means that news that occurs in America is likely to dominate foreign coverage in UK news titles. Similarly, well-known subjects and celebrities are likely to receive the attention of editors.
- **Frequency.** Events that happen over short periods of time are more likely to be reported than long-term social trends. A murder event, for example, gains more news attention than the long-term economic inequalities of a particular region.
- **Unambiguity.** Stories that offer readers clarity or that lack confused multiple meanings are more likely to be featured. A decisive political vote in the House of Commons, for example, is more likely to be reported than an open-ended political enquiry that lacks a decisive outcome.
- **Meaningfulness.** Subjects that connect to readers' experiences are more likely to be selected. A natural disaster in a distant country, for example, is more likely to be reported if UK citizens are directly affected. A wildfire event that requires UK holidaymakers to be evacuated,

for example, is more likely to be reported or given front page prominence.

- **Consonance and unexpectedness.** News events that can be predicted or, conversely, events that happen without forewarning are more likely to command news agendas. The proceedings of a pre-scheduled murder trial, for example, or the outcome of a general election date provide reporters with consonance. Sometimes referred to as on-diary stories, consonant events can be easily calendared into the itineraries of reporters, their predictability commanding the attention of news producers. In some cases, on-diary stories might be written by journalists in advance of any scheduled outcome. Off-diary or unexpected stories, conversely, provide breaking news opportunities where live feeds can manufacture crisis-driven narratives that command audience attention.
- **Negative references.** Negative news stories, Galtung and Ruge argued, are more likely to gain traction than positive news. A personal scandal that affects a notable politician, for example, is often considered more newsworthy than a political briefing that reports falling unemployment figures or improved economic forecasts.

Box 6.2   Apply it: identify representational codes used in your newspaper set texts

News stories create representations of real-world events through the careful selection of language, layout and design. These representations can:

- Lead audiences to a predetermined opinion – so, perhaps, they form the same conclusions as the producers of the product(s) being consumed.
- Reflect the editorial viewpoint of the paper – offering a politically biased view of real-world events.

- Be sensationalised to create reader engagement.

Use the following questions to help you decode the representational effects constructed by the front pages of your set text newspapers:

Language analysis

- Do headlines or copy use emotive language? What connotations do specific words convey?
- Are stories constructed using emotive semantic fields (collections of words that are themed – for example, war, gun, enemy, destruction)?
- Does the article use sibilance (repeated 's' sounds), cacophony (harsh or discordant sounds) or euphony (gentle sounding words – usually using the letters 'f' or 'l')? What connotations are constructed because of these sounds?
- Is the story reported from a specific point of view? Who is quoted in the story? Why have those contributors been chosen?
- Who is the reader guided to empathise with in the story? Who gets more airtime or copy dedicated to their viewpoint? Whose view is presented first and last?
- Who is the reader guided to blame? How does language create distance or demonise article subjects?
- Are statistics or facts used to create selective impact?
- What kinds of sources are used to evidence the story and with what impact?

Image use

- Why has the image used been chosen? What story does it tell?
- How does the composition of the image assist in creating a specific effect? Think in terms of eyelines, tilt and camera distance.

- What connotations are suggested through body language, setting, costuming and colour use?
- How is the meaning of the image anchored by accompanying captions or headers? How does this secondary information guide the reader towards a predetermined conclusion?

Layout

- Are keywords emboldened or underlined?
- What colours dominate within the layout and with what connotative effect?
- How does layout suggest the importance of the news event reported?

Exemplar: *Daily Mirror* **(all boards).** Stuart Hall tells us that newspapers use selection processes to present a version of news events, a process that often reinforces the editorial biases of news producers – what is clearly evidenced by the *Daily Mirror* front cover on the 19 July (Figure 6.1) is their determination to place global warming centre stage in its editorial mix and to use emotional storytelling to underline the importance of the current climate crisis. A hellish semantic field is used via the inclusion of emotive header words – inferno, hell, blazing and terrifying – that help to convey the intensity and chaos of the wildfire reported. The careful selection of a photograph of a helpless child also constructs an image of sympathy, personalising the abstract concept of climate change and its effects on real people. That image of pathos is further intensified by the caption description of the child as an even more helpless 'toddler', the anguished facial gesture of the police officer connoting the desperate struggle of those trying to battle the fire and its effects. The use of vignetting at the bottom of the page also helps to darken the tonal effects of the article with orange text laid on top of that vignetting to connote the heat of the event.

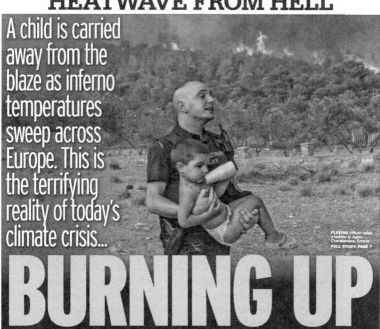

Figure 6.1 Daily Mirror 19 July 2023. © Mirror newspaper.

Concept 2: stereotypes and power

In short, Hall tells us that media products do not just reflect reality; their meanings are shaped by media producers whose work can have a profound influence on audience thinking. In this sense, Hall argues, media products have a discursive effect – in other words, they produce ideological inferences for their readers and viewers.

Hall's own research was particularly interested in the media's portrayal of Black masculinity, initially investigating newspaper reportage in the 1970s in which Black mugging stories were a staple feature. He concluded that media stereotyping during the period firmly linked Black masculinity with criminality and, moreover, that the media's reliance upon such stereotypes had a profound and complex effect on wider social attitudes.

Hall argues that the discursive effect of stereotypes more generally are as follows:

- **Media stereotypes reflect social attitudes.** Hall argues that media stereotypes reflect the wider views of society – by studying the media we can gain a sense of what wider society thinks about those groups that are routinely stereotyped. Hall's work looking at Black youth culture identified, for instance, that the stereotypes associating Black males with criminality reflected a deep-seated anxiety about real Black crime. Journalists who reported Black criminality were therefore reacting to the genuine fears of their audiences when writing and publishing these stories.
- **The media contributes to the construction of stereotypes.** Media stereotyping, Hall further argues, significantly shapes social attitudes regarding specific groups. For example, he concluded that Black youths internalised the criminal stereotypes constructed by the media in the 1970s and, as a result, engaged in real criminal activities. The demonisation of Black youths by newspapers also meant that white audiences were reluctant to trust young Black males, significantly hampering their employment prospects and further channelling young Black males to engage in criminal activities to survive.
- **Stereotypes can be reshaped or repurposed.** Hall also identified that media stereotypes can be guided towards more positive representations of key groups. Indeed, the changing nature of Black representation within the news since the 1970s is testament to the idea that media stereotyping processes are highly fluid.

The essentialising, reductionist and naturalising effect of stereotypes

Hall suggests that stereotypes are incredibly powerful and that their widespread use guides audiences to associate specific groups with negative traits. Stereotypes, moreover, infer a symbolic social power, helping to position some groups as social outcasts, or, as Hall suggests, as social 'others' (Hall *et al.*, 2013, 215). Stereotyping is thus a form of symbolic violence for Hall – an efficient means to hold socially undesirable groups at bay without using actual physical action. Stereotypes, Hall further argues, are an unusually effective means of ideological control because:

1 **They increase the visibility of key groups:** stereotypes usually depict groups by referencing a few key negative features – behaviours, physical appearance and so on. This highlights the undesirability or 'otherness' (Hall *et al.*, 2013, 215) of those groups and enables that sense of 'otherness' to be efficiently communicated to the rest of society.
2 **They infer that negative traits are natural:** the few key ingredients used to construct stereotypes are repeated so often by the media that those ingredients are interpreted by audiences to be fixed or natural qualities. Stereotypes, for example, might infer that Black males are *naturally* lawless or that dumb blondes will *always* lack intelligence.

Hall argued that stereotypes accordingly construct what he calls 'closure and exclusion' effects (Hall *et al.*, 2013, 248) – that their use fixes and perpetuates the boundaries of what or who is socially acceptable. By making stereotyped groups more visible, Hall tells us, they can become excluded and othered in the real world. Criminalising Black male stereotypes, for example, exclude Black males from the normal workings of society – they are positioned as a group to be feared and avoided. Hall further tells us that social exclusion means that stereotyped groups have more limited access to economic or cultural power: Black males, for example, might not be employed because of the imagined fears that employers might have regarding their criminality. And because stereotyped groups have limited economic or social power, they have equally limited means to fight the representations constructed on their behalf. Stereotyped groups might have fewer connections with media producers, or limited opportunities to make media products.

This process leads Hall to conclude that media stereotyping creates power 'circularity' (Hall *et al.*, 2013, 251): those groups with economic or cultural power get to create stereotypes, while the impact of stereotyping effects makes it impossible for powerless groups to escape their lowly social positions.

Box 6.3   Know it: why are stereotypes used by the media?

Stereotypes are universally deployed by the media for the following reasons:

- **To help audiences to understand characters.** Using stereotypes provides a visual shortcut that enables audiences to instantly decode a character's purpose or narrative function. The body language, costuming, behaviours or dialogue of stereotyped characters, as such, provides a set of instant messages – hugely important in products where media producers have to create quick audience interest.
- **To help audiences build character relatability.** Stereotypes build audience empathy, sympathy or antipathy very quickly. We can usually work out whether we like or dislike stereotyped characters within the first few seconds of seeing them.
- **To signpost audiences.** Stereotypes help audiences gain a sense of the potential direction of a story – we understand that certain events will happen to certain characters: princesses will fall in love, dumb blondes die first in horror movies, male action heroes always triumph in the face of adversity.
- **To reinforce genre expectations.** Genres, too, use stock characters that can be quickly inferred using stereotypes. The gay best friend trope, for example, was a staple ingredient of the romance genre.

Box 6.4   Research it: identify common negative stereotypes used by the media

Work with your classmates to research how the following groups are represented by the media – use your own knowledge to supplement the list of areas suggested for study.

Ability-based stereotypes

Possible areas to investigate: groups with physical disabilities, representations based on mental health.

Age-based stereotypes

Possible areas to investigate: teen girls, teen boys, teen subcultures, representations of the elderly.

Class/region-based stereotypes

Possible areas to investigate: single mothers, northerners, southerners, working-class representations.

Ethnic stereotype

Possible areas to investigate: Black males, Black women, Asian men, Asian women, Muslim groups.

Gender-based stereotypes

Possible areas to investigate: dumb blondes, the bitch boss, the nerd, fathers, mothers.

LGBTQ+ stereotypes

Possible areas to investigate: gay men, butch gays, lesbian stereotypes, transgender representations.

For each of the six clusters above:

- Identify the visual cues, costume codes and behaviours that are used by the media to construct the stereotypes within each group.
- Identify media products that contain examples of the stereotypes listed above.
- Create a collage for each of the groups above to help you identify the visual cues used to construct stereotypes.
- What ideas do stereotypes naturalise about the groups they represent?
- Which social groups are immune to media stereotyping?

Challenge question

- In what ways do the stereotypes uncovered help to maintain the economic powerlessness of the groups they represent?

Visit www.essentialmediatheory.com to explore the stereotypes listed above in more detail

Box 6.5   Apply it: what are the effects of the stereotypes used in your set texts?

Identify stereotypes constructed of marginalised groups

- What stereotypes do your set texts create?
- What behaviours or physical traits are used to identify those stereotypes?
- What ideas about these groups are naturalised as a result of the use of stereotypes?

- How do the stereotypes used reinforce existing power structures or help to exclude key groups from mainstream society?

Diagnose the 'internalising' effect of stereotypes

- How might set texts lead marginalised groups/ individuals to internalise attitudes or beliefs that are problematic?
- What particular moments in the set texts might lead to internalisation?

Challenge question

- In what ways might we apply Hall's idea of 'power circularity' to give further weight to arguments regarding the potentially negative impacts of media stereotyping?

Exemplar: *Peaky Blinders* (**Eduqas**). The start of episode 1 might be construed as reproducing a problematic set of Asian stereotypes, serving up a nameless Chinese girl as the anonymously titled character of the 'fortune teller'. The girl's role in blessing Shelby's Kempton entrant here reinforces a sense of Asian exclusion. Her slow-motion powder blessing is underlined with a discordant drone and the girl's isolation from the rest of the Birmingham women, investing the girl with a sense of magic and stereotypical oriental otherness. Stereotypes like these, Hall might argue, produce instant characterisation, drawing upon the audience's familiarity with magical Asian characters in films like *Doctor Strange* or *Karate Kid*, but they also help to produce visibility and exclusion, associating a specific ethnic group with a set of easily definable characteristics that set that group apart from mainstream society.

Further set text help is available for a range of products for all exam boards at www.essentialmediatheory.com

Transcoding and stereotypes

Despite the difficulties faced by socially excluded groups in combating negative stereotypes, Hall tells us that cultural representations are not fixed. The process of representation, he infers, can be thought of as a battleground with each articulation of a stereotype reaffirming or reseeding the suggestions of that stereotype. Representations can and do change as a result, their meanings slide or transform. Stereotypes, moreover, can be contested and their meanings subverted.

Hall argues that media producers who want to challenge pre-existing negative stereotypes generally must graft new meanings onto those existing presentations. He calls this process 'transcoding' and outlines three important strategies that makers can deploy to shift negative stereotypes:

1 **Appropriated representations:** by commandeering negative stereotypes, their meaning, Hall argues, can be devalued or subverted from within. Musicians like Stormzy, for instance, have purposefully appropriated the hyper-masculine stereotypes associated with Black masculinity – repurposing this negative stereotype as iconic or powerful for Black male audiences.

2 **Counter-typical representations:** this process combats negative connotations by producing representations that reverse stereotypes. Butch gay representations, for instance, invert traditional gay representations of male homosexuality as weak or passive.

3 **Deconstructed representations:** stereotype contestation can be achieved by narratives that explain or lay bare the effects of stereotyping. Deconstructed stereotypes add contextual information that helps audiences to forge a deeper understanding of the experiences of the group being stereotyped. Social realist texts and films, for example, often deconstruct class-based stereotypes by exploring the difficulties and problems of unemployment or having very little money.

Box 6.6   Apply it: locate moments of transcoding in your set texts

Use the following questions to help you locate moments of transcoding in your set texts and to diagnose their effect on audiences:

- Do any of your set texts appropriate stereotypes? Where is appropriation most visible and what effect might its use have on the product's audience?
- Which products deploy countertypes? What stereotypical attributes are reversed by the countertype? What assumptions are challenged by any countertypes used?
- Which products explore stereotypes through deconstructions? Which moments in the text could you use to provide the examiner with relevant analysis?

Exemplar: Sam Fender, *Seventeen Going Under* (Eduqas). Sam Fender's tender portrait of growing up in Tyneside in *Seventeen Going Under* offers us a music video that's full of what Hall would call stereotype transcoding. The emotional vulnerability of Fender's performance hints at an underlying masculine identity crisis, the long shot isolation of the video's opening a countertype to the more usual cheeky chappie Geordie stereotypes offered by more mainstream media performers like Ant and Dec or the reality television stars of Geordie Shore. Fender's social realist-tinged music video also offers us a gritty deconstruction of northeastern working-class life, depicting the desaturated economic depravity of Wallsend and the effects of poverty on his life as a teen. The counter topical use of female-on-female violence is interesting, again transcoding the objectified and usually passive representations of femininity found in more conventional pop music videos.

Exemplar: Lil Nas X, *Sun Goes Down* (OCR). Lil Nas' emotive autobiographical music video *Sun Goes Down* generates an unusually counter-typical representation of Black masculinity, expounding the problems of growing up as a gay Black teen – a representation that Stuart Hall might describe as stereotype transcoding. Nas' soft-spoken performance revels in its night-time setting to suggest the depression of his interior anxieties. He is unafraid to depict his teary isolation at his Prom or the loneliness felt as a burger-flipper, using a combination of glidecam camera tracking and slow-motion editing to invest the video with the dreamy disconnectedness of his teen experience. The vulnerability depicted offers us a distinctly different representation to the assertive gay Black masculinity constructed in Nas' video *Montero* and, more generally, an inversion of the hyper-masculine Black male stereotypes routinely offered up by more traditional Black music videos.

Further set text help is available for a range of products for all exam boards at www.essentialmediatheory.com

Table 6.1 Speak Stuart Hall

Closure and exclusion	Media products exclude groups from power through representation – often positioning marginalised groups as unworthy or uncivilised.
Internalisation	Internalisation occurs when marginalised groups or individuals assimilate the behaviours of negative media representations.
Naturalisation	The repeated messages of stereotypes can suggest that groups have a natural disposition towards certain types of behaviour.
Other	Hall suggests that those groups who are excluded from social power or mainstream culture are 'others'.
Power circularity	Stereotypes both reflect social attitudes and simultaneously reinforce them through processes such as internalisation.
Symbolic violence	Stereotypes that demonise groups offer us moments of symbolic violence in that they lead to the exclusion of those groups from social power.
Transcoding	Refers to representation strategies that resist or invert negative stereotypes.

Table 6.2 Stuart Hall: ten-minute revision

Concept 1: *media representation processes*

- The media does not mirror real-world events but produces an edited version of the events depicted.
- Media representations are constructed through codes – using language, imagery, layout, sound and editing to convey a version of real-world events.
- The media plays a vital role in shaping our views of the wider world. Media products can be seen to have a discursive effect on audiences, persuading readers to believe in a specific set of ideologies or beliefs.

Concept 2: *stereotypes and power*

- Stereotypes are used by media producers to create instant characterisation.
- Stereotypes reduce social groups to a few key traits or visual cues and suggest that those groups are naturally inclined towards a specific set of negative behaviours.
- Stereotypes are mostly found where there are huge social inequalities. They exclude and demonise groups in a manner that both reflects and reinforces existing social hierarchies.
- Social groups can internalise the behaviours and outlooks authored by stereotypes.
- Stereotypes can be contested through transcoding strategies.

Challenging Hall's thinking

Hall's writing was groundbreaking in that it provided one of the first attempts to assess the representational power of the media and the way that products constructed different social groups. We also must remember that Hall was writing and researching in the 1970s and 1980s, a time when the media landscape looked very different from that of today.

We might argue that contemporary digital media, for example, provides audiences with the means to contest negative representations – to use social media platforms to quickly call out those media producers who use stereotyping in a problematic way. The sophistication of contemporary media audiences has prompted producers to fashion ever more complex and challenging representations of ethnicity, gender, ability and class – resisting the use of simplistic stereotyping formulas as a means of capturing audience interest.

The media production landscape, too, is more diverse, with more opportunities available for media makers from all social groups to self-represent. This inevitably means that more and more products contest stereotyping practices, offering us narratives that originate from the lived experiences of diverse social groups.

(Continued)

Table 6.2 (Continued)

Two named theorists who might challenge Hall's thinking

- **Stuart Hall:** Strangely, Hall himself provides a substantial challenge to his own ideas. His reception theory model suggests that audiences can resist the effects of the media through the production of oppositional or negotiated readings.
- **Paul Gilroy:** In many senses, Gilroy's work picks up on many of the themes of Hall's arguments – his analysis, however, suggests that racial stereotypes are framed by the wider cultural/historical forces of empire. This makes it much harder for the media to contest Black stereotypes because they are so deeply entrenched within the British cultural psyche.

7 Postcolonial theory

Paul Gilroy

Like Hall, Gilroy explores the construction of racial 'otherness' as an underlying presence within print media reporting during the 1970s and 1980s, arguing that criminalised representations of Black males regularly stigmatised the Black community.

By the 1990s, however, Gilroy shifts his attention to consider the mass media's construction of British identity in post-industrial Britain, diagnosing the existence of a media induced 'postcolonial melancholia' as a representational response to the UK's declining global position in the late 1990s. That decline, Gilroy tells us, is realised because of the loss of the post-war Empire – a loss that the media cushions with stories that are infused with Union Jack-waving nostalgia. For Gilroy, problematically, those stories are also underscored by racial misrepresentations and the amplification of multicultural disharmony in the UK.

Concept 1: racial binaries, otherness and civilisationism

Racial otherness

Gilroy's hugely important study of Black representation, *There Ain't No Black in the Union Jack*, traces the story of UK race relations from the Second World War onwards, in which the post-war wave of immigration from the West Indies produced a series of anxieties regarding immigrant behaviour. He draws attention to, 'Lurid newspaper reports of Black pimps living off the immoral earnings of white women' (Gilroy, 2008, 95) arguing that the public's association of post-war immigrants with substandard living conditions produced racial representations that were 'fixed in a matrix

DOI: 10.4324/9781003361220-7

between the imagery of squalor and that of sordid sexuality' (Gilroy, 2008, 97). Such representations, Gilroy argues, marginalised the immigrant Black community from the outset – constructing them as a racial 'other' in the predominantly white world of 1950s Britain.

In the two decades following the Second World War, media stories regarding the Black community, Gilroy suggests, intensified fears that immigrant communities might swamp white Britain. Those fears were further concentrated in the late 1970s and the 1980s through news coverage that routinely associated the Black community with assaults, muggings and other forms of violent crime. 'It is not then a matter of how many Blacks there are,' Gilroy writes of the period, 'but [of] the type of danger they represent to the nation' (Gilroy, 2008, 105). Blackness and criminality, Gilroy argues, thus became a 'common sense' feature of the media.

During the 1970s and 1980s, newspapers related stories concerning the many community riots of the period, often depicting these multi-ethnic disturbances as Black only events, and further suggesting the Black community was naturally lawless and incompatible with white British values. The Notting Hill Carnival riot of 1976 serves as a particularly poignant example, with the rioters described by various newspapers as 'an angry army of Black youths' and 'as coloured men in screaming groups' (Gilroy, 2008, 122). The anxieties, Gilroy argues, surrounding individual acts of Black criminality – muggings, assaults and so on – tilted towards more generalised descriptions of Black criminality, while the political concerns of the Black community regarding heavy-handed policing tactics were largely ignored.

Gilroy, too, points to other articles of the period that inferred that Black culture had a corrosive effect on white youth during this period. In 1982, for example, the *Daily Mail* reported the detention of several Eton pupils on drugs charges, suggesting that the boys' descent into criminality was prompted by Rastafarian influences. For Gilroy, the story is emblematic of the kinds of racial binaries that the media constructed during the period in which the traditions of white civility – in this case Eton – were increasingly subject to the corrupting influence of a Black 'other'.

Civilisationism

For Gilroy, the 9/11 World Trade Centre terrorist attack in 2001, and its aftermath, radically altered both the tone and the nature of media-oriented representations regarding race and racial difference. The Anglo-American response to the attack is perhaps best summed up by then US president George W. Bush's 2002 State of the Union Address in which he declared that North Korea, Iran and Iraq constituted 'an axis of evil, arming to threaten the peace of the world' (Bush, 2002). For Gilroy, Bush's speech consolidates a deeply troubling and imperialist view of global politics that justified foreign intervention on the grounds that Western democracies were morally superior to other nations. Gilroy's further disquiet surrounding 9/11 is that the media readily accepted and repeated Bush's 'axis of evil' worldview. Gilroy collectively labels these post-9/11 representations as civilisationism. Civilisationism, he argues:

- **Constructs a binary worldview:** President George W. Bush famously declared, 'Either you are with us, or you are with the terrorists': civilisationist depictions construct similarly stark worldviews, positioning media audiences to internalise a simplistic binary that divides the globe into the opposing forces of fundamentalist terrorists and a morally superior West.
- **Has a racist subtext:** for Gilroy, the 'war on terror' rhetoric of the post-9/11 era perpetuates a long-standing racial hierarchy in which Muslim subjects are positioned as inferior.
- **Nurtures cultural incompatibility:** because the media is so focused on global conflicts and terrorist action, an inference is made that European and Muslim groups are incompatible communities. Yet, Gilroy reminds us, the generalised inference of racial incompatibility is a media fabrication. Real-world racial integration, or 'cosmopolitan conviviality' (Gilroy, 2004, 9) as he calls it, is wholly different from the racial binaries presented by the media. Indeed, racially diverse communities live with few, if any, day-to-day effects of racial difference.
- **Nurtures fear:** for Gilroy, the political repercussions of civilisationism have enabled the construction of a 'securitocracy' (Williams, 2013, 44) – the use of repressive measures by Western democracies that are designed to keep nation states terrorist free. In this way, the inhuman treatment of prisoners in Guantanamo Bay, for example, or the torture of terrorist subjects are justified as necessary measures.

Box 7.1   Think about it: representations of 'otherness' in the contemporary media

We can sum up Gilroy's main points as follows:

- Second World War immigrants were seen as an alien 'other' to an imagined white Britishness.
- Black immigrants were perceived to be 'swamping' white communities.
- Black communities were demonised through representations that associated them with individual acts of criminality – knife crime and muggings were particular media concerns. These representations construct a 'common sense' notion of the criminal Black male.
- Later representations constructed the Black community in general, and Black youths in particular, to be naturally lawless and incompatible with British white values.
- Later representations suggested that Black otherness had a corrosive effect on white youth culture too.

Are the representational anxieties outlined above constructed by the British media today?

- Do contemporary media products continue to produce stories that communicate 'swamping' themes?
- Are some communities constructed as 'other' by the media? Who and how?
- Are some communities associated with criminal behaviours?
- Are some communities constructed as having a corrupting influence?
- What evidence could we use to suggest that the media has moved on from the kinds of representations of the Black community that were created during the 1970s and 1980s?

Exemplar: *Daily Express*, 7 March 2023 (all exam boards). Gilroy argues that the media uses a well-worn set of strategies that construct negative representations of non-white communities by depicting ethnic groups as uncivilised others who threaten to swamp Britain. The *Daily Express* front page from 7 March (Figure. 7.1) perhaps exemplifies much

Figure 7.1 Daily Express front page (Tuesday 7 March, 2023). © Reach PLC.

of that approach, constructing a racial binary that pits 'hard-working Brits' against an unchecked influx of 'Channel Migrants'. Inside the body of the paper, the story further alludes to, 'a surge in crossings', echoing Gilroy's observation that the impact of ethnic others is often exaggerated by language that suggests they are swamping the country. The association too of the Channel migrants with 'criminal gangs' who need 'cracking down on' hints at an underlying sense of criminality, helping, perhaps, to lock in an inference that those entering the UK are naturally lawless groups – an 'other' to the civilised inhabitants of Great Britain.

Box 7.2   Apply it: do your set texts construct a civilisationist subtext?

Media depictions that construct contrasts between Western readers and Islamic fundamentalism can be located in news and TV drama. Use the following questions to assess the effect of set texts that deploy representations of this nature:

- How do the representations nurture audience fear?
- How do representations dehumanise extremist subjects?
- What effect do these representations have in constructing racial hierarchies?
- Do any of your set texts deconstruct civilisationist assumptions or offer alternative modes of address?

Exemplar: *Tehran* (Eduqas). *Tehran*'s depiction of the fundamentalist state of Iran in many ways delivers what Gilroy would call a civilisationist set of connotations, constructing a binary view of the world that pits a civilised West against the forces of uncivilised Islamic fundamentalism. Tamar's disquiet when passing the aftermath of an Iranian execution, for example, reinforces the regime's barbaric Sharia laws, more so when the taxi driver explains exactly how the criminals were dispatched. The series at this point delivers a conventional representation of Iran as an uncivilised other, not that surprising given that the drama was originally built for a Jewish-Israeli audience whose relationship with Iran is politically volatile. The binary presentation continues in other moments when the Israeli tourists voice their fear of landing in Iran and their subsequent interrogation by Faraz, again, producing a sharply delineated 'Western freedom' versus 'Iranian totalitarianism' binary, yet that presentation is tempered by the arrogant behaviour of an Israeli couple, Yoni and Shira, when boarding the flight, constructing a more complex set of East/West depictions. A more nuanced set of representations is also constructed when we are introduced to Zhila's husband, whose concerns for his wife construct a more human portrait of the everyday Iranian populous. Ultimately, these complexities muddy the representational effects of the drama, offering a challenge to Gilroy's notion that the media routinely constructs a simplistic presentation of non-Western countries.

Further set text help is available for a range of products for all exam boards at www.essentialmediatheory.com

Concept 2: the legacy of Empire and British identity

In his 2004 book, *After Empire*, Gilroy suggests that we live in a 'morbid culture of a once-imperial nation that has not been able to accept its inevitable loss of prestige' (Gilroy, 2004, 117). The British, he argues, are undergoing a crisis of national identity: the loss of the British Empire, further compounded by the devolution of Northern Ireland, Scotland and Wales, has forced a collective question regarding British identity. 'Is Britain's culture now Morris dancing or line dancing?' Gilroy asks, 'Are we Gosford Park, Finsbury Park or the park and ride?' (Gilroy, 2004, 130).

The loss of British colonial prestige and the resulting contraction of the UK's global influence have largely been airbrushed from public discourse, Gilroy argues, yet that contraction in national importance has simultaneously affected a deep-rooted cultural anxiety accompanied by a sense of national rootlessness and guilt. For Gilroy, moreover, the immigrant population has become an outward symbol that perpetually reminds the UK of its loss of global power. Empire immigrants and their descendants, he argues, are a visible representation of British power as it once was. Post-war racism, he further suggests, acts as a covert attempt to recover the social order of Empire England – to restore the English nation to its pre-war state.

The immigrant, Gilroy argues, is also a symbol of British exploitation and of the racial violence perpetuated in the name of Empire, reminding us that colonial expansion and the British imperial project gave birth to the British slave trade and to the brutal repression of indigenous populations across the colonies. The Empire, as such, represents more than the loss of sovereign power. It is a stain on the collective British identity, the ramifications and extent of which have never been fully explored or acknowledged by the nation.

World war victories and Albionic Englishness

Gilroy tells us that the twin pull of Empire guilt and the loss of British global power has resulted in a national postcolonial melancholia – a sort of collective depression that both absorbs and blinkers the British outlook. The media, Gilroy suggests, compensates for this collective depression by routinely invoking the mythic victories of the Second World War to distract the national populous from its loss. Indeed, Gilroy reminds us that numerous other British military campaigns and over 70 years of history have elapsed since 1945, yet the Second World War remains a potent media symbol that is routinely invoked by the British media.

The Second World War, Gilroy argues, acts as a powerful set of signifiers that enables us to turn the loss of the British Empire into a moment of significant historical and ideological victory. As such, the media routinely conjures up the spirit of the Blitz and the bulldog mentality of Winston Churchill to remind us of our once important historical significance. The media's mythologising of the Second World War, Gilroy further argues, revels in the isolation of Britain and the preservation of an imagined English purity. Wartime allusions, as a result, are routinely invoked in sports and news reportage, with a nostalgic English nationalism adopted as the standard response to World Cup fixtures, Olympic coverage and European politics.

Gilroy, too, draws attention to the media's preoccupation with British tradition as a further response to postcolonial melancholia. The print news' obsession with the Royal Family and television's routine depictions of the quintessential English rural landscape invoke,

Gilroy suggests, an inward-looking Albionic Englishness. The media manufactures a long-lost imagined England untouched by the demise of Empire – an England, more importantly, in which racial diversity and multicultural conviviality are strangely absent. Albionic England is the film world of Bridget Jones; it is the English summers that abound in advertising, the Proms, the wall-to-wall television coverage of Queen Elizabeth's death and King Charles' coronation. It is also the English rurality of historical drama – of ITV's *Downton Abbey* and of Netflix's *The Crown*. Albion, too, is traceable in *Emmerdale*, *Midsomer Murders* and *Vera*. But, Gilroy warns, Albion England is nothing more than a distracting fantasy that disguises the reality of what Britain is really like – a country that remains crippled by regional poverty and an ever-widening economic social divide.

Box 7.3 Discuss it: to what extent are we infected by postcolonial melancholia?

- Is the British media obsessed with the past? Are we a backward-looking nation that cannot come to terms with our diminishing global role? What evidence from the media could you present to support or contradict this idea?
- Why are British newspapers so obsessed with the Royal Family? Do they represent order in a chaotic modern world? Do they represent British tradition?
- Does the media construct an Albionic representation of Britain – a largely white, rural version of England that is celebratory? What products have you seen that construct this imagined version of England?
- Why do you think the media constructs these idealised representations of Albion?

Box 7.4 Apply it: diagnosing postcolonial melancholia in your set texts

Search for moments that affirm Gilroy's view that the UK has been paralysed by postcolonial melancholy. Use the following to help you construct relevant analyses:

- Do any of your set texts create an Albionic representation of the UK? Do they foreground an idealistic or traditional view of England?
- Do the set texts use traditional English institutions to assert an Albionic view? Are they overly concerned with the Royal Family? Do they invoke a traditionally Christian representation of England? Do the set texts defer to English tradition in an idealised way?
- Do the set texts invoke nostalgia or, more specifically, war-oriented nostalgia?
- Are the set texts used to explore/search for an English identity? Do the texts foreground identity anxiety?
- Do the set texts use immigrants as a means of prompting Empire guilt?
- Do the set texts explore hostile attitudes towards immigration?

Exemplar: *The Times*, 9 September 2022 (Eduqas). *The Times* front page (Figure 7.2) exemplifies the approach taken by several newspapers in the wake of the Queen's death, using an archive image as a front-page splash to mourn the passing of the late monarch. The choice of imagery presents the Queen in her youthful prime, a photograph chosen because it represents the stoic innocence of the Queen during her 1953 coronation, a historical milestone and marker for the Queen's 'Life in Service'. The choice of image, and, perhaps, newsprint's wider interest in royal stories might also reinforce Gilroy's observations that the UK media routinely constructs representations of Albionic Englishness via royal family reportage. That archive images like those of *The Times* front cover are used to invoke audience nostalgia, pointing us to an imagined past where perceived social stability and the English Empire brought prestige, certainty and sovereign power. Gilroy tells us that such imagery compensates for the UK's demise as a global power, distracting us from what he calls 'postcolonial melancholia'.

Further set text help is available for a range of products for all exam boards at www.essentialmediatheory.com

Figure 7.2 The Times front page (Friday 9 September 2022). Source: UrbanImages / Alamy Stock Photo.

Table 7.1 Speak Paul Gilroy

Albionic nostalgia	A representation of Englishness that is marked by nostalgia and generally produces a whitewashed version of an idealised/imagined rural England.
Civilisationism	A stark representation of the world in which Western democracy is pitted against extremist others.
Cosmopolitan conviviality	A term that describes real-world multiculturalism and the high levels of racial harmony that mark most people's day-to-day existence. Conversely, the media portrays racial disharmony as the norm.
Postcolonial melancholia	A term used by Gilroy to describe the deep-rooted shame felt because of the loss of the British Empire. That loss is deflected through media nostalgia and a widespread anxiety surrounding British identity.

Table 7.2 Gilroy: ten-minute revision

Concept 1: *racial binaries, otherness and civilisationism*

- Black communities were constructed as an 'other' to white culture and were routinely associated with criminal activity and lawlessness.
- The media reflects civilisationist attitudes through simplistic reportage and the demonisation of Muslims – media products nurture fear and the idea that Muslims and Europeans are incompatible.

Concept 2: *the enduring legacy of the British Empire on English identity*

- A deep-seated postcolonial melancholia infects the media as a result of Britain's diminishing global importance.
- Postcolonial melancholia prompts a nostalgic construction of Englishness.
- Postcolonial melancholy produces a sense of English rootlessness and an anxiety surrounding British identity.

Challenging Gilroy's thinking

Gilroy's concepts work best when exploring media texts that serve a UK audience or with products that originate in the UK. It could also be argued that Gilroy's approach, much like Stuart Hall's representation theory, presents an overly critical view of the UK media, zoning in on the problematic representations constructed by producers in the past.

We might argue that today's mainstream media takes a more complex view of race-relations resulting in rarer instances of the kinds of racial binaries reported in Gilroy's writing. That shift, perhaps, has been driven by audience demands for products that foreground diversity, tilting UK media producers to author savvier representations of different ethnic groups.

(Continued)

Table 7.2 (Continued)

We might also argue that more traditional or right-wing news producers have evolved their approach to target what is ambiguously called 'woke' subjects, critiquing proponents of gender, race and ability diversity as today's 'others' to a civilised traditional Britain. Such stories often name trans or climate activists as swamping influences, citing critical race theory as a corrupting social force.

It could, however, be suggested that the influences of Albionic Englishness are waning. The cold reality of post-Brexit Britain, perhaps, is engineering a collective realisation that sovereign Britain has a diminished global role. The death of Queen Elizabeth II, too, pushes us further away from our Second World War glories, with coverage of the Royal Family tilting towards a soap-opera voyeurism of Harry and Meghan's self-imposed exile in America.

Two named theorists who might challenge Gilroy's thinking

- **David Gauntlett:** would present a far more optimistic picture of the media's capacity to effect change or to enable positive identity construction. He would suggest that the variety of media representations available to contemporary audiences is far greater than that outlined by Gilroy.
- **Henry Jenkins:** again, would present a far more optimistic view regarding the current media landscape than Gilroy's postcolonial assessment – suggesting that new technologies enable audiences to engage in participatory culture and to form online communities that are actively challenging racial injustice.

8   Feminist theory

Liesbet van Zoonen

Central to van Zoonen's feminist concerns is the idea that culture – art, film, literature and the media – plays a crucial role in informing audiences of the gender-based roles that they ought to assume. Her concern in investigating contemporary culture is to isolate the processes that have allowed patriarchal ideals to become the dominant ideological force that shapes gender expectations today – a force, van Zoonen argues, that has resulted in the widespread subjugation of women across society.

Concept 1: the female body as spectacle

'A core element of western patriarchal culture,' van Zoonen writes, 'is the display of woman as spectacle to be looked at, [and] subjected to the gaze of the (male) audience' (van Zoonen, 1994, 87). Using Laura Mulvey's psychoanalytic feminist readings of Hollywood, van Zoonen argues that the dominant representation of femininity in Western media is one that objectifies women. From TV game shows to consumerist advertising, from fashion photography to television drama, the sexualised portrayal of women has had, van Zoonen tells us, a powerful and profound effect on male and female understandings of our gendered identities. The widespread practice of objectifying women, she argues, degrades and dehumanises females, while also giving male viewers, for whom women are sexualised, an unspoken exploitative power that spills into real-world relations.

Objectified representations, van Zoonen tells us, are formed using a range of highly specific creative practices, including:

DOI: 10.4324/9781003361220-8

- **Male gaze invites.** Female sex appeal is traditionally inferred through direct appeals to viewers using fourth wall breaks. Often those appeals are softened by head tilts or other submissive gestures to create female passivity. Use of the male gaze also extends to products that have a predominantly female audience (female lifestyle magazines, female-oriented advertising, etc.) – thus suggesting the extent to which female subordination might be internalised by female consumers.
- **Restricting females to secondary roles.** Women are consistently led or controlled by stronger male presences in media texts. In television they play romantic interest characters or assume supporting roles, while in magazines women are consistently positioned to pursue male-based dependence through advice and relationship-oriented content.
- **Constructing women as passive participants.** Onscreen, females are saved, they do not do the saving. Sports coverage in magazines and news, too, predominantly focuses on male performance, while advertising narratives traditionally position males in more active domestic roles such as DIY or gardening.
- **Framing women differently.** The powerlessness of women in the media is constructed through cinematic tilt downs, low eyeline compositions or soft-focus framing, while costume and makeup conventions further sexualise females for the male gaze.
- **Reinforcing narrow beauty ideals.** Western beauty ideals further restrict female participation in the media to a limited number of roles. Women tend to be excluded beyond a certain age or have to conform to tightly controlled conventions governing physical beauty.

The female spectator

Van Zoonen acknowledges the potential power of female objectification, but also questions the idea that women simply adopt a masculine view of femininity through media consumption. She argues that a variety of audience effects might result:

- **Female identification.** Van Zoonen suggests that female spectators might internalise traditional gender stereotypes that are acted out on screen and that women might come to regard media beauty myths – the narrow definitions of ideal woman-hood presented to us by the media – as something to aspire to.

- **Reading against the grain.** Van Zoonen suggests that the objectification of women by the media does not necessarily lead all women to internalise the male gaze. Audiences, she tells us, 'are no longer … subjected to the vicious intentions of patriarchal power and ideology, but are considered to be active producers of meaning' (van Zoonen, 1994, 149).
- **Female genres.** Van Zoonen acknowledges that some media products communicate narratives, character types or gender-based representations that fall outside of the usual patriarchal mould. She draws particular attention to the theoretical work and research that has sought to examine female media forms such as soap operas and romances – acknowledging that these texts might provoke alternative readership patterns that challenge patriarchy. Romances, for example, often present softened forms of masculinity, generating alternative ideals of how men ought to behave.

Box 8.1   Apply it: detecting female objectification in your set texts

Use the following questions to help you construct exam-ready analysis that examines the scope and impact of female objectification in your set texts.

- Do the texts limit the roles that women play?
- Are women active or passive in the set texts?
- Do the texts objectify women through composition, costuming or acting decisions?

Exemplar: *Kiss of the Vampire* (Eduqas). Hammer Horror's *Kiss of the Vampire* was produced in a period where patriarchal norms were beginning to be challenged – an important contextual influence that helped to determine the design of the marketing poster for the film (Figure 8.1). The lifeless blonde draped over the lead vampire's arms, for example, presents as a passive secondary character, her exposed cleavage and body language producing an objectifying sexual invite for audiences. She is framed, van Zoonen would argue, to satisfy the male gaze, reflecting patriarchal norms of the period that women ought to play a subservient role to male desire in media texts. However, the central female presents in a radically different way: her high eyeline inducing fear on the lead vampire's part, her black hair and provocative sexual power working to produce a femme fatale stereotype. This stronger – and perhaps vilified representation of femininity – potentially reflects wider social fears regarding the rising influence of youth culture in the swinging sixties. The year 1963 signifies the start of the baby boom era, a period of intergenerational flux where younger audiences were beginning to challenge the gender-based norms of the past. The poster's interpretation of female agency as something to be feared reflects, van Zoonen might argue, patriarchal anxieties that male social dominance was being questioned.

Exemplar: *Woman's Realm* (Eduqas). *Woman's Realm* repeatedly reinforces patriarchal ideals throughout the set text pages selected for study. The front cover's demure model offers us a conservative female ideal – a passive set of beauty standards that can only find fulfilment through the child- and domestic-oriented activities outlined in the adjacent sell lines. Those messages are repeated in the accompanying illustration to 'The Sunday Cook' article that depicts an ideal nuclear family of the period, the mother serving her centrally posed business-suited husband with a look of cheery acceptance. Here, van Zoonen might argue that the magazine exemplifies the kinds of representations of passive femininity that so dominated in the 1960s, a set of representations that placed males in central positions of power and that consistently positioned women in secondary roles.

Further set text help is available for a range of products for all exam boards at www.essentialmediatheory.com

Figure 8.1 Kiss of the Vampire (1963). Source: Everett Collection, Inc./ Alamy Stock Photo.

Economic context

Van Zoonen argues that a clear gender imbalance exists in terms of media-oriented production opportunities, with women often sidelined to administrative rather than technical or creative roles. Some pockets of the media are staffed more prominently by women but, van Zoonen argues, even these are symptomatic of wider social gender inequalities. Radio production, for instance, provides an interesting exception to the male-dominated nature of the industry, but only because of its perceived secondary status within the sector.

Similarly, media forms that deal with issues that are connected to traditionally female roles – motherhood or domesticity – tend to be made by women. As a result, children's television, educational programming and consumer journalism tend to be made by female practitioners, while more serious media output – news, political journalism and drama – are dominated by male media makers.

Box 8.2   Research it: who made your set texts?

Research the people who made your set texts and answer the following questions to help you identify the impact of those production teams on the representations created.

Television, music video and radio: who managed the production? Identify writers, directors and producers.

News and magazines: what genders are the journalists who wrote the stories in your set texts? Who are the more senior managers of the set text? Identify editors-in-chief, news editors, section editors and so on, if you can.

- Is there a noticeable gender imbalance in terms of who made your set text products?
- What are the potential effects of that imbalance on story content?

Political context: second- and third-wave feminism

Van Zoonen's writing is emblematic of a wider range of feminist activities that took place during the 1970s and 1980s – a disparate movement of thinkers, academics and social commentators that have been collectively labelled the feminist 'second wave'. Where the feminist 'first wave' fought for the female vote in the early 1900s, second-wave feminism paved the way for equal employment legislation, educational opportunities and cultural empowerment. In highlighting the patriarchal undertones of media objectification and production practice, van Zoonen was hopeful that the media industry would open more opportunities for female participation and female cultural empowerment.

However, the political fervour of the feminist second wave gave way to a generation of female commentators in the late 1990s who viewed the radicalism of their predecessors as too prescriptive. The resulting 'third wave' of feminism advocated a softer feminist agenda, arguing that women themselves were best placed to choose whether they wanted to pursue traditionally female roles or seek career-orientated goals. Third-wave feminism, sometimes dubbed 'girlie' feminism, suggested, too, that women could be both mothers and managers and that the decision to objectify oneself, to use one's body for the purpose of the male gaze, was an individual choice.

Third-wave feminism gathered momentum in the 1990s – the Spice Girls gave us 'girl power' whilst Destiny's Child told their female fans that they could both be 'Independent Women' and beautiful. Third-wave female representations have subsequently become a staple feature of the media, compelling the media landscape to include more powerful female representations, while also tempering those representations with values, ideals and outlooks that are traditionally feminine.

The feminist fourth wave

There is considerable evidence to suggest that the more radical agenda of second-wave feminism is making a comeback, with audiences using social media, primarily, to voice their criticisms regarding media objectification and to agitate for wider social change. The #MeToo movement, for example, responded to the

Harvey Weinstein sex abuse allegations – with women from across the globe using social media to share their own experiences of workplace sexism and male exploitation. Similarly, the online Everyday Sexism Project invited women around the globe to catalogue their experiences of sexism and to call out inappropriate behaviour.

In the media, there is some evidence to suggest that fourth-wave feminism is radicalising female representations. Mainstream music stars like Beyoncé are articulating increasingly politicised pop personas, while TV dramas and sitcoms are giving space to a whole new generation of female writers such as Phoebe Waller-Bridge (*Fleabag* and *Killing Eve*) and Lisa McGee (*Derry Girls*, *Indian Summer* and *Being Human*) – both of whom have been universally applauded for their uncompromising female characters.

Box 8.3 Apply it: third-wave feminism or radical feminism?

It is, perhaps, too simplistic to suggest that contemporary media is wholly saturated with objectified versions of femininity. Use the following questions to help you diagnose which of your set texts challenge traditional gender representations:

- Which of your set texts construct third- or fourth-wave feminist representations of women? In what ways do these representations construct more positive versions of womanhood?
- How do cinematography, *mise en scène*, lighting or other media language features sustain these positive representations?
- Are representations fostered by female media talent? Who are these influential female creatives?

Exemplar: *The Killing* (AQA). Van Zoonen would suggest that the crime drama genre traditionally invokes female powerlessness. Lone wolf male detectives are often positioned as central characters who resolve cases that conventionally feature female-oriented victims. Objectified female support characters might also provide that lone wolf character with a romance story arc, again reinforcing van Zoonen's conclusion that the media routinely authors active/male and passive/female binaries. Third-wave depictions of women, however, have tilted the media landscape towards the creation of more complex female characters. *The Killing*'s Sarah Lund, for example, maintains a traditionally female role through her family-oriented depiction, while negotiating a career-oriented role. Her jumper-clad, middle-aged characterisation, moreover, provides a further contrast to the conventional objectification strategies of the crime genre – offering audiences an alternative to the narrow beauty ideals found elsewhere in the media landscape, and, in doing so, offering us a much-needed example of gender diversity within television fiction.

Exemplar: *Killing Eve* (Eduqas and OCR). Van Zoonen might argue that the spy thriller genre is traditionally dominated by active masculinity. James Bond and Ethan Hunt, for example, lead the charge in their respective franchises, with female characters often providing their alpha male superiority with Proppian Princess rewards via romance story strands. In contrast, *Killing Eve*'s marginalisation of active masculinity provides a subversive set of gender-based representations. Villanelle's sexually charged role, initially perhaps, outlines a third-wave feminist representation, balancing the character's power and control against more traditionally aligned female interests in fashion and style. Yet even here, Waller-Bridge offers us a critique of her third wave's feminist-light villain, revealing that beneath Villanelle's patriarchally controlled Paris existence there lays an emptiness that she seeks to resolve. The drama, too, invokes unlikable male control figures in the form of the creepy, father-like presence of Konstantin, and Eve's traitor boss Frank Haleton – both of whom are rejected by the show's leads so that they can find narrative freedom.

Further set text help is available for a range of products for all exam boards at www.essentialmediatheory.com

Concept 2: masculinity in the media

Van Zoonen tells us that the patriarchal ideologies of Christianity banished the male form to the margins of culture. 'From the Renaissance onwards,' van Zoonen writes, 'the representation of the male nude body became exceptional, always causing uproar and prohibitions' (van Zoonen, 1994, 98). Within patriarchal societies, masculinity is constructed to be the socially dominant gender and, as a result, is more likely to be constructed as an active participant within media texts. Moreover, to allow the male form to be subject to a female gaze is censored or controlled, because, van Zoonen suggests, the act of looking castrates power. In short, to look or to gaze, she argues, is to assume a position of control. To be looked at suggests, conversely, passivity and weakness.

The dominance of men within society thus leads the media to produce radically different presentations of males than it does of females. Of course, van Zoonen acknowledges the presence of sexualised male imagery in the media, and that some of those images objectify the male body, but she also argues that the male form in contemporary Western culture is, by and large, depicted in ways that allow the male subject to retain authority over the spectator. Van Zoonen highlights the following features and processes associated with male representation by the media:

- **The male body is predominantly celebrated through sports imagery.** Sports photography produces representations of masculinity that are designed to connote strength and power, emphasising movement and skill to reinforce a sense of male dominance over the reader. Perfume adverts, male fashion and so on thus draw upon sports personalities to model products – thus allowing male spectatorship to proceed without erotic objectification.
- **Male eroticisation is romanticised.** Male objectification for female audiences exists, van Zoonen tells us, but is rarely expressed in mainstream forms. When such imagery is produced, moreover, the subversive threat of male eroticisation is often limited by contextualising the imagery within a romantic as opposed to a sexual setting. In women's lifestyle magazines, for example, men are described in terms of their

potential as relationship partners rather than as objects of sexual consumption.

- **The active gaze.** Van Zoonen argues that male subjects rarely construct invitational poses. The male gaze, if directed at the viewer at all, is framed by harder body language, offering confrontation or strength rather than passivity. Masculine depictions, too, avoid objectification by directing the subject's gaze to the edge of the frame, or directing it upwards in a show of spiritual strength.
- **Strength not weakness.** Van Zoonen draws attention to the ways in which masculine ideals in media imagery are associated with bodily strength. 'The male pin-up's lack of passivity is one of his important features,' she writes, while 'various signs of activity' (van Zoonen, 1994, 101) are encoded into male imagery to further neutralise any potential for eroticisation.

Box 8.4   Apply it: are masculine ideals constructed by your set texts?

Use the following questions to construct exam-ready analysis that considers the impact of masculine representations created by set texts.

- How are the male characters within your television, video game and music-based set texts constructed? Do they conform to van Zoonen's assertion that males are normally encoded as active?
- In what ways do *mise en scène*, composition and lighting sustain the representational effects of set texts?
- How significant is sports-related imagery of males in newspaper/magazine set texts?
- Do any of your set texts construct a subversive version of masculinity? How?

Exemplar: *GQ* (AQA). *GQ*'s photographic treatment of men provides evidence to support van Zoonen's argument that male representational processes are radically different from those applied to women. The dynamic fourth wall break cover shot of Robert Pattinson, for example, constructs a hard-edged portrait of the actor. Pattinson is caught in a red-eyed growl, his chains and costuming an intertextual reference to the pouting derision of punk icons like The Sex Pistols. Pattinson, as such, is given agency, meeting the viewer's gaze with a confrontational riposte rather than the invitational poses that are conventionally applied to female cover stars. Similarly, the Jonathan Bailey profile uses the returned gaze coupled with tilt to invest the *Bridgerton* star with power, or, in more whimsical shots, is directed to stare out towards the photographic framing, couching the star in a mystical contemplative pose. Bailey, as such resists the spectator's gaze, returning it or redirecting it to the edge of the frame – a set of photographic strategies, van Zoonen tells us, that are readily applied to male subjects, strategies that reinforce masculine and patriarchal ideals.

Further set text help is available for a range of products for all exam boards at www.essentialmediatheory.com

Table 8.1 Speak Liesbet van Zoonen

Active/passive representations	Media products, van Zoonen suggests, encode women to be passive and males to be active within media imagery. Depictions that construct gender in this way reinforce male social dominance.
Male gaze	A stylised depiction of women that invites viewers to take erotic pleasure while viewing the female form. The female gaze is constructed through invitational poses and passive body language.
Objectification	An image that demeans or degrades its subject.
Patriarchy	A society in which males exercise more power than females.
Subversive representation	A media representation that challenges or undermines an idea or set of ideas that are widely held within society.

Table 8.2 Van Zoonen: ten-minute revision

Concept 1: *the female body as spectacle*

- The roles that females are expected to play within society vary enormously across different cultures and historical periods.
- The dominant representational mode in Western culture positions women as an erotic spectacle.
- Second-wave feminism challenged the dominance of men in society, lobbying for equal rights in the workplace, in education and in the home.
- Third-wave feminists have reasserted the right of women to occupy traditional female roles.
- Fourth-wave feminists continue to challenge male privilege using both mass media and social media forms to draw attention to female marginalisation.

Concept 2: *masculinity in the media*

- Masculine depictions are not subject to the same objectification processes as females.
- Male social dominance is reinforced using active representations of masculinity.

Challenging van Zoonen's thinking

Van Zoonen acknowledges that audiences don't necessarily internalise any patriarchal ideals constructed by the media, and that both males and female consumers are active decoders of products. We might also argue that female producers are no longer restricted to those areas of media production that are considered secondary (radio production, for example) or with media forms associated with more traditional female subject matter (consumer affairs, education, health).

As such, female-driven concerns are increasingly being voiced in television drama, news output and film production. Reuter's Institute, for example, estimates that women in 2023 accounted for 40% of journalists in the 240 major news brands it surveyed, up from just 21% in 2022 – an encouraging sign that the male stranglehold on the news media market is finally diminishing.

Two named theorists who might challenge van Zoonen's thinking

- **David Gauntlett:** would argue that contemporary media products, both online and mass media oriented, offer audiences a much wider diversity of gender-based identities than is suggested by van Zoonen. This enables audiences to shape their own identities and to resist the ideological pull of patriarchy.
- **Judith Butler:** would agree with much of van Zoonen's thinking but would suggest further that the use of gender-based labels like 'male' and 'female' mask the complex nature of sexuality. She would also argue that individuals have resisted those conventional labels by engaging in 'gender trouble'.

9   Intersectionality

bell hooks

hooks' writing drew attention to the silence of commentators and academics alike regarding the Black female experience. She contextualises that silence against the wider backdrop of cultural change in America, prompting some awkward questions as to how and why Black femininity has been so readily sidelined.

The Black civil rights movement of the 1960s, for example, paved the way for Black male equality, but, for hooks, neglected to explore the experience of ordinary Black women. Similarly, the feminist movement of the 1960s gave women – white women – the power to strive for gender equality in the workplace and across society, but again the Black female experience was left undiscussed. In response, hooks places Black femininity centre stage, seeking in the first instance to explain why Black women were so readily silenced during these two crucial emancipatory moments, while also offering up a call to action to communities of all colours and genders across the globe: a political plea to women and men of all ethnicities and nationalities to realise that oppression, in all its forms, is driven by a set of historically entrenched social and cultural conditions.

Concept 1: interconnected oppression

The legacy of slavery

hooks' passionate and highly emotive analysis of the airbrushing of the Black female experience is rooted in a historical evaluation of Black femininity within the American slave system. She argues that contemporary Black female representations – over-sexed Black female stereotypes and the Black 'mammy' – are the indirect result

DOI: 10.4324/9781003361220-9

of the horrific abuse enacted on Black women by their white slave masters.

Rape and sexual abuse were a routine feature of female slave life on the plantations in America, with girls as young as thirteen subject to endemic sexual violence. Sadistic floggings were delivered for any number of minor misdemeanours: for not working hard enough, for burning breakfast or, more disturbingly, if those Black slave women and girls tried to resist the sexual advances of their white overseers. Black slave women, hooks tells us, were regarded as little more than a physical commodity, used, she further explains, to breed slave children and to expand the unpaid workforces who maintained the American plantations.

Significantly, hooks argues, the mistreatment of Black women was sanctioned, and sometimes encouraged, by the wives of plantation owners. The sexual violence perpetrated on Black slaves was ignored because it often deflected unwanted attention away from plantation wives themselves. The religious ideals of the white plantation wives, too, fostered sexual purity as a female idea. As such, the Black women who toiled bare breasted in cotton fields were easily disregarded as unchristian and heathen by the white plantation wives. Black females were, accordingly, considered to be fallen versions of womanhood, naturally over-sexed, and, as such, considered complicit or culpable when plantation husbands raped them.

The contemporary Black female experience

And so begins, hooks argues, a cultural process that associates Black femininity with overly sexualised stereotypes. Black women, when they do appear in cultural products, hooks tells us, often feature as prostitutes or repulsive characters who prey upon weak white masculinity. 'One has only to look at American television,' hooks writes, 'to learn the way in which Black women are perceived in American society – the predominant image is that of the "fallen" woman, the whore, the slut, the prostitute' (hooks, 1982, 52).

Perversely, the nineteenth-century white abolitionists who campaigned to end slavery echoed the same sentiment. The abused position of Black women was well known, but their experiences were quietly sidelined as a result of the middle-class abolitionists' reluctance to discuss sexual abuse in public. Moreover, hooks suggests, the hierarchical position of Black women within the slave system and their subservience to all others (including the white wives of plantation owners) made them a less worthy cause. Much of that plantation-based social structure persists today, hooks argues, with white males ascending to economic, social and political positions of power, while beneath them, white females, then Black males and finally Black women fight for the scraps.

White feminism as covertly/overtly racist

Black women, hooks tells us, sought to escape their lowly social positions and the stigma of over-sexualisation by constructing outlooks that mirrored the feminised conservative ideals of their white counterparts. In the 1950s, Black women, accordingly, embraced motherhood and domesticity and were subsequently reluctant, hooks tells us, to join the white-dominated feminist movement of the 1960s and 1970s because they had so embraced these conservative female ideals.

hooks further argues that white feminism itself was equally complicit in omitting Black women from women's liberation politics. The suffrage movements of the 1920s, for example, reflected white supremacist ideologies by openly refusing to admit Black women as suffrage members; feminist writers in the 1960s and 1970s similarly sidelined the female Black experience, jettisoning racial concerns because they were considered too controversial and might have derailed any emancipatory progress that could be negotiated with white male power brokers. Thus, while white feminism might have suggested that it was advancing the cause of all women, in reality those writers who preached equality knew nothing, nor did they attempt to discover anything, about the experiences of Black American women.

Absent representations

hooks suggests that the legacy of Black female cultural subordination has resulted in their wholesale absence from mainstream media. Magazine beauty ideals, on the whole, are constructed to be white, while in television, advertising and drama, she argues, the few tokenistic Black representations who are allowed to break through are dominated by male actors. As a result, Black masculinity, she suggests, has come to represent the Black community as a whole.

That domination is reflected even today, with the 2022 University of California, Los Angeles (UCLA) diversity report providing concrete evidence of the continued marginalisation of Black female roles in American television. Only 81 Black male actors, UCLA claim, played a top scripted role in US shows broadcast during 2020/2021. Conversely, 218 lead roles were played by white males and 176 by white women. The number of Black female actors playing top roles was just 58 (UCLA, 2022).

Negative Black female stereotypes

The historical mistreatment of Black women has informed a range of media stereotypes of Black femininity. hooks outlines the following representations that persist in contemporary cultural products:

- **Jezebels.** Over-sexualised representations of Black femininity have significantly shaped perceptions of Black women since slavery. They remain common in hip-hop music wherein Black women are consistently served up as sexualised side-dressing for Black male artists. The widescale presence of the Jezebel in Black male music videos, moreover, leads hooks to argue that this stereotype has been internalised by Black women themselves.
- **Aunt Jemimas.** Black women have always been associated with domestic service – their role as house slaves on the plantations and their subsequent restriction to domestic roles in America during the 1950s has helped build the Black mammy stereotype. Aunt Jemimas are overweight asexual representations of Black femininity, often depicted as maids or servants who loyally serve their white employers without complaint.
- **Sapphires.** The sapphire stereotype is a comedic depiction of Black women and is a common staple of talk shows and reality television output. Sapphires usually appear as angry mothers who cannot control their emotions, producing a vilified representation of Black women who have power. The sapphire also critiques Black women who do not conform to the passivity of the mammy stereotype.

Box 9.1 Apply it: absent Black femininity in your set texts

Set texts that lack female Black representation can be linked to bell hooks' ideas very quickly. Use these questions to help you diagnose the effects of those absences:

- Which of your set texts contain no representations of Black femininity?
- Does that absence suggest that Black women are excluded or marginalised? Does that absence reinforce the 'otherness' of Black femininity?
- Are Black females excluded at the expense of Black male counterparts?
- Does the exclusion of Black women symbolise their lack of power?

Exemplar: *Kiss of the Vampire* (Eduqas) and *Score* (AQA). Both posters articulate the dominance of white masculinity over white femininity via layout and proxemics. In *Kiss of the Vampire*, the blonde damsel in distress is figuratively subordinated by the lead male, while active femininity is villainised in the form of the central femme fatale. In the 1967 advert for *Score*, the objectification of white femininity is more explicit – a crowd of scantily clad women clamouring for the attention of the all-powerful white colonial male is a photographic representation of late 1960s patriarchy. The total absence, moreover, of any Black representations in either poster is more problematic. The invisibility of Black femininity in advertising of the period, bell hooks might argue, mirrors the marginalisation of Black women within society at the time. She further tells us that absent representations allowed white femininity to represent all female beauty ideals, constructing a powerful message that excluded Black women from public discourse.

Further set text help is available for a range of products for all exam boards at www.essentialmediatheory.com

Box 9.2   Apply it: analyse set texts in terms of their potential use of Black female stereotypes

Some set texts might inadvertently offer the stereotypes highlighted previously. Use the following questions to help you locate examples and analysis that you can use in your exam.

- What effect does the stereotype have on Black or white audiences?
- Does the stereotype construct an internalised Black identity?
- Is the stereotype typical of the genre in which it appears?
- How does the stereotype contrast with other representations constructed by texts made by the same or similar producers?

Exemplar: *Formation*, Beyoncé (Eduqas). Beyoncé's career is founded, many would argue, on her willingness to use the Black female Jezebel stereotype. The performances offered within much of her work is, in bell hooks' view at least, highly symptomatic of the disempowering over-sexualised female roles that have been constructed for Black women throughout our recent cultural history. *Formation* repeats much of the Jezebel formula, in which corseted troupes of women parade their bodies in sexually explicit dance sequences, inviting audiences to view Black women as sexually available and highly promiscuous.

Further set text help is available for a range of products for all exam boards at www.essentialmediatheory.com

Concept 2: hooks' call to action

Intersectionality as a political and cultural tool

'To me,' hooks writes,

> feminism is not simply a struggle to end male chauvinism … it is a commitment to eradicating the ideology of domination that

permeates Western culture on various levels – sex, race, and class, to name a few – and a commitment to reorganising U.S. society so that the self-development of people can take precedence over imperialism, economic expansion and material desires.

(hooks, 1982, 194)

hooks' concerns are historically and analytically informed, but to pigeonhole her as an ivory tower academic whose sole concern is to relate the history of the Black female experience misses much of the political thrust of her writing. Indeed, hooks' analysis views all forms of oppression – sexism, racism and class-based subjugation – as symptomatic of the middle-class, white male-dominated world we live in. The subjugation of these oppressed groups, she tells us, is interconnected. Indeed, the intersectionalist thinkers who have followed hooks' lead have similarly argued that homophobia, transphobia and disability-based oppressions are similarly affected as a result of white male oppression.

It is important to understand that hooks' intersectionalist thinking is not just a tool for analysing or describing the world in which we live. Yes, intersectionality points accusingly to problematic media representations, but it is also a political tool – a cultural instrument that seeks to nurture products that actively challenge the many forms of oppression that white male patriarchy produces. In this sense, we can describe some products as 'intersectional media' in that they are knowingly designed to draw attention to the effects of white male power. Intersectional media is constructed to:

- **Explore the interlocking nature of oppression.** Intersectional products explore the connections that exist between different forms of oppression, expressing, for example, how racism and sexism share the same root causes or have similar effects.
- **Highlight white male privilege.** Intersectionality seeks to critique the mechanisms that reinforce white male hegemony.
- **Outline economic oppression.** An increasing number of intersectional media products draw attention to the huge wealth gap that exists between privileged white groups and the rest of society; moreover, they draw attention to the privileges that economic power generates for those groups.
- **Give a voice to invisible social groups.** Intersectional media fills the gaps that absent representations create – telling the

stories and giving weight to the experiences of groups who are 'other' to white male patriarchy.
• **Celebrate otherness.** Intersectional media seeks to construct positive as well as critical effects.

Box 9.3   Discuss it: has intersectional thinking gone mainstream?

• In what ways has racism become a mainstream issue? In what ways have contemporary media producers focused more attention on the Black female experience in recent years?
• What other movements or media products can you name that have tried to shed light on the abuse of power by white males?
• What evidence is there to suggest that white hegemony is still the dominant force in society?

Box 9.4   Know it: #BlackLivesMatter – intersectionality in action

The Black Lives Matter (BLM) movement formed in response to the acquittal of George Zimmerman after he fatally shot Trayvon Martin, an unarmed Black 17-year-old youth; Zimmerman wrongly thought Martin was about to commit a criminal offence. The verdict compounded accusations that the American justice system was institutionally racist. The social media hashtag #BlackLivesMatter subsequently served as a rallying call for state-wide protests following Zimmerman's trial, helping BLM to become a global movement.

Importantly, BLM is deliberately shaped by intersectionalist values in that it exists to provides a space for Black women and Black trans women to express their political voice. Yet the aims of the BLM movement are not simply limited to agitating on behalf of the Black female/queer community. 'We work vigorously for freedom and justice for Black people,' BLM writes, 'and, by extension, all people' (Black Lives

Matter, 2019). The BLM movement and intersectionalist thinking has undoubtedly shaped the cultural output of the media industry over the last five years, having found support from a host of global megastars including Beyoncé and Jay Z.

Box 9.5   Apply it: diagnose set texts that deliberately provide intersectionalist commentary

Set texts across the exam boards incorporate intersectionalist viewpoints. Locating those texts and finding moments that articulate those views can help you gain premium marks in representation, institution or audience-based questions. Use the following to help you produce relevant analysis:

- In what ways do set texts provide a space to celebrate marginalised identities?
- In what ways do set texts draw attention to the social or economic inequalities experienced by marginalised groups?
- In what ways do set texts suggest that those inequalities are shared across different social groups?
- In what ways do set texts call out white male privilege?

Exemplar 1: Sufjan Stevens, *Sugar* (OCR). The Black female presence in Sufjan Steven's *Sugar* provides a powerful intersectionalist subtext, one that gives voice to the Black female experience of everyday family life in America. The video highlights the destructive bent of female domesticity – an ideal, bell hooks argues, that was readily internalised by Black women from the 1960s onwards as a means to neutralise the sexualised stereotypes that were routinely used to depict Black women. The video, however, also imbues Black femininity with a sense of agency, the mother leading the charge to escape the confines and the family's limited world to find hope in the open space of the natural landscape at the end of the narrative. In their escape, the family finally connects with the maternal forces of nature, a liberating presence that the video foregrounds via the fruit symbolism of the mother's cooking. Black femininity is accordingly represented as active, dynamic and nurturing.

Exemplar 2: Beyoncé, *Formation* **(Eduqas).** Beyoncé might provide us with several moments that reflect a white power affirming jezebel stereotype, yet the context of further imagery suggests that those representations are deliberately ironic. *Formation* knowingly references the #BlackLivesMatter movement through the 'stop shooting us' graffiti reference towards the end of the product. The metaphor of the drowning police car similarly critiques the response of the American government during the Hurricane Katrina emergency, pointing an accusatory finger at the treatment of the mostly Black New Orleans residents during the natural emergency. The text not only draws attention to the economic disparities and institutionalised racism of America, but also provides a stream of high key, tilt up images of a diverse range of Black female, Black queer and Black male identities. The video, as such, provokes an intersectionalist ideology – simultaneously critiquing the legacy of Black slavery while celebrating those identities that mainstream American culture marginalises, and, in doing so, asks active audiences to question the overly sexualised imagery at the start of the video. In this sense the video affirms bell hooks' intersectional political intentions by calling out the effects of white male privilege.

Further set text help is available for a range of products for all exam boards at www.essentialmediatheory.com

Table 9.1 Speak bell hooks

Intersectional media	Media products that deliberately include or allude to an intersectional viewpoint.
Intersectionality	The exploration of oppression (sexism, racism, homophobia) as having an interconnected or underlying set of causes.
Otherness	hooks suggests that those who are not white or male are 'others' and, as such, are subject to the various oppressive practices of white masculinity.

Table 9.2 hooks: ten-minute revision

Concept 1: *interconnected oppression*

- Representations of Black women (and men) have been shaped by historical forces.
- Feminist movements of the twentieth century were largely dominated by a white viewpoint.
- A social hierarchy exists that places white men at the top followed by white women, male ethnic minorities, and, lastly, female ethnic minorities.
- Oppression of minority groups (racism, sexism, ableism, homophobia) is a construct of a white male-dominated social hierarchy.
- A lack of Black female power results in absent representations and a range of negative stereotypes that some Black women have internalised.

Concept 2: *from evaluation to action, bell hooks' call to action*

- hooks' intersectional work does not just provide us with an analytical tool, but also prompts media producers to fashion their products in ways that draw attention to social inequality.
- Intersectional media foregrounds the interconnected nature of inequality.
- Intersectional media celebrates social diversity and gives voice to social groups that have been marginalised by white male power.

Challenging hooks' thinking

---

hooks provides us with a set of ideas that are particularly useful when exploring media products made in the USA, her work is less useful when assessing the representational impact and construction of UK-produced texts whose historical, cultural and social contexts are radically different. Other commentators critique the simplicity of hooks' gender-racial hierarchy, questioning whether white masculinity ought to be identified as a root cause of the social inequalities she identifies.

Some criticism, too, has been levelled at intersectional media representations, pointing out that they can associate minority social groups with disempowering victim stereotypes, or, more contentiously, that they demonise white masculinity, compounding the social inequalities experienced by working-class white men and boys, in particular.

Two named theorists who might challenge hooks' thinking

- **Paul Gilroy:** would not necessarily challenge hooks, but his work provides a more UK-specific framework for evaluating the representation of Black people. His analysis highlights the legacy effects of Empire on our notions of ethnicity and national identity.
- **Henry Jenkins:** again, he would not challenge hooks directly, but would suggest that contemporary media products, through participatory culture, can circumvent established media power. Indeed, the online activism of #BlackLivesMatter provides a brilliant example of the power of participatory culture.

10 Gender as performance
Judith Butler

Butler's theoretical work is concerned with unearthing the processes, both cultural and psychological, that shape our identities. She tests orthodox explanations of gender, principally those of the theoretical heavyweights Claude Lévi-Strauss, Sigmund Freud and Jacques Lacan. Her critique of those thinkers is concerned, to a large degree, with the various explanations they give to describe the development of non-heterosexual gendered identities.

Butler concludes that masculinity and femininity are not naturally given states, but instead are maintained by the everyday acts that individuals perform. Our gendered identities, she argues, are not established at birth, nor are they formed in childhood or adolescence, but are instead realised through a continuous performance of gendered behaviour. The media, more importantly, plays a vital role in providing us with a set of gender-based templates that we use to inform those performances. The dominance of heterosexual representations across media forms, Butler further argues, helps to maintain traditional male and female identities as a social norm.

Concept 1: gendered identities are constructed through repetition and ritual

Butler draws attention to Lévi-Strauss' anthropological work on cultural myths, particularly those aspects that deal with incest and sex-based taboos. She critiques his conclusions that myths tend to reinforce male power as the norm because males are the more naturally dominant gender. She also hangs an important question mark over Strauss' arguments that the absence of homosexuality within mythic stories provides evidence that our natural sexual inclinations are heterosexually oriented.

DOI: 10.4324/9781003361220-10

Butler, too, was interested in the work of the influential psychologist Jacques Lacan, who, she tells us, similarly defined male and female genders using a binary straitjacket. Lacan argued that our gendered identities are fixed when we emerge from the dormant state of early infancy, when we realise that we are independent from the world around us. The discovery of the phallus by boys during this transition, Lacan suggests, prompts a symbolic awakening – a moment when males realise that they effect sexual power. That awakening, he further argues, translates into masculine social power. Female infants, conversely, are defined through the symbolic discovery that they are phallus free and the subsequent realisation that they are castrated and socially powerless.

To Lacan, and perhaps comically to us, the realisation of having, or not having, a penis naturally creates the patriarchal social structures in which we live. Importantly, for Butler at least, Lacan further defined homosexuality as an aberration of those symbolic awakenings, or that non-heteronormative identities were anomalies imprinted on individuals as a result of heterosexual disappointment during formative sexual encounters.

Butler also examines the work of Sigmund Freud who similarly explains same-sex affection as a form of melancholia, formed by boys through an unnatural rejection of the mother during the Oedipal phase, or, for girls, as an over-identification with the mother figure during the Electra stage (see Box 10.1 for further explanation). Freud suggests that these key moments in infancy inform lifelong behaviours and, moreover, that homosexuality produces a mental aberration as a result: a kind of depressive melancholia that forms because of the realisation by gay individuals that conventional heterosexual satisfactions will never be realised.

Butler's gender revolution

Butler offers a complex and devastating critique of these three cornerstones of twentieth-century thinking. Her principal objections run as follows:

- **Male and female identities are not naturally configured.** Butler's critique of Lévi-Strauss points to the array of gender-based identities that exist in addition to heterosexuality. Butler tells us that these non-heterosexual identities, and the relationships that non-binary individuals form, are built on desires that are just as valid as those experienced by heterosexuals. Their exclusion from myths and other cultural products reflects, Butler infers, the marginalisation of these groups in society.

- **Gender does not exist inside the body.** Butler critiques the notion that gender – whatever it is – is stored within the body as if it were something akin to a soul. Freud's assertion that our sexual identities are internalised during the Oedipal phase is illusory – our gendered identities, Butler argues, are realised through our desires, sexual contacts and physical expressions of love. Butler argues that our gendered identities are not fixed objects, but that they form because of our behaviours.
- **Gender is not solely determined by primary experiences during childhood.** For Butler, the Lacanian and Freudian idea that our gendered identities are fixed during infancy is a myth that serves to reinforce heterosexual ideals. Those ideals aren't natural states, they are social constructs. Our genders, Butler further argues, are far less stable than Freud or Lacan suggest – that we continuously form and reform our sexual identities throughout our lives.

Box 10.1   Help box: what is the Oedipus/Electra complex?

Freud argued that children become very aware of their genitalia at the age of three – this stage leads to the development of intense emotional attraction to the parent of the opposite sex and to feelings of jealousy towards the parent of their own sex. Put more simply, boys (through the Oedipus complex) fall in love with their mothers and hate their fathers, while girls (via the Electra complex) become attached to their fathers and develop intense jealousy of their mothers.

For boys, the intense rivalry for their mother's affection leads to an internalised fear that their fathers will castrate them as punishment. Boys, Freud suggests, must reposition their fathers as role models to avoid being emasculated, and, in copying their father's masculine behaviour, they assume a male identity. Girls, conversely, will eventually realign their love for their mothers (thus creating their female identity) but will also retain their love for father figures.

Box 10.2 Discuss it: what are the problems with the arguments used by Lévi-Strauss, Lacan and Freud to explain how we construct our gendered identities?

Claude Lévi-Strauss

- What criticisms could be made of the idea that our genders are fixed by nature? What other factors might contribute to the creation of our sexualities or gender-based notions?
- If our genders are not naturally fixed, why do so many cultural stories construct heterosexuality as the norm? Can you identify any myths or fairy tales in which homosexuality even features?

Jacques Lacan

- Does the discovery of a penis really invest men with a sense of internal power?
- Lacan argues that homosexual desires form because of heterosexual disappointments – does this theory describe a natural process? Is this idea formed, perhaps, because of his own heterosexual vantage point?

Sigmund Freud

- Can we really explain adult same-sex sexual attraction as the result of rejecting or over-identifying with our parents at a very early age?
- In what ways is Freud's description of homosexuality as 'melancholic' problematic?

Butler's alternative gender model

Butler puts forward an alternative view of our gendered identities that can be summed up as follows:

- **Our genders are culturally rather than naturally formed.** Butler tells us that our biological anatomies do not determine our genders. The normalisation of heterosexuality is established, she further argues, because of long-standing social rituals that orientate us towards traditional male and female roles.

- **Our genders are not stable but are constructed through repeated actions.** Rituals and performative actions constantly reinforce our identities: the act of wearing makeup, for instance, or dressing in female or male clothing fosters an illusion that we have a seamless and permanent male or female identity. Similarly, our mannerisms and behaviours work as learned micro-performances that continuously signal our gendered identity to ourselves and to others. Importantly, those gender-based cues can be learned or imitated from media products.

Concept 2: gender subversion and gendered hierarchies

Butler might argue that our identities are an open story, but she also acknowledges that heterosexuality is the dominant identity mode in Western culture. To maintain an identity that falls outside of the heterosexual norm in our society is, she suggests, a subversive act that takes a great deal of effort to maintain. Subversion is difficult Butler argues, painful even, because heteronormative ideals are so deeply entrenched within the fabric of language and other cultural practices.

Box 10.3   Challenge it: challenging heteronormativity is painful

Butler argues that it is incredibly difficult or painful to assume a non-heteronormative identity. Media narratives mirror this assertion, often constructing gay characters who must seek acceptance from friends and family or who have to confront homophobic intolerance.

- Can you name any media products that use storylines that reinforce the idea that gender subversion is difficult?

- Are non-heteronormative representations still as subversive as Butler argued in the 1990s?
- Can you think of any media products that offer us more positive or normalised representations of non-heteronormativity?
- In what ways do the target audiences of products affect gender representation? Are subversive representations more prevalent in products aimed at specific demographic groups? Does the age, class or gender of audiences affect non-heteronormative representations?

Gender subjugation

Butler argues that non-heterosexual identities – male homosexuality, lesbianism, transgender identifications – are socially suppressed in favour of heteronormativity. Heteronormativity privileges traditional male and female identities while also promoting heterosexuality as a default relationship model. The subjugation of identities that fall outside of conventional heteronormativity, Butler tells us, can be affected through physical coercion: gay men, for instance, can be compelled to attend conversion therapy by concerned family members. In extreme cases, punitive physical deterrents can be deployed to prohibit same-sex relationships – in Somalia, for example, the death penalty is used as a deterrent for homosexuality.

More importantly, heteronormativity and male patriarchy are reinforced through cultural practices that position non-heterosexuality and female empowerment as a social taboo. Butler draws our attention to the following media processes that commonly marginalise female power and LGBTQ+ groups:

- **Absent representation.** The sheer lack of non-heteronormative representations in the media helps to reinforce heterosexuality as the prevailing social norm. In 2022/3, for example, analysis by the Gay and Lesbian Alliance Against Defamation (GLAAD) located only 596 LGBTQ+ characters in total across all US broadcast, cable and streamed scripted originals, a decrease of 41 characters from the previous year. More worryingly, GLAAD projects that 175 of those characters will not return in 2023/4 due to series cancellations and character culls. Only 27 of the 596 LGBTQ+ total were categorised as transgender representations. Butler would argue that reduced levels of LGBTQ+ representation recorded here allow straight relationships to take centre stage as a behavioural norm. Interestingly, 359 of the LGBTQ+ tally were disproportionately found in products made by streaming providers (Apple TV+, Amazon Prime, Disney+, HBO Max, Hulu, Netflix, Paramount+ and Peacock).

- **Abjected representations.** Butler acknowledges the theoretical work of Julia Kristeva (see Box 10.4) in suggesting that heterosexuality and male power are reinforced through the suggestion that alternatives to those identities are disturbing, repellent or unnatural. Narratives, for instance, that focus on sex change operations create physical abjection of the trans community through the presentation of graphic surgical procedures. Depictions that focus on castration and so on have a deeply unsettling effect.

- **Parodic representations.** Media presentations of homosexuality often use exaggerated masculine or feminine behaviours in a comedic way, using, for example, overtly camp presentations of gay men. Parodic characterisations of this nature produce questionable humour while reinforcing the idea that homosexuality is an aberration. Yet, for Butler, parodic representations also create what she calls 'gender trouble' and draw audience attention to the performative nature of gender per se. The drag queen, for example, who represents anatomical masculinity yet performs a traditionally feminine role reveals to the audience a sense that all our identities might similarly be constructed or, in Butler's words, that 'the inner truth of gender is a fabrication' (Butler, 2007, 186).

Box 10.4   Help box: Julia Kristeva and female abjection in film

Film theorist Julia Kristeva famously argued that horror films rely on a range of well-worn strategies that repulse audiences by using female-oriented depictions that are intended to be disturbing or unsettling. Films like *Carrie* or *Teeth*, for example, create their horror effects by referencing and distorting female bodily functions (menstruation, birth or female sexuality). For Kristeva, the cultural effect of such depictions is to reinforce the idea that the female body is somehow taboo or needs to be hidden from public view, which, as a result, consolidates patriarchal power.

Box 10.5 Discuss it: how does the media present gender subversion?

Absent representations analysis

- How many of your set texts contain prominent LGBTQ+ representations?
- Why do you think that LGBTQ+ representations are missing from media products?
- Why do you think streaming services lead the field in terms of including characters that are gender diverse? Could this be related to the target audience of Netflix?

Hierarchical subjugations

- Can you think of any mainstream products, including your set texts, that have constructed problematic LGBTQ+ representations? In what ways are these portrayals negative?
- Can you think of any products that deliver abjectified LGBTQ+ representations?
- Can you think of any products that construct comedic or parodic characters who are non-heteronormative?

Box 10.6   Apply it: using Judith Butler to explore representation effects in set texts

Use the following questions to help you find moments in your set texts that can be explained or interpreted using Butler's ideas:

Concept 1: gender as performance
- Are there moments in the text in which characters openly perform a gender-based identity?
- Do the set texts give advice to their audience on how they might perform their genders?
- How do magazine set texts help their readers/viewers adopt traditional male or female roles?
- Do the set texts provide alternative models of gender or sexuality?

Concept 2: reinforcing hierarchical binarisms
- Are the set texts dominated by heteronormative representations? Are lead characters presented within conventional family units? Do lead characters follow heteronormative love interests?
- Does the set text give space to marginalised or non-binary identities? How much space is given to these moments? What is the effect of any absent representations?
- Do the set texts present marginalised identities in a way that creates abjection?
- Do the set texts offer moments that subvert traditional heteronormative expectations? Are these moments constructed as painful or difficult? In what way do those representations reinforce hierarchical binaries?

Exemplar 1: *Mail Online* (OCR). The *Mail Online* routinely reports on stories that contain trans content strands, identifying, for example, trans victims of crime, criminal cases where the perpetrator is named as transgender, trans teen suicides, and, more recently, detransitioning stories of people who regretted the surgeries they undertook during their gender transition journey. Butler might argue that victim-based narratives might produce readings of non-heteronormativity as a singularly painful or tragic experience, representations that suggest that maintaining a subversive gender-identity comes at great cost or risk. Singling out criminal cases that involve trans perpetrators, conversely, outlines non-heteronormativity as abjectifying – potentially associating the trans community with criminality or anti-social behaviour. The *Mail* headline on 2 August 2023, 'Jealous transgender woman murdered three sex workers', is typical of the newspaper's output in this regard, foregrounding the 'trans' identity of a 2017 US case in ways that could lead readers to asociate criminality and gender transitioning as mutually connected factors.

Exemplar 2: *Killing Eve* (Eduqas and OCR). *Killing Eve* offers audiences a series of representational effects that Butler might find interesting. Eve's relationship, for example, with Villanelle, finally consummated in season 3, is prefigured by a cat-and-mouse tease of longing looks, confessional intimacy and smouldering sexual attraction. The two central characters' subversion of heteronormative expectations is hinted at from the outset, their first encounter in episode 1 producing Villanelle's double take of Eve in the hospital toilet mirror. The scene, problematically perhaps, queer codes the spy villain as an uncivilised other, but also sows the seeds for Eve's romantic repositioning as her gay love interest, helping to assert a Butler-like subtext that gender is fluid or changeable rather than a fixed or natural state.

Further set text help is available for a range of products for all exam boards at www.essentialmediatheory.com

Table 10.1 Speak Judith Butler

Abjection	The process of constructing an object or person as repulsive. Abjection is used, Butler infers, to suggest that non-heteronormative identities are unnatural.
Compulsory heterosexuality	A phrase used by Butler to describe the deeply entrenched social expectation that we assume male/female identities and that we engage in heterosexual relationships.
Gender/sex	Butler differentiates between gender and sex. Gender, she argues, is the socially constructed identity that we assume, while sex refers to the body we are born with.
Gender trouble	A representation or identity that falls outside of heteronormativity. Gender trouble might be inferred through asexuality, bisexuality, homosexuality, lesbianism, pansexuality, transgenderism or transvestitism. Butler suggests that the performance of gender trouble is a difficult and sometimes painful process.
Gender performance	The repeating of acts or rituals that continuously define our gender. Butler argues that our gender is not innate but constructed through the continuous repetition of micro-rituals.
Gender subversion	A representational process that undermines heteronormativity.
Heteronormativity	The dominance of heterosexuality as a normal or preferred identity – usually accompanied by a view that gender is binary (either male or female).
Parodic representation	An imitative gender representation usually constructed using exaggeration or dissonance. Drag queens are parodic in that they offer us a highly exaggerated version of femininity. Parodic representations can be used to subjugate marginalised identities, but they also simultaneously sketch the performative nature of gender for all of us and are therefore subtly subversive.

Table 10.2 Butler: ten-minute revision

Concept 1: *Our gendered identities are not naturally given but constructed through repetition and ritual.*

- Our bodies or sex do not define our gendered identities.
- Genders are not fixed by childhood experiences.
- Gender is constructed through the continuous repetition of micro-rituals.

Concept 2: *Contemporary culture reinforces a traditional gender binary – identities that fall outside of that binary are constructed as subversive.*

- Heteronormativity is entrenched within society.
- Non-heteronormative identities are marginalised or subjugated.
- The media assists in the marginalisation of subversive identities through absent representations, abjection and parody.
- The performance of gender trouble is a difficult, sometimes painful, process given the entrenched nature of heteronormativity.

Challenging Butler's thinking

Discussions regarding gender and identity in the contemporary media landscape are often accompanied by fiercely polemic commentary. Butler's writing, in many senses, encapsulates the dynamic of one side of that discussion, advocating the notion that our gender-based identities are fluid, socially constructed, and, potentially, subject to personal choice, that our anatomical bodies don't necessarily dictate our gendered identities.

Opponents of that view assert a connection between the anatomical-self and gender-identity, arguing that menstruation, pregnancy and childbirth, for example, are gender-defying processes that define the female experience. 'The anti-gender ideology movement,' Butler comments, 'is a global movement, [that] insists that sex is biological and real, or that sex is divinely ordained … This movement is at once anti-feminist, homophobic and transphobic, opposing both reproductive freedom and trans rights. It seeks to censor gender studies programs, to take gender out of public education – a topic so important for young people to discuss' (Gleeson, 2021).

Less contentiously, we might draw attention to the progress that's been made in terms of LGBTQ+ representations since Butler wrote *Gender Trouble* in 1990. We now live, for example, in a media landscape where *Ru Paul's Drag Race* and *Queer Eye* have equal billing space to more heteronormative offerings, a media landscape in which, arguably, LGBTQ+ representations are constructed a little less painfully or comedically than they were thirty years ago.

(*Continued*)

Table 10.2 (Continued)

Two named theorists who might challenge Butler's thinking

- **David Gauntlett:** acknowledges much of Butler's writing as an influence but would suggest that heteronormativity does not completely dominate in terms of gender representations. He might also suggest that contemporary media consumption practises allow audiences to author diverse or fluid identities.
- **Liesbet van Zoonen:** would agree with Butler's assessment that gender is a social construct but would suggest that the media reinforces male power as a result of women internalising the male gaze and assuming the same passivity that on-screen depictions of femininity construct.

---

11 Media and identity
David Gauntlett

David Gauntlett has been included in the list of prescribed A-Level theorists primarily for his work regarding identity theory. Heavily influenced by the thinking of the sociologist Anthony Giddens, Gauntlett constructed a timely critique of mass media consumption models and their effects on audience thinking. He was particularly interested in the impact of the media proliferation boom of the 1980s and 1990s that gave audiences access to more media products and broadcast channels than ever before. The resulting diversity of choice, in Gauntlett's view, fundamentally changed the way that audiences use media products, turning viewers into active rather than passive consumers, and, as a result, giving those audiences the ability to craft their identities via media consumption.

Concept 1: traditional and post-traditional media consumption

Anthony Giddens: traditional and post-traditional culture change

To explain Gauntlett's ideas it is necessary to take a preliminary detour and explore Anthony Giddens' analysis of the far-reaching social changes currently affecting Western societies. We are transitioning, Giddens argues, from a society in which our identities were constructed via rigid traditions to a distinctly different phase that he calls 'late modernity'.

In social structures in which tradition dominates, the notion of who we are is heavily determined by long-standing social forces. The roles that men and women are expected to fulfil, for example, are tightly regulated and heavily moderated by social customs,

DOI: 10.4324/9781003361220-11

family expectations and rigid social codes. Thus, cultures based on 'tradition' produce fixed identities that are hard to escape from. Men are expected to assume stereotypically masculine identities, to adopt the role of the primary earner, while women are expected to look after children, to cook and to keep the family home clean. These rigid roles, importantly, are reinforced by the ideological stances taken by wider social institutions such as education, religion and, importantly, the media.

The period that Giddens calls 'late modernity' begins to take shape in the years following the Second World War and is characterised by a relaxation of the rigid social roles expected in the traditionally ordered society of the pre-war years. Individuals in 'late modernity' realise, in short, that they can shape their own outlooks and beliefs. This transition is partially enabled, Giddens argues, via the liberating effects of globalisation – by exposing individuals to values and identities that are different from those they experience at the local level.

Globalisation, in brief, allows individuals to transcend the rigid expectations of their immediate communities. By watching, for example, an American soap opera that contains powerful female characters, women in traditionally ordered communities might perceive that an alternative identity exists other than the one that their society has prescribed for them.

Giddens and the reflexive project of the self

As a result, Giddens suggests that individuals who live within 'late modernity' can engage in what he calls the 'reflexive project of the self' (Giddens, 1991, 164). The 'self' in 'late modernity' is not fixed, but fluid. In short, we have far more control over who we are in 'late modernity'. We can revise or deconstruct our identities. We can escape the narrow gender or class-based roles prescribed by traditional social structures.

Importantly, David Gauntlett openly acknowledges Giddens' arguments, using them to explore the effects of the contemporary media landscape and arriving at the conclusion that the variety of media products available for us to consume allows us to 'create, maintain and revise a set of biographical narratives – the story of we are, and how we came to be where we are now' (Gauntlett, 2008, 107).

Box 11.1   Discuss it: can you find evidence of social change in your own family?

Giddens suggests that the transition to 'late modernity' accelerated towards the end of the twentieth century. Think about the gender-based roles that your parents and grandparents assume in your own family:

- Who is responsible for cooking, cleaning or childcare in your immediate family? Who goes out to work?
- Do your parents assume traditional or post-traditional gender roles in your immediate family?
- Do your grandparents have a more fixed notion of their gender roles?
- What expectations do you have of yourself and the role you expect to play in your own future family?
- How do your families and your classmates' families compare? Is there evidence to suggest, as Giddens argues, that we are moving from traditionally ordered identities to a less traditional set of expectations?

Concept 2: reflexive identity construction

David Gauntlett: self-help books and consumer-led identities

Gauntlett connects Giddens' notion of the 'reflexive project of the self' to the proliferation of media content in the 1980s and 1990s. He argues that the sheer diversity of new products and channels, both niche and mainstream, facilitates the process of identity editing by audiences.

Gauntlett cites the growth of self-help manuals during the 1990s as evidence of our desire to manipulate the way we engage with the world at large. These self-help guides, he tells us, 'describe aspirational but reasonably realistic (as opposed to utopian) models of how we might expect women and men to present themselves in today's society' (Gauntlett, 2008, 233). Self-help books tell us that we can remedy the personality flaws that hold us back from the jobs we want or the relationships we desire. A whole new you, whatever that 'you' is, can be realised at the flick of a self-help page found in your local bookshop.

Lifestyle magazines and transformation narratives

Gauntlett suggests that a similar dynamic can be identified in contemporary lifestyle magazines where advice columns and inspiration articles prompt audiences to realise their true callings. The front covers of magazines such as *Vogue* and *Men's Health* are shop windows to a sexier, more successful future self for their readerships. Inside, lifestyle-oriented contents pages invite their readers to assimilate aspirational ingredients from the diversity of articles and glossy (but not too perfect) imagery that adorns their pages.

Multi-protagonist television and music

In television, too, it could be argued that the arrival of new programme formats in the 1990s facilitated further identity play. Reality television shows of the period drew contestants from a wide social spectrum, asking audiences to reject or embrace candidates based on nothing more than mediated backstories or the narrative journeys those contestants crafted during a show's transmission. The birth, too, of multi-protagonist TV drama further enhanced the notion that identity was fluid. Where traditional drama formats focused audiences on the identities of a single hero protagonist, multi-protagonist hits such as *Friends* and *Sex and the City* asked audiences to pick their favourite character – to identify with the on-screen presence they felt most akin to. In today's on-demand oriented television landscape, the multi-protagonist drama format rules. From *No Offence* to *The Returned*, most of the television set texts required for exam study contain a rainbow of protagonists that facilitate the same effect.

We might argue that solo music artists have also provided audiences with a set of useful narrative templates as to how identity might be repurposed. Music thrives on identity experimentation, on blurring gender and racial stereotypes and, in doing so, has connected impressionable young audiences to a roll call of global stars who have successfully affected identity change. From Michael

Jackson's plastic surgery-driven resculpting to Beyoncé's regeneration as a radical feminist, the identity U-turns of music artists provide audiences with a stream of stars who model identity fluidity that they themselves can copy.

Advertising and the alternative you

Likewise, Gauntlett suggests that marketing and advertising agencies construct multiple possibilities of who we might be through product branding, providing us with 30 second glimpses of who we might become – of the ideal versions of ourselves and our loved ones.

Of course, we have the power to reject those images, yet, equally, we can also be seduced or inspired by them. These lifestyle narratives, the life-hack impulse of our age, Gauntlett suggests, have gathered further momentum in the digital era – repackaged and repurposed by everyday users in self-penned webzines and DIY YouTube tutorials (Gauntlett, 2008). In the globalised multi-channel media landscape of the 2020s, audiences are now in charge of the remote control. Audiences gatekeep the identities they are exposed to, and if they do not like what they see, they have the power to change channels or, more interestingly, use contemporary digital media platforms to create their own channel.

Box 11.2   Interview with David Gauntlett (January 2019)

MD: *Your book* Media, Gender and Identity *(2002, second edition 2008) was hugely optimistic about the capacity of audiences to use media in shaping their identities. Do you still feel that the contemporary media landscape affords the same opportunities?*

DG: Back then, it was still exciting to talk about people using popular culture within the process of constructing their sense of self-identity. But that was people making use of material that was generated by others – a professional elite, essentially.

Nowadays, that sounds awful. The positive thing we have now is the online culture made by everybody, which – while far from perfect – is definitely much richer and more diverse and exciting than what you got from traditional media.

Of course, traditional media still exists and provides us with big, visible slabs of popular culture, which remains a battleground for representations – the questions about who gets represented, and how. But in 2017 I criticised the then new UK A-Level syllabus for 'making young people study their grandparents' media preferences', which some teachers seemed to think was harsh, but it's true. The 'mass media' perspective – the shared culture where everyone watches the same stuff – is very twentieth century. It made sense then, but not now. You really want to be talking about the present diverse, digital world.

MD: *You are a passionate advocate of digital technologies and their capacity to stimulate a DIY culture. What potential does this culture have to positively transform society?*

DG: The basic point I made in *Making is Connecting* (2011, second edition 2018) is that it's always better for people to be making media, and participating in culture, rather than just being a consumer of it. And the arrival of technologies which enable people to do that quite easily, and engage in highly networked conversations around it, makes a fundamental difference to media studies and, more importantly, to our social and cultural life. For too long our cultural conversations were led by the fortunate elite. Now, it's much more open to everyone, which is obviously better. But recently we've seen more of a toxic spiral of social media nastiness – and the mass-surveillance, advertising-driven business model perfected by Facebook – which is awful. We can still get back to a positive, open, DIY culture, I believe, but it'll take a lot of work.

Box 11.3 Apply it: diagnose the ways that set texts encourage identity fluidity

What evidence is in your set texts to reinforce Gauntlett's idea that the media facilitates identity play? Think about the following:

- Do your set texts construct a single ideal identity or do they offer a number of lead characters, presenting the product's audience with a diversity of identities to choose from?
- What representations of gender, race or class are constructed through the various role models presented in your set texts? Do they reinforce, deconstruct or subvert traditional identities?
- Do your set texts encourage audience identity play? How?

Magazines and online media

- In what ways do the magazines you have studied offer life-changing advice? Which articles promote identity play? What features of readers' lives do the magazines aspire to improve?
- What kinds of aspirational imagery do products present? What effect might ideal imagery have on readers' notions of identity?
- In what ways do the same magazines also construct realism? What is the combined effect of presenting aspiration and realism side by side?
- In what ways do the online set texts you have studied offer life advice or deliver role models that their audiences are encouraged to copy?
- How does characterisation, *mise en scène* or language usage reinforce the aspirational nature of the various role models?

- How does the digital presence of contemporary magazines help facilitate identity play? In what ways do magazines encourage audience engagement?
- How does that engagement help audiences to reshape
  their identity?

Radio

- In what ways do the radio presenters of your radio set
  texts offer their audiences aspirational role models?
- How does programme content help audiences to reshape
  or change their real-world lives?

Television and film marketing

- Do set texts offer multiple protagonists? Do these varied
  protagonists offer a range of identities that audiences can
  use to inform their own identity construction?
- Do set texts provide aspirational role models?
- Do set texts offer a variety of gender-based representations?
- Do set texts actively deconstruct or question traditional
  notions of identity?

Gauntlett: the power of media narratives

Gauntlett also draws our attention to the idea that most story
structures are concerned with the transformation of a central hero,
suggesting that we can 'borrow from these stories when shaping
our narratives of the self' (Gauntlett, 2008, 120). In this sense, the
characters we watch on television shows or follow in online games
offer us examples of how we can transfigure ourselves, of how we
can become something better.

Most products provide their fictional leads with character weaknesses or with quests that need to be completed if they are to gain
happiness. The journeys those characters take – the challenges they
face – might potentially mirror our own weaknesses or provide us
with a template to guide our own goals or desires. At the very least,
the transformations offered suggest that our identities are not
fixed but can be altered for the best if we are motivated enough to
change who we are.

Box 11.4   Analyse it: identify the impact of narrative transformation in your set texts

Use the following questions to provide three-sentence analyses for your set texts to diagnose the effect of character transformation on audience identity:

Fiction-based narratives (TV drama)

- What barriers do central characters face in the wider narratives of the product?
- Do these challenges connect to wider issues of gender, ethnicity, class or ability?
- In what ways does the set text character triumph?
- In what ways do characters transform themselves?
- What are the potential effects of those triumphs on the product's audience?

Non-fiction narratives (magazines, news, radio)

- In what ways do your set texts encourage identity transformation?
- What positive benefits are wrought by transformations?
- What are the potential effects of those narratives on the product's audience?

Use the exemplars below to help structure your responses:

Exemplar 1: *Deutschland 83* (AQA and OCR). Moritz's mission in *Deutschland 83*, to assume the identity of a West German first lieutenant, provides an interesting example of what Gauntlett would call a transformation narrative. Narrative arcs such as these provide audiences with an identity change blueprint. The transformation of Moritz in *Deutschland 83*, for instance, is one of liberation, allowing him to transcend the narrow confines of East German society. The text, moreover, reinforces a sense for the audience that their identities are a reflexive project and that they too can revise who they are to escape their own local conditions.

Exemplar 2: *Huck* magazine (Eduqas). Gauntlett suggests that a range of contemporary media products provide readers with transformation blueprints they can use to legitimise identity play. *Huck*'s 'Beyond Binary' feature clearly provides such a template, with Jacob Tobias' self-penned account of his transgender transition offering a clear challenge to fixed notions of traditional gender roles, while also demonstrating the psychological benefits of that transition. Tobias' call to 'work with me' at the end of the article, moreover, is an open invitation to *Huck*'s readers to accept gender fluidity as the natural condition of our postmodern age and to similarly affect their own identity-oriented experimentations.

Exemplar 3: Beyoncé, *Formation* (Eduqas). *Formation* provides a celebration of Black culture and traditional Black identities via its inclusion of basketball players and references to iconic civil rights activist Martin Luther King. However, it also provides moments of Black identity play – the counter-typical inclusion of a Black cowboy, for example, or shots that celebrate the gay subculture of the New Orlean's bounce scene. Beyoncé, too, models identity change – flipping from hypersexualised and provocative dance routines to the jewellery-heavy power poses offered outside a colonial mansion. This sense of continuous sense of identity fluidity, Gauntlett might argue, provides audiences with a range of signals that tells them that they too can craft and repurpose their identities, inviting them to draw directly upon the many identity cues provided in the video, or, conversely to craft their own identity play.

Further set text help is available for a range of products for all exam boards at www.essentialmediatheory.com

Using Gauntlett, van Zoonen and Butler to develop arguments in long format essays

Gauntlett, importantly, is cautious not to overly exaggerate the potential role that the media plays in enabling identity fluidity. He might assert that audiences play an active role in using media to construct non-traditional identities, but he also realises that the weight and scope of traditional representations constructed through media broadcasting do not necessarily enable limitless or very liberated versions of ethnicity or gender.

Gauntlett clearly acknowledges that the media manufactures 'narrow interpretations of certain roles or lifestyles' (Gauntlett, 2008, 113). Yet his conclusions regarding the overriding effect of the contemporary media landscape are a great deal more optimistic than those suggested by van Zoonen or Judith Butler. For Gauntlett, the diversity of representations available to consume via contemporary media contrasts sharply with van Zoonen's assessment that we are controlled by the dominant pull of patriarchy. He also provides a more upbeat assessment than Judith Butler, whose identification of 'gender trouble' as a subversive act conflicts with Gauntlett's optimism. For Gauntlett, 'gender trouble' is not merely a sideshow or a subversive niche. Indeed, contemporary mass media has helped to mainstream non-heteronormativity (see Table 11.1 for a further comparison of representation theories by van Zoonen, Butler and Gauntlett).

Table 11.1 Quick reference: gender representation theory comparison table

Theorist	Key arguments	Audience effects
van Zoonen	• The media is maintained through patriarchy. • Images of female objectification dominate female representation. • Media makers can challenge dominant representations, but those challenges are viewed as subversive. • Calls on media makers to offer subversive representations.	• Audiences are largely passive. • Audiences, both male and female, internalise female objectification. • Audiences reinforce patriarchal ideologies by subconsciously aligning themselves with the values of a male-dominated society.
Judith Butler	• Gender is socially constructed. • Society constructs a binary view of gender (strict roles for males and females). • Society also presents male/female relationships as the norm (heteronormativity). • The media reinforces heteronormativity through heteronormative representations. • Alternatives to the gender binary exist but are presented as subversive.	• Audiences internalise socially constructed gender norms. • Audiences can seek out representations that offer 'gender trouble'. • Audiences learn how to perform gender via the media. • Audiences can learn alternative models of gender performance – but they are rare and often painfully wrought.

(*Continued*)

Table 11.1 (Continued)

Theorist	Key arguments	Audience effects
David Gauntlett	• Gender is socially constructed. • We now live in a post-traditional society. • Audiences realise they can change their identities. • The media provides a range of products in which a huge diversity of identities is portrayed. • Alternative lifestyles are becoming mainstream.	• Audiences are active. They control the representations they want to engage with and can actively reject those that do not appeal. • Audiences are free to experimen with a variety of identities. Audiences use global media to offer alternatives to the identitie that society constructs for them.

Table 11.2 Speak David Gauntlett

Active audience engagement	Active audiences are in control of the way they watch or interact with the media. Gauntlett would argue that active audiences use – or make – media products to craft their own identities.
Aspirational narrative	A product that offers a means to self-improvement or offers audiences an ideal lifestyle choice.
Fixed identity	Fixed identities do not give individuals a great deal of choice about who they want to be. Identities might be fixed by religiou beliefs, social norms or rigid family roles.
Fluid identity	Our identities can be described as fluid when we realise that they can be changed or that we do not necessarily have to conform to the rigid categories laid down by traditional social structures.
Globalisation	Globalisation, in this chapter, refers to the way that media produc began to be produced and shared across the globe as a result of ownership changes in the 1980s. Globalisation brought audience into contact with a much wider range of identity influences.
Media proliferation	Media proliferation refers to the explosion of media products and channels that started to occur in the early 1980s. Media proliferation meant products were increasingly produced for nich or specialised audiences.
Post-traditional society	A society that does not require individuals to adopt rigid roles or identities.
Reflexive project of the self	A term coined by Anthony Giddens to describe the way that identities are constructed in a post-traditional society. Giddens argu that individuals are able to craft and revise their own identities – th our identities are a constantly evolving and adapting project.
Window to the future self	A product that gives its audience a glimpse into who they could become. Commonly used to describe magazine front covers.

Table 11.3 Gauntlett: ten-minute revision

Concept 1: *traditional and post-traditional media consumption*

- Gauntlett's ideas build upon Anthony Giddens' assertion that society has progressed to a stage that Giddens calls 'late modernity'.
- The conditions of late modernity enable audiences to escape the prescriptive identities that are constructed for them through localised social norms and traditional viewpoints.
- Gauntlett argues that contemporary media has brought audiences into contact with a wider range of representations – and, importantly, that audiences can consciously shape their own sense of self.

Concept 2: *reflexive identity construction*

- The media provides a variety of role models and lifestyle templates that audiences use to guide their own outlooks.
- Audiences are engaged in a continuous revision of their identities.
- Media narratives mirror the process of identity transformation.
- Audiences are in control of the media – adapting and assimilating ideas about themselves through the various representations that the media presents.

Challenging Gauntlett's thinking

Gauntlett might be challenged for providing an overly optimistic view of media consumption, a view, perhaps, that too readily assumes that audiences can successfully resist media messaging. Critics who adopt a more Marxian view, for example, might suggest that media products construct a dominant set of representational effects that audiences can't help but internalise, or that the media tends to be made by elite social groups whose perspectives and biases are readily adopted by more mainstream listeners.

Gauntlett's later work might also be critiqued as overly cyber-utopian. His suggestion that audiences readily use digital media tools as a form of identity expression, perhaps, overestimates levels of audience creativity, where audiences in reality adopt the kinds of passive sit back and listen relationships that are associated with traditional broadcast media forms.

Three named theorists who might challenge Gauntlett's thinking

---

- **Stuart Hall:** would argue that the media landscape is not diverse, but saturated with stereotypical portrayals that reflect wider social inequalities. This leads to a deeply problematic portrayal of minority groups of all persuasions.
- **bell hooks:** hooks would argue that portrayals of Black women are largely absent from the media, and when they are present, they are prone to producing overly sexualised portrayals.
- **Paul Gilroy:** would argue that British media narratives do not offer diversity but are stuck within a colonial mindset that positions non-whites as threatening, primitive or uncivilised.

---

12 Ownership effects

James Curran and Jean Seaton

Curran and Seaton's widely regarded history of the media in the UK, *Power without Responsibility*, is concerned, to a large degree, with narrating the story of how the media landscape has fallen under the control of a handful of global media conglomerates.

Of course, the media landscape has changed considerably since the book's first publication in 1981, and the seventh edition of *Power without Responsibility* (2010) very much reflects contemporary concerns regarding digital media. But at the heart of Curran and Seaton's book remains a core concern – a guiding notion of what the media *ought* to be doing, and it stems, in part, from James Curran's detailed reading of the development of the radical press in the early 1800s.

The numerous radical press pamphlets and small-scale newspapers of the Victorian era, Curran argues, were engines for social and political change. Made by the working class to be read by a working-class readership, they highlighted the plight of the poor, and fostered, Curran tells us, 'an alternate value system that symbolically turned the world upside down' (Curran and Seaton, 2010, 15).

The lifespan of this early media form, however, was short lived. A combination of rising production costs and increased competition from high-quality, professionally produced titles eventually drove the radical free press out of business. Newspapers of the mid-Victorian period, Curran argues, could only be mass produced by those who could afford the extensive start-up costs needed to manufacture products on an industrial scale. Curran, too, points to the corrosive effect of commercial advertising which was sold to offset production costs; the radical press, with its agenda to effect political change, did not partner well with the commercial activities of advertisers who represented the same capitalist system they

DOI: 10.4324/9781003361220-12

wanted to undermine. Without advertising income, the free press could not compete with their commercial rivals, and the process of media concentration – the control of the media by ever-larger organisations – began in earnest.

Curran and Seaton suggest that a second and equally turbulent wave of ownership consolidation took place in the latter half of the twentieth century when economic globalisation and the widespread deregulation of the media industry reduced the number of national press titles in the UK to just 11 publications. This lack of diversity, in Curran and Seaton's view, concentrates too much power in the hands of a small number of newspaper proprietors – an entirely different scenario to the radical origins of the newsprint industry.

Concept 1: media concentration

Creativity versus commerciality

Today, the media industry is driven, Curran and Seaton tell us, by the twin forces of creativity and business. Media creatives – writers, directors, actors and photographers – are tasked to give us exciting, innovative and aesthetically pleasing products, while those we call the media's business managers are responsible for ensuring the profitability and commercial viability of products.

Curran and Seaton suggest that profit-driven motives take precedence over creativity in the world of commercial media – that the agendas of the industry's business managers control creative output. Money wins, while both audience size and audience share determine content. As Jean Seaton explains, 'Commercial broadcasting is based not on the sale of programmes to audiences, but on the sale of audiences to advertisers' (Curran and Seaton, 2010, 90). Because commercial broadcasters need to secure long-term advertising revenue to survive programming, she argues, content is designed to attract economically affluent audiences who can buy the products that are promoted during advertising slots.

As a result, peak-time television schedules (where commercial space is most sought after and costly) are dominated by lighter entertainment formats, while less popular minority interest products are sidelined to secondary channels or late-night slots. Advertising, too, prompts media broadcasters to make content that focuses on capturing a middle-class ABC1 demographic – those audiences who can afford to buy the products that advertisers want to sell. 'The reason why,' Curran tells us, 'approximately 25 per cent of the market sustains half the number of daily [newspaper] titles ... is because this is the most affluent part of the market, and generates a large advertising bounty' (Curran and Seaton, 2010, 90).

Box 12.1   Think about it: the effects of commercial imperatives on set texts

Activity 1: think about advertising effects

Identify which of your set text products are funded through commercial advertising and answer these questions:

- How does advertising affect the content of those products? Do newspapers try to capture a mass market audience by sanitising hard news stories? Do television dramas produce formulaic content? Are characters stereotyped? Is political content softened to appease advertiser needs?
- In what ways are media products and advertising linked? How does editorial content in your magazine set texts, for instance, covertly promote the products that are advertised in the magazine? Do magazines or newspapers use advertorials?
- Do your commercial set texts serve affluent ABC1 demographics because of advertiser needs? In what ways does this need channel content or editorial decisions?

Activity 2: think about the effect of audience size

- Group your set texts by institution, with commercial products in one group and non-commercial products in another. What do the products in each group have in common? What separates the two groups?
- Are Curran and Seaton right in suggesting that mass audience products tend to be sanitised or lightweight?

Activity 3: think about scheduling

Identify the time of the day that set texts were originally broadcast.

- How do broadcast times affect content?
- What do products broadcast at peak time, 7–10 p.m., have in common?

Activity 4: think about time shifting and on-demand effects

Identify which of your radio/television set texts are distributed as podcasts or through on-demand services.

- What effect does podcasting (time shifting) or on-demand distribution have on the content of set texts? Are products allowed to take more creative risks? Are products more political? More experimental?
- Has on-demand distribution allowed producers to make more niche products?
- What effect does the absence of advertising have on texts produced by Netflix? Do subscription services like these give media creatives more control?

Exemplar: *The Times* and *Daily Mirror* (Eduqas). Curran and Seaton argue that the media landscape is dominated by a handful of commercially owned companies that prioritise profit and power. Both *The Times* and *Daily Mirror* provide evidence to support that view. The *Mirror*'s owners, Reach PLC, for example, oversee the production of the *Daily Star*, *Daily Express* and *Daily Mirror* alongside 130+ regional publications and other online interests giving it an estimated monthly readership of 48 million. Similarly, the owners of *The Times*, News UK, a subsidiary of the global conglomerate News Corporation, distributes news and publishing output in the UK, USA and Australia, helping the parent conglomerate to achieve profits of $760 million (USD) in 2021/22.

Curran and Seaton further suggest that the pursuit of profit by such companies skews producers to target middle-class readerships – those readers who can attract significant advertising revenues – and, moreover, that the radical potential of newsprint has been sanitised to secure advertiser interest. It is significant that Reach PLC and News Corporation own subsidiary interests in the form of Reach Solutions and News UK's Bridge Studios – companies that help the news brands in their respective conglomerates to secure advertising income through sponsored content and advertorial creation. The activities here providing significant evidence to reinforce Curran and Seaton's conclusion that contemporary news providers shape editorial content to increase their revenues.

Further exemplars for set texts from all exam boards are available online at www.essentialmediatheory.com

Conglomerate advantages

Most commercial print, film and television-based media in the USA and the UK is now controlled by just six global players: Comcast, Walt Disney, Fox, AT&T, Sony and Paramount Global. The control of the market by a handful of high-profile organisations is fuelled by the ability of those six companies to produce, distribute and market their content as efficiently and effectively as possible. Their size and dominance prevent smaller companies from gaining any significant foothold in the respective markets of the big six. Their conglomerate structures also allow them to use the respective talents of the smaller subsidiaries under their control to market, produce and distribute media products as efficiently as possible. Two expansion patterns worth exploring further include horizontal and vertical integration.

Horizontal integration

Horizontal integration (HI) occurs when a conglomerate acquires subsidiaries that make similar types of products or media output. News Corporation is a classic example of a horizontally aligned organisation in that it owns lots of news titles, including *The Times*, *Sunday Times* and *The Sun* in the UK, as well as the *New York Post* and the Australian broadsheet the *Daily Telegraph*. The benefits of HI can be defined as follows:

- **Production costs can be minimised.** Products can be bought in bulk while production facilities can be brought together to rationalise costs. Owning more than one newspaper title, for example, reduces printing costs through the common ownership of a printing facility or through the bulk buying of paper.
- **Sharing resources.** Horizontally aligned companies have the power and financial means to create resources that independent producers are simply unable to develop. *The Times* and *The Sun*, for example, make use of News UK's social media analysis subsidiary called Storyful – a service that investigates and verifies social media leads, helping News UK brands to identify trending issues on social media. Cost savings can also be achieved by sharing stories across sister publications. *The Times*, for example, often recycles content from News Corporation's Australian and American news outlets, helping the broadsheet to print an extensive global news section every day. Reach PLC also pools resources from across its publications – photography archives, stories, regionally based journalists and so on – in ways that help the organisation make substantial cost savings.
- **Controlling the market.** By owning both *The Times* and *The Sun*, News Corporation uses its considerable news-gathering resources to control a substantial slice of the broadsheet and tabloid markets in the UK. News Corporation products are also strategically positioned so they do not compete with one another while their use of shared resources helps nurture a competitive advantage over rival titles.

Vertical integration

Vertical integration (VI) enables conglomerates to control the production, marketing and distribution of media products by owning subsidiaries that have bespoke functions to fulfil in the media supply chain. Disney is a good example of a vertically integrated company in that it owns or has cultivated subsidiaries that allow all aspects of the supply chain to be controlled inside the Disney conglomerate. They include the following:

- **Production divisions.** Disney owns film production studios such as Marvel Studios, Pixar, Lucasfilm and Twentieth Century Fox, as well as television production facilities such as ABC or ESPN.
- **Distribution services.** In owning Disney+ and Fox Network, Disney can globally distribute their filmic and television content without the need to employ external partners. This allows Disney to retain all profits from distribution processes by minimising the use of rival distributors who would, ordinarily, take a cut of their profits. Owning your own distribution network also gives full control of where and when content is broadcast – helping Disney, for example, to time film releases at optimal points in the year.
- **Subsidiary support.** Film and media products need to be financed, promoted and planned – owning specialist support subsidiaries allows Disney to manage projects effectively. For example, Disney uses a variety of specialist subsidiaries including promotional services (Disney Marketing), merchandising (Marvel Toys) and financial/support services (Marvel Film Finance) to help the conglomerate maximise profits.

The advantages of VI include:

- **Capturing upstream and downstream profits.** Producing and distributing products of your own content creates substantial cost savings. Production subsidiaries do not need to pay distributors to stream their products (thus capturing downstream profits). Likewise, distributor subdivisions do not have to pay external providers for media content (thus capturing upstream profits).
- **Control over all aspects of the production chain.** Owning a satellite network means Disney can release products in ways that maximise profits. Sky subscribers, for instance, are given access to premium movie content during the lucrative Christmas holiday period. VI also allows companies to release or schedule products so that they do not compete with one another.
- **Restricting access to competitors.** By controlling key distribution outlets, Disney can prevent rivals from dominating

broadcast schedules and can even charge competitors who might want to distribute their products through Disney-owned networks.

- **Cross-media ownership synergies.** Owning a variety of media company types enables the conglomerate to distribute product benefits across a range of media forms. For instance, Marvel Television uses the advanced production processes developed for Marvel Films. Characters and storylines developed for the *Star Wars* film franchise can also be recycled into gaming products. The popularity too of big film franchises also helps to nurture interest in their theme park experiences, with Disney Parks generating revenues of $7.78 billion for the second quarter of 2023 alone.

Box 12.2   Think about it: the effect of horizontal and vertical integration on set texts

Use the following questions to identify the effects of horizontal and vertical integration on set texts:

Activity 1: diagnosing vertical integration effects

- How do ownership patterns help in terms of product distribution? What distribution services does the conglomerate own? How do these distribution channels give the product access to mass audiences?
- How do distribution subsidiaries help the set text reach a global audience? How does this increase the profitability of the product?
- What effect does the set text's distribution have on budget constraints? Because the set text is distributed to a mass audience, does it have a bigger budget than if it was made by an independent?
- Do cross-media ownership patterns give the set text an opportunity to be translated into other media formats?

Activity 2: diagnosing horizontal integration effects

- Does the product serve a clearly defined target audience as a result of HI ownership patterns? What audiences do sister companies target? Are audiences differentiated to maximise profits?
- How does the set text use the shared expertise/joint resources of a sister company to make or distribute the product?

Concept 2: effects of concentration on media content

Proprietor control of print news

Media concentration has resulted in the elevation of proprietor power, whereby the owners of conglomerates potentially use their media portfolios to sway public opinion or to lobby political parties. Some news brand proprietors, Curran and Seaton argue, play a significant role in influencing the content and flow of news either directly or indirectly:

- **Direct control.** Proprietor owners, Curran suggests, censor news content that conflicts with their own political views and wider business interests. Large-scale conglomerates that own news titles, Curran and Seaton argue, tend also to have vested interests in a range of other business activities across the globe – banking, engineering, oil and transport, for example. Media divisions might be directed to ignore or downplay news stories if conflicts of interest arise with those business activities.
- **Indirect control** of news content might also be affected through the hiring and firing process, through the installation of editors who are sympathetic to a specific worldview that a proprietor wants to broadcast.

Elitist media/political relationships

James Curran also draws our attention to the relationships that have developed between news groups, big business and government, suggesting that the power of concentrated media ownership has forced political parties to form cosy relationships with media moguls in order to generate favourable press coverage.

The former Labour prime minister Tony Blair, for example, was famously invited to address News Corporation executives in 1995 before his New Labour Party was elected. News Corporation owner, Rupert Murdoch, also forged a relationship with Prime Minister Margaret Thatcher during the 1980s that was close enough, reportedly, that he could affect some influence over crucial policy decisions regarding media regulation. Curran suggests, rather powerfully, that these cosy relationships result in the formation of a news landscape that lacks the critical bite of a fully functioning press establishment.

Mass market news, news depoliticisation and hysterical news values

Media concentration, Curran and Seaton also argue, has significantly reduced the diversity of available news titles, while at the same time increasing the readerships of those titles that remain. Catering for the needs of those huge readerships, Curran argues, has resulted in a watering down of news content to create news brand appeal for mass audiences. Mass readership newspapers are depoliticised as a result – often replacing hard news with entertainment-driven content, while the quality and tone of news coverage is sensationalised in a bid to retain audience share.

Curran and Seaton: a neo-Marxian approach?

Curran and Seaton suggest that contemporary media ownership places the media in the hands of the few and not the many. In this sense, they take an approach that follows in the footsteps of the Victorian economist and philosopher Karl Marx. Marx argued that culture – the arts and so forth – is deployed to make the working poor believe that there is not really much alternative to the drudgery of their appalling working conditions. Marx argued that:

- **Culture is controlled by social elites.** Curran and Seaton likewise suggest the media is controlled by a minority of wealthy institutions and that those institutions often work for the benefit of themselves.
- **Culture acts as a distraction.** Culture, according to Marx, provides a temporary escape from the drudgery of our working lives, and in doing so, distracts us from the true nature of our exploitation. Curran and Seaton would similarly argue that the media offers us depoliticised narratives made by entertainment-oriented companies who author highly formulaic content.

Regulated media pluralism

Yet, to label Curran and Seaton as nothing more than neo-Marxists would miss much of the thrust of their work. They might call out press proprietor abuses, but they also present a strong case for what might loosely be termed 'media pluralism', arguing that the media landscape ought to be populated by a range of company types, both commercial and public service oriented.

Box 12.3 Apply it: media concentration and news-based set texts

This activity is particularly useful for exam-based questions that ask you to identify the effects of ownership on set text news products. Analyse relevant set texts using the following prompts:

- Curran suggests that contemporary newspapers must compete for readers' interests, often using hysterical news values – making them angry or frightened – to attract and sustain mass readerships. Do stories in your news set texts support this argument?

- Is political coverage minimised or sensationalised in contemporary news?
- Does the editorial mix of contemporary print news feature an unusually large element of softer news features, sports coverage or entertainment news?
- Do the editorial biases of your set text newspapers reflect the political views of their proprietors?
- In what ways do set text newspapers rely on official sources for stories? Do they readily challenge those sources or accept them as accurate?
- Are journalists and columnists given the freedom to express ideas that conflict with proprietor views?
- Do newspapers incorporate reader commentary and opinion to broaden the perspectives offered?

Exemplar: *Daily Mail* **(OCR).** The *Daily Mail* exemplifies much of the thrust of Curran and Seaton's arguments that media globalisation has resulted in the domination of the news industry by a handful of proprietor-owned titles that are dependent on advertising and mass audience readership to remain commercially viable. A mass marketisation of news has resulted, Curran tells us, using hysterical news values and softer news content to maintain mass appeal in the face of cut-throat competition.

The Daily Mail and General Trust's (DMGT) aristocratic owner, Lord Rothermere (Jonathan Harmsworth), paid over £3.1 billion to take the news group into private ownership in 2021, placing Rothermere at the head of DMGT as the organisation's chief executive. Lord Rothermere's new role is hugely powerful, giving him full control of the *Daily Mail* and *Mail on Sunday* (26.5 million estimated monthly readers) as well as *The Metro* (20 million monthly readers). Some estimates also suggest that DMGT commands over

10% of news traffic online in the UK (Ponsford, 2022). Something of Rothermere's political views were revealed at a *Daily Mail* celebration dinner in 2022 when he told the party's assembled group of politicians and journalists that, 'We must not be afraid to stand up for decency and the traditional values that have stood the test of time' (Greenhill, 2022). Those views, perhaps, help to guide the middle-England values of the paper's well-known editorial direction. Yet, the *Daily Mail* also needs to target a commercially lucrative ABC1 demographic, using a softer editorial mix that foregrounds royal stories and celebratory gossip in its 'showbiz' version of the online Mail – a clear effect of the need to provide advertiser-friendly content that has mass market appeal.

Further exemplars for set texts from all exam boards are available online at www.essentialmediatheory.com

Certainly, Curran and Seaton highlight the need to protect UK public service broadcasting to counterbalance the forces of the free market. In this sense, they are media pluralists, suggesting that media audiences are served best when a range of different institutions contribute to the media landscape.

The internet and ownership concentration

Certainly, there was much to celebrate at the outset of the internet's invention in terms of its potential to challenge the top-down nature of traditional media. Yet, Curran and Seaton suggest, the web landscape of today is increasingly commercialised, with large-scale traditional media companies having invested huge amounts of time and money to develop equally huge web presences. These companies, Curran tells us, 'had enormous assets: back catalogues of content, large reserves of cash and expertise, close links with the advertising industry, brand visibility and cross promotional resources' (Curran and Seaton, 2010, 265). As a result, the natural advantages of media conglomerates meant that they were able to affect a sizeable web presence very quickly.

Box 12.4   Think about it: the creeping commercialisation of the web

Do your online set texts provide evidence that the radical potential of the internet has been curtailed by commercial pressures?

Questions to test the level of commercialisation of online set texts

- Which parent companies make your online set texts – are they part of an established media conglomerate? Have producers partnered up with commercial organisations to make their product?
- Is the online set text financed, either wholly or in part, by commercial advertising? What is the potential effect of advertising on the content of the product?
- Does the set text openly, or even covertly, market products to its audience?

Questions to diagnose public service benefits of online set texts

- Do your online set texts invite commentary from its users? Is commentary designed to prompt debate?
- Do set texts give marginalised groups a voice?
- Do products foreground information over product sales?
- Are products designed to nurture an online community?

In 1996, the internet was a relatively advert-free interface; fast forward 20 years and we barely register the presence of all those web cookies logging our browsing activity. Social media sites and search engines mine our personal data so that we might receive personalised advertising. YouTube monetises user uploads, turning cat videos and vlogs into spaces that can be prefaced by adverts for soft drinks, cars and hair products. The web has become a place of commerce rather than a space to share and discuss. But, Curran argues, the web is still a contested space. Enough cyber-mavericks exist, he suggests, to ensure that the world's digital networks have not been completely overtaken by major corporations just yet.

Concept 3: diverse ownership creates diverse products

The free market effect

UK government policy, Seaton and Curran argue, is partly responsible for the domination of the media landscape by huge conglomerates. Jean Seaton points to the prevailing neo-liberal viewpoint of politicians who oversaw media policy from the 1980s onwards, with both Labour and Conservative politicians championing a 'free market' media landscape – an approach that allows media companies to operate without overbearing regulatory measures or other governmental controls. Free market neo-liberalism is intended to produce, in Jean Seaton's words, 'conditions of the greatest possible competition' (Curran and Seaton, 2010, 371), in which media audiences, not politicians, determine content and where companies that provide the most popular content are allowed to flourish.

As a result of neo-liberal government policy, commercial media output has bloomed. In 1980 just 300 hours of television programming was broadcast each week; by 2000 that number had grown to over 40,000 hours (Curran and Seaton, 2010, 246). The problem, Curran and Seaton highlight, is that without suitable controls, commercial media companies readily abandon commitments to public service broadcasting and content diversity. We might have more television content, they argue, but the pursuit of mass audience appeal has produced a landscape that is dominated by format-driven products.

Media formats that are successful are replicated to deliver mass audiences. *The Great British Bake Off*, for instance, has morphed into *The Great British Sewing Bee*, while the dominance of prime-time talent shows such as *The Voice* and *Britain's Got*

Talent have spawned a stream of shows that share remarkably similar formats. Channel 4, too, mines formats relentlessly – *24 Hours in Police Custody, 24 Hours in A&E, Countdown, 8 out 10 Cats Does Countdown*, etc. The need to produce mass audiences means that the television industry replicates rather than originates.

It could be argued that the television streaming revolution spearheaded by Netflix, Apple and Amazon might have broken the formulaic approach taken by terrestrial television broadcasters. Certainly, the production budgets of streaming giants dwarf those of traditional UK terrestrial broadcasters like Channel 4 and even the BBC, yet the need to retain global audience appeal drives streamers to commission products that command mass interest. New content is routinely devised on the basis that storylines replicate the popularity of pre-existing narratives. Far from increasing consumer choice, media proliferation has generated products that lack invention. The jarring pace and plot twists of Apple TV's *Tehran*, for example, reuses storytelling strategies forged by *Homeland* or *24*. Likewise, the domination of Nordic Noir's world-weary, slow-paced, crime-based storytelling was a staple streaming genre in the late 2010s because of the unexpected success of shows like *The Killing, The Bridge* and *Wallander*.

Public service broadcasting as a counter influence to commercial media

Curran and Seaton remind us, however, that commercial media has not been allowed to dominate UK television and radio markets completely. The BBC as a public service broadcaster, for example, is funded via the television licence – a charge levied to all households in the UK who want to watch or record any television channel. Licence fee funding allows the BBC to operate without the need to attract advertising revenue, enabling the provider to create content for minority audiences. Licence fee funding also enables the BBC to fulfil its public service remit – its founding Reithian values – to not only entertain their audiences, but also provide programming that both informs and educates – content strands that traditionally attract lowers levels of advertiser interest within commercial radio and television.

Unsurprisingly, the BBC's alternative funding structure has been subject to much criticism by many. Key arguments include:

- **Reduced audience engagement.** Critics cite the BBC's dwindling audience share in today's digital media landscape, suggesting that audiences ought not to contribute to BBC funding if they don't watch or listen to BBC output.
- **The BBC's monopoly of license fee income.** Providers like Channel 4, for example, whose broadcasting licence also tasks them to provide public service content outline the unfairness of the current system, arguing that their obligations to produce diverse content would be more easily met with the guaranteed income of the licence fee.
- **The license levy restricts commercial competition.** Others point to the commercial advantages that the license fee generates for the BBC, arguing that its guaranteed income stream prevents competitors from maintaining a presence in key markets. Critics, for example, point to the demise of local news brands in the UK, arguing that the BBC's heavy regional presence makes it difficult for local newspapers to compete.
- **Technical convergence challenges.** The range of devices that can record, live-stream or broadcast television programming makes it increasingly difficult for the BBC to police or enforce licence fee controls. Audiences, for example, are using device blurring to opt out of the licence fee, with a drop of 500,000 licence renewals recorded in the year leading up to July 2023. Some argue that this trend will inevitably force the BBC to abandon its current funding model and adopt a subscription-based pay-per-view service.

The BBC's non-commercial funding model, however, has survived – its reach and popularity securing enough public support to ward off, thus far, any life-threatening reforms. However, the current Royal Charter agreement – the BBC's deal with the government that allows it to levy the licence fee – is set to expire in 2027. The pressure to reform, perhaps, will mean that the terms and conditions of the next Royal Charter are likely to be subject to significant changes.

Box 12.5   Think about it: is the media dominated by format-driven products?

Curran and Seaton suggest that commercial media broadcasters copy rival products that are successful or rely on trusted television formats to deliver safe programming. Think about the following questions to test the truth of Curran and Seaton's arguments today:

- In what ways do the schedules of major broadcasters offer similar products during peak viewing slots?
- Can you think of some examples of television programmes/formats that have been successful and have produced copycat products as a result of that success?
- How far do you agree with the argument that streaming services like Netflix rely on a formulaic approach?

The benefits of diverse ownership

Undoubtedly, Curran and Seaton are champions of the BBC, arguing that its diverse funding model enables the broadcaster to do things that commercial media providers would find too risky or niche to invest in. Freed of its need to garner mass audience appeal, the BBC can take a more experimental approach in production content. It can take risks in nurturing new talent, invent new kinds of programming or relate stories that are politically uncomfortable for readers or advertisers. The following three overarching benefits are cited by Curran and Seaton that derive from the BBC's unique funding status:

- **All programming standards are raised.** Because, for example, the BBC is not part of a larger cross-industry conglomerate, it approaches news with impartiality. The BBC's impartial approach, furthermore, sets high standards that other commercial broadcasters have to copy to compete with.

- **High-quality minority interest programming is provided.** Without the need to make a profit, the BBC can serve minority audience interests through programming and scheduling. The BBC's commitment to the arts, for instance, is evidenced via BBC 4, while minority ethnic and regional audiences are engaged via BBC Asian Network and the BBC's regional radio portfolio.
- **It is a unifying organisation.** The BBC brings the UK together, functioning as a collective voice during moments of national importance. The BBC, for example, plays a critical role in reporting national elections and global sporting events. It also provides vital support during moments of national crisis – pandemics, wars, acts of terrorism or financial turbulence. It also reflects the nation's voice during moments of national tragedy, helping us negotiate, for example, the death of the Queen in 2022. In this sense, we might argue that the BBC is a vital social glue that binds the UK with a sense of common purpose.

Box 12.6   Revise it: BBC Radio and public service broadcasting

BBC Radio output provides an excellent illustration of the organisation's non-commercial remit to inform, educate and entertain. With 10 national radio stations and over 39 local stations, the BBC provides a range of niche and majority interest radio programming. Freed from profit-driven motives, the BBC can also deliver a diversity of content that would not ordinarily survive if it were funded through advertising.

Exemplar: *Have You Heard George's Podcast?* **(Eduqas).** Radio 4 is one of only a few UK-based radio stations that are dominated by spoken word broadcasting. *Have You Heard George's Podcast?* (HYHGP) is an experimental product that challenges us to reflect upon the politically charged audio mixes of George the Poet.

Issues that you could relate to Curran and Seaton in an exam might include:

- **The programme's format:** the show's collages of poetry, urban soundscapes, political musings, rap, jazz and hip-hop produce a hugely unconventional audio mix. The podcast's refusal to also follow a repeatable format is interesting, with George's personal reflections intertwined with bigger news stories in different ways across each episode. The use, moreover, of the Common Ground website as accompaniment to the show allows audiences to connect with aired issues in ways that aren't readily apparent in more mainstream radio output.
- **Content issues:** the focus on a range of always controversial issues evidences the BBC's commitment to impartiality, and, moreover, to using content that celebrates minority voice concerns. George's unabashed criticism of government policy in terms of the Grenfell disaster (episode 3) or the criminal justice system (episode 1) provide a personal perspective that is hard to find in more commercial radio output.

Further set text help is available for a range of products for all exam boards at www.essentialmediatheory.com

Table 12.1 Speak Curran and Seaton

Commercial media	An organisation that makes or distributes products for economic gain. Commercial media usually make products for entertainment purposes.
Horizontal integration	Ownership of subsidiaries that produce similar types of products.
Hysterical news values	Sensationalist news content used to drive mass market sales.
Mass market news	News designed to appeal to huge readerships, often critiqued for its lack of analysis or for its entertainment-driven values. Also known as news depoliticisation.

(Continued)

Table 12.1 (Continued)

Media concentration/ media convergence	A term used to describe the reduction in the number of media organisations that produce products.
Media pluralism	A media landscape with a healthy balance of products made by different media company types. Typically, these might include public service broadcasters, commercial media and citizen-generated media.
Public service broadcasting	A media producer who is not reliant on advertising to fund production or does not make products for commercial gain. Public service broadcasting products usually seek to inform and educate their audiences as well as to entertain.
Vertical integration	Ownership of subsidiaries that enable a media company to produce, promote and distribute products without external support.

Table 12.2 Curran and Seaton: ten-minute revision

Concept 1: *the media is controlled by a small number of companies that make products to create profit*

- Globalisation has concentrated media ownership into the hands of a few companies.
- Media conglomerates are horizontally and vertically integrated to maximise profit.
- Large-scale media producers rely on advertising to generate income.
- Advertising drives media companies to produce products that have mass audience appeal.

Concept 2: *media concentration adversely affects media content*

- The business function of the media industry takes precedence over its creative/ public service capacities.
- Profit-driven media is softened to create mass audience appeal.
- Minority interest content is pushed to the margins of broadcast schedules.
- Free market competition produces format-driven products.

Concept 3: *diverse ownership creates diverse products*

- Curran and Seaton highlight the damage that free market ideologies have had on the media landscape.
- Public service broadcasting provides impartial news, serves minority audiences and champions national unity by offering inclusive rather than exclusive content.

Challenging Curran and Seaton's thinking

Undoubtedly, the work of Curran and Seaton is open to extensive criticism. The idea, for example, that the news agenda is controlled by a handful of proprietors stands at odds with the reality of news production where editors and journalists often work with considerable independence. Curran and Seaton's thinking, perhaps, also downplays the needs and cues of audiences in terms of production approaches.

Arguably, consumers – rather than proprietors or advertisers – play the most important role in shaping the editorial mixes and political bias of media brands, and audiences respond very quickly when the values of brands don't readily fit with their own. Forecasters, for example, predict a drop in X's user count (formerly Twitter) of some 32 million by the end of 2024 in the wake of Elon Musk's $44 billion takeover, attributed in part to Musk's reinstatement of controversial right-wing figures like Jordan Peterson and Andrew Tate

We might similarly argue that diverse funding doesn't always lead producers to make diverse content. Indeed, BBC television and radio schedules are awash with output that foreground the same kinds of celebrity-oriented lightweight editorial mixes found in the popular press. *Strictly Come Dancing*, *Celebrity MasterChef* or *The Graham Norton Show*, for example, don't readily partner with the political and social concerns of *Woman's Hour* or *Have You Heard George's Podcast?*

Three named theorists who might challenge Curran and Seaton's thinking

- **Clay Shirky**: argues that the media industry is increasingly driven by audience feedback systems rather than the top-down control of proprietors.
- **Henry Jenkins:** would acknowledge that Web 2.0 enables big business to exploit the web for commercial reasons, but would also argue that the internet retains the capacity to work as a social good and that online communities created via 'participatory culture' have the power to change the world for the better.
- **Steve Neale:** would critique the idea that media proliferation has resulted in a narrowing of product types or the dominance of formula-driven media. He would argue that audiences prompt producers to continuously adapt and finesse genre-driven material.

13 Regulation

Sonia Livingstone and Peter Lunt

Sonia Livingstone and Peter Lunt's academic work constructs a critical analysis of the changing regulatory landscape in the UK over the last 30 years. Central to that analysis is an exploration of how the UK's approach to media governance has served the needs of audiences as both consumers and citizens.

Consumer-based regulation, Livingstone and Lunt tell us, is realised when audiences are given the freedom to consume the widest possible range of content – where, in practical terms, media regulation by government is minimised and consumption decisions regarding problematic content are devolved to audiences. A consumer-based media system also provides benefits for producers, generating opportunities for media makers to create as wide a range of products as possible. The only limits placed on media makers in a consumer-based regulatory landscape is whether products can garner enough audience take-up to be commercially viable. In short, a consumer-based regulatory framework seeks to guarantee audience choice and promote product diversity.

A citizen-based regulatory system, conversely, shapes media output to play a significant role in shaping society and its citizens – pushing television output, newspapers, radio, etc. to educate and inform their audiences, while performing a pivotal function in maintaining the democratic health of the nation. In a citizen-based regulatory model, governments and government policy play a critical role in defining the kinds of content that the media ought to broadcast or publish.

Crucially, Livingstone and Lunt argue that media policies affected by successive governments over the last 25 years have worked in ways that have protected, by and large, the commercial interests of media producers, and, as a result, that we have

DOI: 10.4324/9781003361220-13

moved from a regulatory system that was more concerned with citizen-oriented motives to a more consumer-based approach.

Concept 1: citizen and consumer models of media regulation

The consumer-oriented approach

A consumer-based regulatory approach offers the following advantages and features:

- **Regulation champions consumer choice.** Consumer-orientated regulation is designed, principally, to encourage media plurality and to ensure that a diversity of broadcasters operate within the media landscape. A consumer-led market allows audiences to be able to access a broad range of content, opinions and ideas.
- **Relies on consumer-led policing of programme content.** Content monitoring, Livingstone and Lunt argue, plays a secondary role within a consumer-based regulatory model, with audiences having to 'rely much more on their own judgements of quality, truthfulness and enjoyment' (Livingstone and Lunt, 2012, 16).
- **The state plays a minor role in determining media regulation.** A consumer-based regulatory model minimises the role that government plays in pushing media providers to make content that has specific benefits – news, factual programming, educational content, programming for children, etc. Media schedules aren't determined by government-led quotas or overbearing content codes that police language use, sexual references or matters of taste and decency.

The citizen-based approach

In contrast, the citizen-oriented approach provides the following features and advantages:

- **Regulation promotes civic-minded media content.** Livingstone and Lunt argue that citizen-based regulation provides a content-focused framework that directs media makers to 'contribute to the enrichment of cultural and social life and the potential for self-development of individuals, groups and communities' (Livingstone and Lunt, 2012, 39). Civic-minded media providers serve audiences not just with entertainment-based content, but also with education and information – television schedules, for example, ought to include content that prompts political debate or that nurtures audience understandings of the world via documentary output. The civic-minded media model directs producers to serve a diversity of audience types, both mainstream and minority, niche and broad.

- **Citizen-based regulation foregrounds content issues.** Maintaining acceptable standards of content is a primary focus for citizen-based regulation. Content makers are tasked to ensure that news accuracy is maintained and that programmes deal with issues in a fair and objective manner.
- **Encourages a media landscape that can critique governmental power.** Livingstone and Lunt argue that a central function of the media sector, if it is working properly, lies in its ability to hold the government and other sources of authority to account. A citizen-oriented approach champions investigative journalism and consumer affairs programming, and scrutinises government decisions.

Box 13.1   Discuss it: do you favour a consumer-based or citizen-based approach?

- Should media producers be compelled to provide educational content?
- Should we censor media content so that audiences are protected from seeing material that is offensive? To what degree should the government play a role in deciding what we should or should not watch?
- Should the media play a significant role in reinforcing democracy? What might happen if the media did not inform us through political coverage?

Communications Act 2003

The Communications Act 2003 was designed by the then Labour government to modernise the UK's regulatory systems and help the UK television industry become competitive in the globalised media landscape of the late twentieth century. The 2003 Act, among other things, promoted independent television production by requiring the BBC and Channel 4 to commission more content from smaller production companies.

Crucially, for Livingstone and Lunt, the replacement of the Broadcast Standards Commission (BSC) and the Independent Television Commission (ITC) with the new super regulator Ofcom through the Communications Act 2003 significantly diluted the public service requirements of television broadcasting. As a result, independent television production companies were freed up to produce content that was more commercially viable, but this also resulted, some critics suggest, in the production of programming that lacks the civic-minded republicanism that had been fostered by the ITC's civic-minded framework. Livingstone and Lunt argue that Ofcom 'established institutional structures and roles relating to consumer policy ... Strikingly, little equivalent activity or accountability was forthcoming regarding actions to further citizen interests' (Livingstone and Lunt, 2012, 50).

More general criticism is levelled at the UK's current regulatory infrastructure regarding the way that the various regulatory bodies (see Table 13.1) responsible for media oversight are managed. Livingstone and Lunt remind us, for example, that the organisations tasked to regulate the media are often overseen by staff who are drawn from the very industries they seek to police, prompting accusations of industry bias. The codes of practice enforced by regulatory bodies are further criticised as unduly lenient – existing, to a large extent, to protect the interests of vulnerable audiences and children. Key concerns of the various codes used across the different media sectors include:

- **Protection of under eighteens.** Both the British Board of Film Classification's (BBFC) film classification system and the Games Rating Authority's use of PEGI rating labels, for example, are designed to help parents identify depictions of violence, sexually explicit content and taboo language use. Similarly, Ofcom guidance for television and radio broadcasters provides closely defined rules to ensure that depictions of harmful or imitable behaviour, sexualised imagery and violence are limited to post-watershed broadcast slots.

- **Accuracy.** The Advertising Standards Authority's (ASA) codes, for example, identify inaccuracy as a significant issue with the power to force advertisers to withdraw materials that make misleading or false claims. The Independent Press Standards Organisation (IPSO) – the UK's magazine and newsprint regulator – can also launch investigations where magazines or newspapers are accused of including misleading, inaccurate or distorted reporting.
- **Protection of privacy.** Ofcom, the ASA and IPSO all contain detailed guidance to help prevent unwarranted intrusions into privacy by the media. Ofcom, for example, stipulates that television and radio makers must not use material recorded without the consent of subjects, while IPSO includes a specific clause in its code that photographs must not be taken of individuals, 'in public or private places where there is a reasonable expectation of privacy' (IPSO, 2021).

The Leveson Inquiry and the formulation of IPSO

One of the most significant prompts for regulatory reform since the Communications Act 2003 came in the form of the Leveson Inquiry, a report into the culture and ethics of the UK press. Lord Justice Leveson's 2012 investigation was prompted by accusations that newspapers were illegally hacking the phones of celebrities and crime victims to secure headline stories. Leveson concluded that newspapers had shown 'recklessness in prioritising sensational stories, almost irrespective of the harm the stories may cause and the rights of those who would be affected' (O'Carroll, 2012). His recommendations included the setting up of a new press watchdog to be policed by non-industry personnel and backed up by government legislation.

A watered-down and much criticised version of that watchdog was set up in the form of IPSO in 2014, a new independent regulatory body that was granted the power to levy fines of up to £1 million for newspapers and magazines judged to have broken its editorial code of conduct. IPSO, however, has issued no financial penalties in its lifetime, leading some commentators to be critical of the regulator's agenda to clean up UK news practices. Membership of IPSO, moreover, is voluntary with some titles (*The Guardian, The Independent* and *Financial Times*) opting out because they impose their own much tougher codes of conduct via self-regulation.

Self-regulation

In the absence of extensive state-sponsored regulation, media producers are left, to a large degree, to independently decide upon their own moral or ethical direction. As a result, most media organisations construct their own editorial codes in addition to those outlined by regulatory bodies to guide the creative personnel working under their remit. Of course, these editorial codes vary enormously from one institution to the next. *The Sun*, for example, adopts a much looser approach to sexually explicit content than *The Guardian*, while the BBC's commitment to producing citizen-oriented content is far more extensive than its commercial rivals. Broadcasters and publishers will invariably use the following factors to help them define the editorial standards that their output should maintain:

- **Independent regulator codes of conduct:** most producers will apply the editorial codes of their sector-based regulator (see Table 13.1).
- **Audience-based factors:** producers and editors are sensitive to the needs and tastes of their target audiences and will invariably mirror those standards to retain readerships.
- **Advertiser needs:** commercial producers are mindful of the impact that editorial content will have on advertising revenues. Advertisers invariably place adverts in products that match their own brand values and will readily pull advertising if content does not match their own ethical steer.
- **Institution-oriented factors:** some organisations – the BBC and Channel 4 in particular – are obliged to provide citizen-oriented content as a result of their broadcasting licence agreements.

Table 13.1 Quick reference: key regulators operating in the UK

Regulator	Responsible for	Primary responsibilities	Sanctions
Ofcom	• Commercial radio and television. • Video on demand (NOW TV, Amazon Prime but not Netflix). • Jointly responsible for regulating the BBC alongside the BBC's board of governors.	• Tries to ensure that the media landscape is not dominated by a single organisation. • Oversees complaints from members of the public. • Protects those under 18 years old from exposure to harmful content.	• Can direct broadcasters to not repeat problematic material. • Can demand a correction or apology. • Can impose a fine in very extreme cases or even revoke a broadcaster's licence.
Advertising Standards Authority (ASA)	• Print advertising (newspapers, magazines). • Ambient advertising (billboards, bus hoardings). • Radio advertising. • Online advertising. • Television advertising. • Internet advertising (including YouTube). • Social media content in which online advertisers promote products.	• Oversees complaints made by members of the public regarding adverts. • Applies a standards code – mostly concerned with protecting vulnerable groups and to ensure accuracy in advert claims. • Pre-clears screen-based advertising. • Encourages self-regulation.	• Can force broadcast advertisers to withdraw or amend problematic advertising. • The ASA's powers online are limited to naming and shaming repeat offenders.
Independent Press Standards Organisation (IPSO)	• Regulates a voluntary membership of over 1,500 print (newspaper and magazines) and 1,000 online news titles. • Some newspapers have refused to sign up to the voluntary code, including *The Guardian*, *The Observer and Financial Times*	• The semi-official press regulator for the UK – oversees reader complaints that infringe its editorial code of conduct. • Complaints are overseen by an adjudicating panel made up of industry-based experts.	• Can levy fines of up to £1 million but has never issued any financial penalties. • Most adverse judgements result in retractions or printed apologies.

British Board of Film Classification (BBFC)	• UK film and video distribution.	• Operates a co-regulatory code that classifies films according to age-appropriate criteria. • The key focus of the BBFC is to protect children from harmful content and to help parents make informed viewing choices for their children.	• No sanctions needed – films are pre-vetted before distribution.
Games Rating Authority (GRA)	• Games sold as physical copies including console-related online gaming content. • Games developers initially self-certify content using the PEGI classification system with checks carried out later by the GRA to certify content.	• Operates a content code that enables age-related classification of games. • Like the BBFC, the GRA's primary aim is to provide reliable information to guide parents when purchasing console games.	• Again, no sanctions needed – games are pre-vetted before distribution. • Retailers supplying physical copies of 12-, 16- or 18-rated titles to underage buyers can be prosecuted. Supply of digital or downloadable material is not illegal.

Box 13.2   Apply it: using Livingstone and Lunt to answer regulation-oriented questions

Livingstone and Lunt suggest that the UK is dominated by a consumer-based approach to regulation. Regulation impacts on products in the following ways:

1 A consumer-oriented regulatory approach has created product diversity in which audiences play a vital role in regulating their own media consumption.
2 Media producers are trusted to police their own content (guided by the 'light-touch' editorial codes of independent regulators).
3 Some media producers choose to include citizen-oriented content – social diversity, educational elements, etc. – as a result of following a public service broadcasting ethos.
4 Consumer-oriented regulatory codes exist, primarily, to protect vulnerable audiences.
5 Media producers face light-touch sanctions when editorial codes are infringed.

Use the following questions to help guide your analysis of the consumer impact:

Consumer choice

• Does the product contain material that is controversial?
• In what ways does set text content meet the demands of the target audience?

Self-regulatory effects and citizen-oriented content

• In what ways does the set text police its own content? What prompts this self-policing?
• How do target audience/advertiser needs affect self-regulatory decisions?
• Does the product deliberately contain material that exemplifies a civic-minded approach? Why?

Protection of vulnerable audiences

- How do the set texts protect vulnerable users from potentially problematic content?
- Does the set text broadcast content that contains material that is problematic for vulnerable users? How?
- In what ways does the set text comply with regulatory codes to protect vulnerable audiences?

Infringement issues

- Has the set text ever infringed regulatory guidelines? What were the repercussions of those infringements?

Exemplar: *Assassin's Creed* Franchise (Eduqas). Livingstone and Lunt's argument that the media landscape is dominated by a consumer-based regulatory approach can certainly be applied to the video games sector. That approach is hugely permissive, ultimately devolving content-policing decisions to audiences, with regulatory controls principally concerned to protect the needs of the young and vulnerable.

The Games Rating Authority (GRA), for example, provides parents with age-based ratings of content using PEGI classifications. The PEGI system enables parents to identify violent or graphic content while also providing a legal framework to limit sales of physical copies of games (DVDs and cartridges) to underage buyers. *Assassin's Creed Odyssey*, for example, is classified by the GRA as an adult-only title due to graphic depictions of violence and torture in gameplay as well as cut scenes that include unmotivated attacks on innocent characters. Language issues elevate the title to an 18 certificate because of the use of frequent extreme taboo phrases, outlining the game as unsuitable for younger players.

Further set text help is available for a range of products for all exam boards at www.essentialmediatheory.com

Concept 2: regulation in the globalised media age

Livingstone and Lunt tell us that the global nature of contemporary media production and distribution has weakened the UK's ability to effect meaningful control of media content. They further identify the following factors that make it difficult for governments to effectively regulate digital global media output:

- **The relatively recent expansion of online services.** Today's tech giants have expanded their reach at an extraordinary rate. Anticipating and reacting to the regulatory issues thrown up by that expansion has been hugely difficult.
- **Tech giants do not author their own content.** Because Meta, Google, Tik Tok and X publish user-generated content, it makes it almost impossible for them to pre-vet problematic material. YouTube, for instance, claims to have over one billion users with some estimates suggesting that over 300 hours of footage are uploaded every minute. Companies have had some success in deploying content-vetting algorithms to automate their gate-keeping processes, but they currently lack the sophistication to solve meaningful regulatory issues in a satisfactory way.
- **Online media providers lie beyond the reach of UK regulation.** Regulation of the internet's major content distributors is made more difficult because their operations are based outside of the UK. To a lesser extent, the same is true of global television streamers who operate beyond the control of the UK's broadcast regulator Ofcom. Netflix stands as a useful exemplar here in that its European base in the Netherlands means that it is regulated by the Dutch-based Commissariaat voor de media and not Ofcom, while other on-demand distributors like Amazon Prime, Disney+ and Paramount+ are subject to a lighter set of Ofcom guidelines than those outlined for the UK's domestic broadcasters. Ofcom's On Demand Programme Service rules, for example, are less defined in terms of what constitutes harmful or offensive content, nor do they put in place a suitable alternative to the broadcasting watershed to prevent younger viewers from accessing harmful material.
- **The internet is decentralised.** Attempts to regulate social media giants may succeed, but regulation of the wider content of the net is a hugely difficult task given the extent of material available and the number of authors manufacturing content.

- **Online anonymity.** The anonymous authoring of content makes it hard to identify individuals and to take meaningful action if content contravenes expectations.

Attempts to regulate digital content

The failure of the Communications Act 2003 to address online media and the hesitance of subsequent UK governments to tackle online regulation has prompted widespread dissatisfaction. The ASA, however, effects some limited reach in policing online advertising, while also declaring an interest in the activities of social media influencers in 2018, outlining guidelines that require vloggers and influencers to label content that contains sponsored material. The volume of online marketing posts, however, make it all but impossible for the ASA to effectively monitor all online content, and when infringements are spotted, ASA sanctions are limited in scope due to the organisation's lack of power to control online distributors who operate outside of the UK.

The Online Safety Bill of 2023 outlines a significant move to regulate the activities of the online sector, giving Ofcom a new set of powers to make the internet a safer space for children. The Bill seeks to make social media platforms:

- delete illegal or harmful content and to identify measures that will prevent problematic material from being published at all.
- devise ways to stop children from accessing harmful or overtly sexual material.
- enforce strict age limits for signing up to social media platforms.

Box 13.3   Discuss it: should the internet be regulated?

- What evidence can you present to support the argument that the internet should be regulated?
- Have you ever seen any problematic online content?
- Does the internet pose a particular problem for vulnerable users? In what ways?

Table 13.2 Know it: key regulatory themes in different media sectors

Medium	Key themes
Television and radio	• **Self-regulation and the BBC.** BBC products exemplify a civic-minded approach to production, readily applying a citizen-based ethos to their products. • **Self-regulation and Channel 4.** Channel 4 was initially constructed as a public service broadcaster, and still retains much of that civic-minded ethos, yet a combination of budgetary constraints and a reliance on advertising has pushed the broadcaster towards what many would regard as a consumer-based production agenda. As a result, Channel 4 increasingly commissions content that promotes entertainment values over public service. • **Increased competition for terrestrial broadcasters from global media.** The relatively weak regulatory approach by the UK government in terms of protecting UK content has allowed global media producers to dominate UK television viewing. The European Union, in contrast, sets a 30% quota to ensure that streaming providers make European content.
Newspapers and magazines	• **Weak press regulation.** The failure of the Communications Act 2003 to include the print news sector within the remit of Ofcom is seen to be particularly problematic. The creation of IPSO in the wake of the Leveson Inquiry, moreover, has prompted a great deal of criticism regarding the new regulator's failure to encourage citizen-based news values across the print sector. • **Broadsheet self-regulation.** Broadsheet newspapers, however, have tried to maintain their reputations by constructing their own citizen-oriented editorial codes.
Online	• **Limited regulation of online content.** The failure of the Communications Act 2003 to address internet-based content has resulted in a regulatory approach to online media that is relatively weak. Social media platforms lack effective regulation. • **Online extremism.** The failure of social media to control fake news and extremist content is the result of a regulatory model that does not adequately take account of audiences as citizens.

(*Continued*)

Table 13.2 (Continued)

Medium	Key themes
	• **Protecting vulnerable users.** The capacity for social media to influence youth audiences is particularly concerning. The 2023 Online Safety Bill seeks to remedy that by making online platforms more accountable for published content. • **Regulating online influencers.** The ASA, however, does regulate online advertising and has taken action to make sure that online influencers who endorse products declare any payments received to their followers. • **The difficulties of policing global online media.** Online media provides a further difficulty in that most content is delivered by tech giants who fall beyond the reach of the UK's regulatory system. The power and size of online media giants makes it incredibly difficult for the UK government to create applicable legislation.
Film and gaming	• **The creation of advisory bodies designed to protect vulnerable audiences.** Both the BBFC and the GRA play an advisory role in terms of informing parents about the content of products. In the case of gaming, the application of PEGI classifications by the GRA has had a limited effect on controlling the sale of problematic content to children.

Table 13.3 Speak Livingstone and Lunt

Citizen-based regulation	Citizen-based regulatory systems outline a civic role for the media and encourage media makers to produce content that contributes to the social and cultural health of the societies in which they operate.
Consumer-based regulation	A regulatory system in which choices regarding content are largely devolved to audiences and where media makers are given as much freedom as possible to make the media that audiences want to consume.
Digital literacy	Sonia Livingstone advocates that audiences should be adequately informed about online content in a way that allows them to effectively evaluate the material they are presented with online.
Self-regulation	Self-regulation devolves regulatory decisions to industry practitioners.

Table 13.4 Livingstone and Lunt: ten-minute revision

Concept 1: *citizen and consumer-based models of media regulation*

- Citizen-oriented regulation is concerned with content-based issues.
- Citizen-based regulation is a positive form of regulation that directs media content so that it can improve the lives of citizens and contribute to the well-being of wider society.
- Citizen-based regulation promotes forms of media that can hold powerful groups to account.
- Consumer-based regulation seeks to ensure that the media landscape contains a variety of different producers so that audiences have choice.
- Consumer-based regulation seeks to ensure that the technological infrastructure that provides media to the public is fit for purpose.
- Consumer-based regulation creates an environment in which audiences themselves make judgements about the kinds of media that are appropriate for their consumption.
- A consumer-oriented approach has dominated the media landscape because of the Communications Act 2003 and the creation of Ofcom.

Concept 2: *the challenge of regulation in the age of globalised media*

- Globalisation has reduced the power of national governments to control the media – global companies operate beyond the scope and boundaries of any one country.

Challenging Livingston and Lunt's thinking

Some commentators might suggest that Livingstone and Lunt's assessment of media regulation, particularly digital regulation, doesn't go far enough. Christian Fuchs, for example, points to the growing power of corporate digital monopolies, arguing that the size, power and reach of tech giants like Meta (Facebook) have an insidious effect on th globe's democratic capacity and ought to be subject to tighter controls. He highlights, for example, Cambridge Analytica's improper use of Facebook user data by the Trump campaign to build voter profiles and Mark Zuckerberg's repeated refusal to give evidenc when called to a UK House of Parliament inquiry that sought to investigate Facebook's role in the scandal. Regulating digital content is a sideshow, Fuchs suggests, and the rea challenge facing governments is to devise mechanisms that can regulate the monopolisti control of big tech.

Sonia Livingstone herself has shifted direction, focusing her research energies on issues like digital literacy, arguing that UK audiences – parents and teachers in particular – need more help in their battle to equip young people with the necessary skills to negotiate digital content issues. A tacit admission, perhaps, that government control of digital content is all but impossible in today's ever-expanding online world.

Two named theorists who might challenge Livingstone and Lunt's thinking

---

- **Henry Jenkins:** would emphasise the benefits that the global digital media landscap offers. He would argue that digital media allows audiences to freely construct their own products and to make connections with like-minded individuals across the world. This process has also enabled some groups to effect deep-seated social change
- **David Gauntlett:** again, would emphasise the benefits of globalisation. Globalisation, he might argue, has brought audiences into contact with a wide range of identities that they did not previously have access to. This has helped audiences to perceive their identities as fluid and not fixed.

---

14 The culture industry
David Hesmondhalgh

Hesmondhalgh's 'cultural industries' approach explores the media from the perspective of commercial production practices and makes two enormously important observations regarding the necessities of product development:

1 **Products exist within an economic context.** Hesmondhalgh, first and foremost, tells us that media products are made within a commercial context. Much like any other business product, media content is manufactured to create profit, or, in the case of public service broadcasting, to maintain audience engagement. To gain a full understanding of the media industry and its impacts, Hesmondhalgh argues, we must appreciate the extent to which media-making decisions are guided by the need to be profitable as opposed to prioritising creativity.
2 **The media industry is a high-risk business.** 'All business is risky,' Hesmondhalgh writes, 'but the cultural industries constitute a particularly risky business' (Hesmondhalgh, 2019, 31). The impossibility of predicting audience tastes coupled with the high costs of production and the effects of mass competition mean that the business of making commercially successful media is very difficult. The reduction of those risks, Hesmondhalgh argues, has compelled the media industry to be structured in highly specific ways with risk minimisation, importantly, playing a crucial role in directing the design and marketing of media content.

DOI: 10.4324/9781003361220-14

Concept 1: maximising profits and minimising risks

The high-stakes nature of the media industry is exemplified, perhaps, by the enormous problems that film production companies face when trying to distribute a new release. The British Film Institute's analysis, for example, of the 834 films released in the UK in 2022 reported a total gross revenue of £945 million in cinema ticket sales for the period. The top 20 releases, however, monopolised over 67% of that total, with the number one hit of the year, *Top Gun: Maverick*, taking £83.7 million alone. The UK independent film sector accounted for just 7.9% of total ticket sales, with just one UK independent film, *Belfast*, making it over the £10 million mark.

Such figures underline the 'winner takes all' nature of commercial media, in which a relatively small number of big hits capture a disproportionate share of the available profits. Predicting the success of those big hits, Hesmondhalgh tells us, is hugely difficult, if not impossible. Hesmondhalgh (2019) outlines these difficulties as follows:

- **Media businesses are reliant upon changing audience consumption patterns.** Audience tastes continuously adapt making it incredibly difficult to produce material that guarantees satisfaction.
- **The media industry is reliant on marketing and publicity functions.** Products need the oxygen of publicity if they are to thrive, but controlling the messages delivered by reviewers or publicity partners of other companies is very difficult – even if such organisations are owned by the same parent company as the producer.
- **Media products have limited consumption capacity.** Unlike other businesses, films, television and music-based products tend to be consumed as 'one off' purchases. The 'one off' nature of production means that the huge sums of cash invested to create media products results in a one-time reward.

Hesmondhalgh argues that the risks associated with media creation leads the culture industry to employ a highly tuned range of production and organisational practices. Moreover, because the media industry is sustained, by and large, using the enormous profits achieved from the industry's winners – top grossing films, hit

TV dramas and so on – it must employ an economic model that deliberately overproduces content.

In short, media companies create as many products as they can in the hope that one or two projects will be hits. Only large-scale companies can successfully engage in this overproduction model given the enormous sums required to finance multiple projects simultaneously and the requisite need to absorb the huge losses of failed products while companies search for big hits.

The ways in which media organisations expand

Hesmondhalgh argues that overproduction has compelled media companies to expand through mergers or the acquisition of smaller companies. Growth in the media sector has traditionally centred on the following three strategies:

1 **Horizontal integration:** acquiring media companies that operate in similar sectors enables large-scale institutions to achieve scale-based cost savings, while also allowing them to maximise profits by positioning brands so they do not compete with one another. (The benefits of horizontal integration are covered in more detail in Chapter 12.)
2 **Vertical integration:** by acquiring production, distribution and marketing specialist subsidiaries, media conglomerates can control all aspects of their supply chain while also achieving significant cost-saving efficiencies. (Again, a more detailed discussion of the benefits wrought through vertical integration are covered in Chapter 12.)
3 **Multi-sector integration:** buying companies across the culture industry allows for further cross-promotion opportunities and the deployment of brands across media platforms. Most films, for instance, create cross-brand profits through the sale of soundtracks and, in the case of Disney, through their theme park experiences.

Expansion strategies and brand acquisitions

Hesmondhalgh, like Curran and Seaton, is careful to distinguish between those personnel in the media industry who are responsible for producing creative content – the 'symbol creators' as

Hesmondhalgh calls them – and those who oversee the wider business-oriented functions of media distribution.

Traditionally, Hesmondhalgh tells us that, 'symbol creators are granted considerable autonomy within the process of production – far more, in fact, than most workers in other forms of industry' (Hesmondhalgh, 2019, 32). Writers, directors, journalists and designers, he tells us, are given enough artistic freedom to create products that excite audience engagement. Yet, Hesmondhalgh argues, these loose controls are giving way to tighter business models in which creativity increasingly plays a secondary role to marketing needs and brand development.

Box 14.1   Discuss it: what impact does internationalisation have on media?

Hesmondhalgh suggests that media expansion is often pursued so that producers can develop the ability to distribute their products on a global scale (internationalisation). Global distribution, of course, generates the capacity to exponentially increase the profits made from any single investment, but can also result in media products that sacrifice local flavour to maximise global appeal.

- In what ways are today's mainstream media products crafted so that they can appeal to international audiences?
- Does today's globalised media landscape mean that we consume a disproportionate number of products that originated in the USA? Is this problematic?
- Do audiences suffer when their media stops being local?

This process is evidenced, in part, by the kinds of acquisitions that have dominated media expansion in the past decade. Yes, conglomerates continue to expand both vertically and horizontally, but they are growing in ways that enable them to acquire lucrative brand-driven content. Disney's $4 billion takeover of Marvel in 2009 and the 2012 purchase of Lucasfilm, also for $4 billion, was pursued, in part, to give Disney exclusive access to the hugely successful film brands cultivated by both companies. Those acquisitions have yielded not only filmic content, but also a steady stream of new television titles to promote their Disney+ global streaming service. Here, Disney's creative teams have been tasked to minimise the commercial risk of launching a new streaming platform by targeting the inherited audiences of the *Star Wars* and *Marvel* franchises, developing serialised content in the form of shows like *The Mandalorian* and *Ms. Marvel*.

'The increasing presence and status of marketing,' Hesmondhalgh argues, 'represents a shift in the relations between creativity and commerce' (Hesmondhalgh, 2019, 243). Product-branding decisions, for instance, are increasingly channelled by audience research and focus groups. Product content, too, is pushed in directions that consumption data suggests will generate the most engagement. The consumption of products using digital platforms has enabled media distributors to mine audience data in new and extraordinary ways. Netflix, Amazon and Apple+, for example, understand in microscopic detail the engagement patterns of their subscribers, gathering data about what kinds of audiences are watching and where, for how long those audiences are watching, and when they are hitting their stop buttons. Data harvesting of this kind informs decisions about which pitches will be commissioned, or, more cruelly, whether existing series will be recommissioned. Detailed audience data also produces statistics that help them determine which stars, directors, genres or show formats are working, and which aren't.

Product formatting and risk reduction

Media makers, Hesmondhalgh tells us, control commercial risks through the careful supervision of distribution and promotion practices, affecting what he calls 'artificial scarcity' – restricting access to products by limiting their availability to platforms that are owned by the parent company of the product (Hesmondhalgh, 2019, 31). Disney, for example, restricts access to its film back catalogue to its vertically integrated distribution services (principally its cable broadcasting infrastructure and its Disney+ streaming service). This allows Disney to preserve the mystique of its classic films while also preventing competing broadcasters from using Disney content to grow their own audiences.

Hesmondhalgh draws our attention to the following formatting strategies also used by the media industry to reduce risk:

- **Star formatting.** It takes, Hesmondhalgh suggests, 'considerable marketing efforts, in order to break a writer or performer as a new star' (Hesmondhalgh, 2019, 31). Yet star power, once enabled, can deliver ready-made audiences for products.
- **Genre-based formatting.** Labelling media content using genre-based categories allows audiences to identify the potential rewards of consuming a particular media product in advance of consumption. In this sense, genres, Hesmondhalgh argues, operate as a pre-promise of consumer satisfaction.
- **Serialisation.** The use of sequels and prequels are well-established techniques that are deployed to maximise audience engagement and that allow producers to fully realise their investments in serialised material (spin-offs, sequels, etc.). Serialised media needs less investment in marketing activities to create audience visibility. Prequels, too, piggyback on pre-existing audience successes, while also enabling institutions to nurture new star power through the introduction of unknown talent within an established, and relatively risk free formula. The success of serialisation as a production strategy is evidenced by the sheer volume of franchised output that dominates streaming releases and film charts. In 2022, for example, 9 out of the top 10 grossing films released in cinemas in the UK were part of a pre-existing franchise.
- **Remakes.** The media industry further reduces risk by recycling archived material that has enjoyed prior success. Retellings often seek to recapture audience engagement through nostalgia-based appeals, while also rebranding content so that it fits the needs of a contemporary audience.
- **Independent labelling.** Hesmondhalgh points to the use of 'independents' to produce and market media goods. Independents, he argues, provide a useful means of engaging audiences that are reluctant to consume mainstream media. Conglomerates delegate production to independents to shield themselves from the impact of content failure on their brand identity. Companies that are truly independent, of course, use their non-mainstream status as a marketing tool, deliberately stylising and formatting their products in ways that make them look and feel alternative.

Box 14.2 Apply it: how do film marketing products use established formatting techniques to reduce risk?

Hesmondhalgh's approach can be applied to questions that ask you to consider how products are styled or format-ted in order to create audience interest. Use the following questions to help you construct Hesmondhalgh-oriented analysis:

- **Star power.** In what ways does the product use star power? For what is the star best known and for what sorts of audience will the star create appeal? Remember that stars can include writers, directors and journalists as well as performance-oriented stars.
- **Genre-based formatting.** What genre does the product invoke through marketing decisions? How is the product stylised to make its genre explicitly visible? What narra-tive satisfactions does genre formatting convey to the product's target audience?
- **Remakes and serialisation.** Does the product piggy-back on previously successful products? How does it invoke product nostalgia to recapture existing audience interest? In what ways is the product reshaped for a new audience?
- **Independent stylising.** Does the product deliberately invoke a non-mainstream aesthetic? For whom does this create appeal?

Exemplar: *Black Panther* **(Eduqas).** Hesmondhalgh's as-sertion that media creativity is subservient to the business and marketing function of the industry is readily visible in *Black Panther*. The movie's use of a predominantly Black cast initially looked like a high-risk strategy in terms of delivering a mainstream audience, yet the use of the Kendrick Lamar soundtrack and the selection of Michael B. Jordan (*Creed*) as a frontline presence helped secure recognisable star power.

The further choice of Martin Freeman (*The Hobbit* and *The Office*) as Everett K. Ross also helped deliver wider European and UK audience appeal. Interestingly, Freeman is the first character we see in the UK general release trailer. Hesmondhalgh would similarly draw attention to the heavy presence of Marvel Studio branding within the trailer and the repetition of the hugely successful and in vogue superhero formula as a means of reducing the commercial risk through product serialisation.

Further exemplars for set texts from all exam boards are available online at www.essentialmediatheory.com

Concept 2: the effects of the internet revolution are difficult to diagnose

A great deal of academic writing that has tried to diagnose the impact of technological innovation has, Hesmondhalgh argues, done so using overly simplistic formulas. The reality of the digital revolution, he suggests – if it can be described as a revolution at all – is highly complex. More importantly, Hesmondhalgh tells us, the various practices that are seen to constitute 'Web 2.0' in reality represents a continuation of the activities of traditional mass media provision.

The faux benefits of cyberspace

Hesmondhalgh suggests that the often-cited positive effects of the digital revolution stem from an overly romanticised view of technology as an anti-authoritarian counterweight to traditional power sources. In contrast, he argues that the internet's 'many minor forms of subversion, insubordination and scepticism don't cancel out the enormous concentrations of power in the cultural industries' and further diagnoses those subversive effects as 'representing a disturbance' (Hesmondhalgh, 2019, 361). Hesmondhalgh's relegation of the digital revolution to the status of a mere 'disturbance' centres on a critique of the following two claims regarding technological innovation:

1 That the digital revolution gives power to audiences by enabling cultural participation and that audience control is enabled through feedback mechanisms.
2 That the digital revolution has weakened the power of the mass media.

In many ways, the benefits outlined above are very similar to the 'participatory culture' and 'end of audience' arguments presented, respectively, by Henry Jenkins (Chapter 18) and Clay Shirky (Chapter 19). Hesmondhalgh offers the following three criticisms:

1 **The web gives unequal user access and depends on user skill levels.** When we refer to the internet, we are really describing its capacity to provide a host of benefits, including email functionality, social networking, data storage and entertainment provision. Hesmondhalgh argues that users mostly access internet services in a relatively simplistic manner and usually for information-retrieval purposes only – reading online news, browsing the weather and so on. Only a relatively small number of advanced users deploy, or have the skills to deploy, the 'participatory culture' skills that Shirky and Jenkins celebrate.
2 **The internet is dominated by a relatively small number of providers.** Hesmondhalgh points to the dominance of search engines and their ability to point users to a small number of sources. In this sense, the near monopoly of Google as the world's search engine flatly contradicts the notion that the internet has eroded media concentration.
3 **The internet is increasingly dominated by commercialised activity.** Hesmondhalgh argues that the democratising impact of the internet has been further damaged by the adoption of an internet model that relies on advertising revenue. 'Much web content,' Hesmondhalgh argues, 'is permeated by advertising to the extent that it is sometimes difficult to tell where the advertisements end and the content begins' (Hesmondhalgh, 2019, 331). Thus, the neutrality of the information provided by the internet is compromised by commercial imperatives.

Hesmondhalgh also suggests that the various forms of technological advances of the digital era are often packaged together in ways that suggest the digital revolution is a singular force. He argues, in response, that technological advances have had varied effects on different media forms. Hesmondhalgh identities the following sector specific trends:

- **Digital games.** Despite technological advances, the games sector is still dominated by an oligarch of hardware companies (Sony, Nintendo and Microsoft). Smaller independent production has grown, but those companies are largely responsible for software development (with the exception of Electronic Arts). As a result, Hesmondhalgh suggests, the digital revolution has not really influenced the games sector – larger companies are still able to forge cross-media synergies with the film and music sectors, while formatted franchises (*Call of Duty*, *Assassin's Creed*, etc.) are used to maximise audiences and reduce risk.
- **Newspaper industry.** Hesmondhalgh suggests that technological developments have had a significantly adverse impact in this sector. Online media has eroded readerships and forced newspapers to adopt free-to-view online models. Some titles have tried to mitigate the effects of plummeting advertising revenues by implementing pay-per-view firewalls (*The Times*), while other publications such as *The Guardian* have turned to supplementary activities – using their brand recognition to sell dating services, books, holidays, music and other add-ons.
- **Television.** Hesmondhalgh points to the hybridisation of television and the internet to produce on-demand services and to enable time-shifted consumption patterns; however, he also argues that television viewing figures have not reduced greatly. The winners of the analogue to digital broadcast migration, he argues, are more likely to be the small number of global organisations that own the archives of content needed to fill on-demand services. Disney's global streaming service, Disney+, is a case in point here. Hesmondhalgh also points to the continued use of star power to attract audiences to streamed television products, with remakes and serialised content dominating the schedules of on-demand television services.

Box 14.3   Discuss it: what is the real impact of the so-called 'digital revolution'?

- Do you think that modern audiences fluently engage in participatory culture?
- Is participatory culture more likely to be used by a limited number of social groups? Think here in terms of age, gender and class.
- Which groups are likely to be excluded from the benefits of participatory culture?
- Are audiences still passive consumers?

Box 14.4   Apply it: assessing the revolutionary impact of digital innovation on your set texts

Hesmondhalgh's diagnosis of the digital revolution as a 'disturbance' can be integrated in exam responses that ask you to consider the way that digital consumption has impacted on audiences. Discussion that centres on the following three criticisms could be applied to these questions:

1 Digital products continue to engage passive viewing responses.
2 Digital products tend to be made by a relatively small number of providers.
3 The commercialisation of the web weakens the suggestion that the web is a democratising medium.

Exemplar: *Daily Mirror* (Eduqas). Hesmondhalgh tells us that the effects of the digital revolution aren't singularly beneficial, highlighting the newsprint industry as a hard-hit sector that has had to overcome significant issues because of the migration of readers from print to digital consumption. The *Daily Mirror*, like all other national news titles, has experienced a dramatic drop in print circulation, losing 15% of its readers in 2021 alone (BFI, 2023). Like most UK red top titles, the *Daily Mirror* has responded by shifting its distribution focus to a free-to-view online access model – a move that has presented it with significant advertising revenue issues because of the much-reduced income achieved from pay per click ad placement. That shift means that the *Daily Mirror* has had to increase its online readership numbers using smaller production budgets, necessitating the use of churnalistic content production in a bid to keep costs low and repeat visits to its website high, recycling press releases, rehashing stories from other publications, and sourcing click bait content from celebrity social media feeds. The *Mirror Online* foregrounds a much lighter editorial mix than its print counterpart, attempting to gain youth reader interest via celebrity news features, while also foregrounding family-oriented content to widen its reach to a more upmarket female audience.

Further exemplars for set texts from all exam boards are available online at www.essentialmediatheory.com

Table 14.1 Speak David Hesmondhalgh

Creative business managers	Those workers who look after the marketing, distribution and financing of media products.
Creative symbol makers	Hesmondhalgh suggests that those workers who create media products (scriptwriters, directors, etc.) are the media's creative symbol makers. Traditionally, creatives were given lots of freedom in the media industry, but, Hesmondhalgh argues, creative decision making is increasingly sidelined in favour of a business-oriented approach.
Genre formatting	Promoting products using genre formatting helps audiences to understand the narrative satisfactions that a product can offer prior to consumption.
Internationalisation	Internationalisation refers to strategies adopted by media makers to maximise their profits and audience reach using global distribution.

(*Continued*)

Table 14.1 (Continued)

Serialisation	Serialisation enables producers to reduce risk by constructing products that have an established audience.
Star formatting	The foregrounding of star power (writers, actors, directors and journalists) in products and promotional material to generate audience interest.

Table 14.2 Hesmondhalgh: ten-minute revision

Concept 1: *maximising profits and minimising risks*

- The media industry is prone to risk because of shifting audience tastes.
- The media industry tries to reduce risk through overproduction.
- Overproduction strategies can only be engaged by large media conglomerates.
- Media conglomerates have expanded to enable them to cope with risk.
- Media products are carefully formatted using several industry-specific strategies to reduce risk: serialisation, star power and genre formatting.

Concept 2: *the effects of the internet revolution are difficult to diagnose*

- The democratising effects of the digital revolution have been over-exaggerated by some academics.
- Digital media is used by audiences in radically different ways, with only a minority of users having the necessary skills to engage in participatory culture.
- The internet is dominated by a handful of very powerful companies.
- The commercialisation of the web has further reduced its democratising capacity.

Challenging Hesmondhalgh's thinking

Hesmondhalgh himself identifies Chris Anderson's long tail theory as an economic model that works in a radically different way to the big-business risk-minimisation dynamic of his own writing. Anderson's theory, for example, sees the internet as a place where high-risk niche products can find big enough audiences to sustain a diverse range of creative practices and practitioners. The internet, Anderson tells us, is a place where niche magazine titles, small-scale musicians and narrowcast documentary filmmakers can garner enough sales over time to sustain themselves. Contemporary media practice, as such, is a place where creative risks can be taken.

Hesmondhalgh's own writing provides a much more detailed picture of how the creative industries work, acknowledging the effects of government policy, sociocultural changes and technological developments as significant factors other than risk management that shape media output. He also acknowledges the shifting nature of audience loyalties 'and the tendency of audiences to shift and flit across different cultural experiences' – a factor, perhaps, that makes serialisation a less certain driver of commercial success (Hesmondhalgh, 2019, 465).

(*Continued*)

Table 14.2 (Continued)

Two named theorists who might challenge Hesmondhalgh's thinking

- **Henry Jenkins:** emphasises the positive effects of the digital revolution – suggesting that digital media cultivates online communities and allows audiences to express themselves in positive and creative ways through fan engagement.
- **Clay Shirky:** might argue that large-scale media providers will be replaced by products that are created by everyday users, or that mass media content will be significantly controlled by audience feedback mechanisms.

---

15 Media modelling effects

Albert Bandura

The exploration of aggression had been a point of interest for psychologists and philosophers long before Bandura introduced the world to his Bobo doll experiments. Sigmund Freud, for example, explained the origins of aggression as an innate and instinctive emotional response. Excessive masculine aggression, he reasoned, was present as a result of the male sex drive, suggesting that male aggression is driven by a latent fear of castration by our fathers.

Post-war psychologists, too, looked inwards to explain the presence of aggression – some connecting outwardly violent behaviour to the genetic disposition of individuals or to hormonal imbalances. Even as late as 1965, the psychologist P. A. Jacobs argued that a disproportionate number of institutionalised men, those committed to prison or mental institutions, were born with an extra chromosome that produced hyper-masculine behaviours. Aggression, Jacobs reasoned, was genetic or the product of innate dispositions that were beyond the control of the individual.

Bandura's experiments, however, led him to a remarkably different set of conclusions and gave birth to a psychological school of thought that was later labelled 'social learning theory'. Bandura's research, in short, suggested that our behaviours are not governed by innate traits or genetic impulses but that our environments – the human environment in particular – shapes the way we behave.

DOI: 10.4324/9781003361220-15

Concept 1: violent behaviours are learned through modelling

Bandura's psychological experiments led him to conclude that behaviours are acquired as a result of the following two processes:

1 **Direct experience.** Individuals, Bandura argued, learn or replicate aggressive acts as a result of their experiences of aggression. Children might learn to be aggressive from the models of negative behaviour provided by parents, or, conversely, they might reject violent behaviours as a result of parent-induced punishments and sanctions.

2 **Modelled learning.** Bandura intuited that direct experience alone could not account for all our human traits. Individuals, he hypothesised, could not possibly have witnessed enough directly modelled behaviour to account for the complexity of their own behaviour. Behaviours, Bandura conjectured, must therefore be learned by watching the actions of others – through what he called 'vicarious learning'. A child, for example, who witnesses the violent behaviour of a classmate might later imitate the actions that he or she sees. Conversely, if a child witnesses the same behaviour being punished, they might be more likely to be inhibited from copying those actions. 'It is evident,' Bandura writes, 'that human behaviour is to a large extent socially transmitted, either deliberately or inadvertently' (Bandura, 1973, 68).

Concept 2: audiences copy media modelling

Bobo dolls and symbolic modelling

Bandura's initial research, in the 1960s, was conducted using nursery-aged children who were made to watch a variety of adult role models execute a series of aggressive acts on an inflatable Bobo doll. The experiments were designed to investigate whether the children would copy the adults' actions when left alone, and, overwhelmingly, the observations that Bandura's team noted from the experiment were that the children did replicate the aggressive behaviours they had witnessed. Aggressive behaviours, Bandura concluded, were most certainly learned through direct modelling.

**Box 15.1   Think about it: from where
have you learned your own behaviours?**

- What influence have your parents had on your behaviours? In what ways have their expectations affected your outlook?
- Have your friends ever affected your behaviour in a negative or positive way?
- In what ways did the rules and expectations of your primary and secondary schools shape your behaviour?

What shocked the Bobo doll research team more was the response of the children when they replaced the adult role models with filmed sequences that depicted the same aggressive behaviour. To the researchers surprise, the children responded in a similarly violent manner, leading Bandura to conclude that behaviours can be transmitted through the representational effects of television.

Bandura's conclusions regarding media viewing, moreover, suggested that media-based representations of violence might have a more concentrated impact than direct modelling. He drew attention to the following three factors that amplify the effects of television consumption on behavioural modelling:

- **Attentional processes.** The effectiveness of a modelled behaviour is dependent on the degree to which the observer's attention is focused on the behaviour being modelled. In the real world, he argued, our attention is less focused on modelled action than when we watch television. 'Indeed, models presented in televised form are so effective in holding attention,' Bandura writes, 'that viewers learn the depicted behavior regardless of whether or not they are given extra incentives to do so' (Bandura, 1973, 70).
- **Role models and social learning.** The effectiveness of modelling is also swayed by the people we are watching. If behaviour is modelled by aspirational role models, Bandura argued, we are more likely to want to copy their behaviour. The level of power and prestige of television-oriented role models therefore makes it more likely that they will have a greater impact on audience behaviours.

- **Retention processes.** Bandura argued that representations of behaviours that are visually vivid or symbolically constructed will be retained for longer periods. Given that television and film products are encoded in a visually rich manner – through costuming, set or acting styles – the resulting effect, Bandura argued, is much richer than real-life modelling.

Box 15.2   Discuss it: how did the media affect you?

- In what ways did watching visual media affect your behaviour as a young child? Did you or your brothers and sisters copy the negative behaviours you saw on television?
- Did you have any media role models that you wanted to be like when you were younger? What effect did those role models have on your behaviour?
- Is television hypnotic? Does it capture our attention in a way that no other media form can?

Television fiction and the commercialisation of violence

Bandura argued that television and film products are rich with violent content, and, as a result, adverse television modelling effects are widespread. Violence is endemic within the media, Bandura argued, because producers, scriptwriters and directors are themselves too desensitised to the effects of screen violence to raise objections to problematic content. Moreover, the media relies on conflict to engage audience attention quickly and effectively, using depictions of violence to produce cheap thrills in stories. Bandura also pointed to the incremental concentration of violent content that results from broadcaster competition, arguing that television producers continuously intensify violent content within their products as a means of poaching their competitors' audiences.

Video violence effects

Even though Bandura's work did not directly comment on the capacity of gaming to produce violent behaviours, it is routinely invoked to suggest that a link exists between real-life aggression and game playing. American mass shootings by teenagers, for instance, are regularly explained as a direct result of violent video game play. Commentators draw attention to the following factors when linking game playing and real-world violence:

- **Attention factors.** Players control and direct gaming avatars to exercise violence, meaning that a direct connection exists between player actions and the resulting violent behaviours that are depicted on screen. This intimate connection is seen to promote violent behaviours in the real world.
- **Players are rewarded for violent actions.** Gaming engines generate scores and rewards for kills. Narrative progression in games is often only revealed once violent episodes are resolved by players. Reward systems of this nature promote violent behaviour as positive modelling experiences.
- **Violence is portrayed without moral justification or explanation.** Games often require players to kill innocent bystanders or to inflict violence on defenceless characters. The casual nature of these acts desensitises players to the effects of real-world violence.
- **Video games are immersive.** Players are thought to consume video games in isolation without the mediating effects of others to help them question their actions.
- **Realistic violence.** Gaming graphics are increasingly capable of producing ever more realistic portrayals, and, in doing so, limit a gamer's ability to distinguish real-world actions from those experienced in gaming narratives.
- **Video games are addictive**. Long periods of gameplay produce sustained negative modelling experiences.

Box 15.3 Apply it (OCR and AQA): violence in television set texts

Both OCR and AQA suggest that students should be able to apply Bandura to their television set texts. Answers could reference the following:

- **Analysis of specific moments within the set texts that offer modelled violence**. What negative behaviours might audiences learn from these moments?

- **Analysis that explores the narrative context of modelled behaviour.** Is the violent behaviour of characters rewarded or punished across story arcs? How might these factors concentrate or inhibit audience responses?
- **Role model effects**. In what ways does star power or the idealised presentation of violent content help concentrate the product's modelling impact?
- **Attentional effects.** Does the way the product is consumed alter any modelling effect it might have? Might on-demand binge-watching result in an intensified modelling experience?
- **Vivid visual encoding effects**. Is modelled negative behaviour likely to have an effect on the product's audience as a result of a heightened aesthetic presentation?
- **Positive modelling effects**. Does the product have the potential to produce positive learning for the audience? How and where?

Arguments and theories you could also use that suggest audiences do not necessarily engage with products in the way that Bandura suggests:

- **Henry Jenkins:** use Jenkins' ideas concerning fan communities to develop discussion concerning any potential positive effects of set texts. In what ways are fans using set texts to explore positive rather negative aspects of their identity?
- **Stuart Hall:** use Hall's encoding and decoding model to critique Bandura's ideas. Not all audiences respond to products in the same way – we decode texts using our contextual knowledge and experience.

Exemplar responses for set texts from all exam boards are available at www.essentialmediatheory.com

Box 15.4   Apply it (OCR): using Bandura in synoptic set text questions

Opportunities to apply Bandura's theoretical perspective are available within the synoptic question of the component two exam. You could connect Bandura's arguments to question types in the following ways:

Questions that have a representation focus

- Representation of violence might be minimised because producers are mindful of modelling effects that products could have on their target audience.
- Representations of violent content might be deliberately minimised because of regulatory codes and wider fears that such imagery might provide modelled behaviour for vulnerable audiences.

Questions that have a language focus

- Genre-based products might contain violent content as a core convention or audience expectation.
- Narratives are conventionally driven by conflict. Conflict inevitably raises issues regarding the effects of violence on audiences in terms of modelling behaviours.

Questions that have an institution focus

- Commercial organisations, arguably, are more likely to include violence as a means of attracting audience engagement.
- Netflix content is not directly subject to UK regulatory codes. Does this make it more likely to produce material that produces modelled violence?
- On-demand broadcasting cannot reduce the effects of modelled violence using scheduling restrictions or watersheds.

Exemplar responses for set texts from all exam boards are available at www.essentialmediatheory.com

Regulatory frameworks as protection

The Pan European Gaming Information (PEGI) rating system has responded to the concerns surrounding gaming content by creating an advisory ratings code – a code also employed by the Games Rating Authority (GRA) to classify video game releases. The code principally protects vulnerable players through an age classification system and works to alert parents to the following types of gaming content:

- **Violent content.** Games with lower age ratings must contain minimal violence. A 12-rated game is allowed to include violent content as long as it is presented in a non-realistic manner. Violence perpetrated on innocent characters is only allowed in 18-rated games.
- **Drugs, alcohol and tobacco use.** Depictions of this nature are limited to PEGI 16-certified games and above. Glamorised depictions of drug taking are only allowed in PEGI 18-certified games.
- **Discrimination.** Games that contain problematic ethnic, religious, nationalistic or other negative stereotypes are again restricted to an 18 certificate.

Box 15.5   Discuss it: video game regulation and imitable behaviour

- How effective do you think the PEGI ratings system is in protecting young people from the harmful effects of gaming? How might young people circumvent that system?
- What evidence would you present to critique the view that video games induce violent behaviour?

Box 15.6   Apply it (Eduqas and AQA): using Bandura in video game set text questions

Eduqas and AQA questions that ask you to apply Bandura's ideas to games and online set texts might be styled as follows:

- **Eduqas.** Explain how audiences might respond to video games. Answer with reference to your video game set

text. (12 marks)
- **AQA.** Media effects theories argue that the media has the power to shape the audience's thoughts and behaviour. How valid do you find the claims made by effects theories? You should refer to two of the Close Study Products. (25 marks)

Answers to the above could focus on the following key areas:

- **Attention and immersion factors.** Gaming technologies produce narratives that are longer and far more complex than other media forms – potentially leading to a more concentrated modelling effect.
- **Graphic content.** Provide knowledge and analysis of moments in set text gameplay and/or marketing materials where graphic violence is depicted. What potential modelling effects might those moments have on audiences? In what ways do these moments glamorise screen violence?
- **Gameplay that provides rewards for violent actions.** Analyse how your gaming set texts reward audiences for violent play. Identify the use of violence to unlock side missions, advance narratives, provide new weapons or advance online multiplayer rankings. What impact do these reward systems have in promoting violent behaviours?
- **Portrayals of violence that have moral justification or explanation.** Discuss moments in set texts where protagonist violence is disproportionate to antagonist actions. These moments might also be found in marketing materials. Does this sort of game violence desensitise players?
- **Video games are targeted at impressionable teenage audiences.** Video games are regulated, but is the PEGI classification system used by the GRA effective in prohibiting under-age game consumption? Discuss the effects of online distribution on teenage consumption and the ease with which young audiences can circumvent age checks.

Exemplar responses for set texts from all exam boards are available at www.essentialmediatheory.com

The arguments against negative video game modelling

In 2008, Henry Jenkins famously rallied to the defence of the video games industry, arguing that the panic surrounding gaming violence was founded on some questionable assumptions (Jenkins 2019). He highlights the following factors in defence of video game playing:

- **Studies that link game playing time and criminal behaviours are flawed.** Advocates of the argument that video games produce violent behaviour often point to studies that identify video game use by violent youth offenders as disproportionately widespread. Yet, Jenkins points out, video gaming is so universally practised among teenagers that any concrete cause and effect link is highly tenuous.
- **Game play is not solitary.** Jenkins points to research that suggests most gameplay takes place within a social context, either physically or across a digital network. Researchers point to the potential benefits of communal play, suggesting that players hone communication skills by working together to solve gaming problems.
- **Audiences can separate gameplay from real life.** Games might indeed illicit violent responses on screen, but research suggests that players are able to distinguish screen violence from their real-world activities.

Box 15.7 Apply it: diagnose the positive effects of video game set texts on their audiences

Video games and moral panics

Critics suggest that video game violence concerns are magnified by the media, and that the moral panic concerning the effects of gameplay are symptomatic of society's wider anxieties about the use of new technologies by young people. Think about the following questions to help you diagnose the positive effects of your video game set texts:

- In what ways do your set texts have a positive effect on audience behaviours?
- Do any of your gaming set texts teach their audiences new skills? How do they do this?

Exemplar responses for set texts from all exam boards are available at www.essentialmediatheory.com

Table 15.1 Speak Albert Bandura

Attentional effects	Bandura argues that media products are more likely to produce modelled behaviour because of the focused attention they command while engaging with them.
Desensitisation	Desensitisation normalises violent behaviours as a result of repeated exposure.
Modelled learning	Bandura suggests that we learn new behaviours by watching other people (direct modelling). Behaviours can be inhibited if we see others being punished; conversely, we copy behaviours when they are rewarded.
Representational modelling	The process of watching behaviours on screen. Bandura concludes that representational modelling can be equally, if not more, powerful than direct modelling.
Role model effects	Bandura argues that watching others we hold in high regard (on-screen stars/heroes) can amplify the impact of any modelled behaviours.

Table 15.2 Bandura: ten-minute revision

Concept 1: *violent behaviours are learned through modelling*

- Humans learn much of their behaviour through social interaction.
- Social learning can occur as a result of first-hand experience.
- Social learning can also occur by watching others' experiences.

Concept 2: *audiences can copy media representations of negative behaviour*

- Representational modelling can have a powerful effect on the behaviours of media audiences.
- Modelled behaviours by role models and the vivid visual encoding systems of media products further concentrate the effects of representational modelling.
- Violence is an endemic feature of media content.

Challenging Bandura's thinking

Alternative explanations of audience effects after Bandura have tried to identify how the media works in the real lives of audiences, observing, for example, the potential effects of television watching in real family living rooms rather than the artificial world of the science laboratory. Such research suspected that Bandura's conclusion that audiences were largely passive receivers of media messaging failed to take account of the social interactions that accompany television viewing – that media watching, for example, is often accompanied by family discussion that shifts, filters or tweaks the messages produced by products.

(*Continued*)

Table 15.2 (Continued)

Other qualitative studies questioned the idea that different audience groups react to media products in the same way – that gender or social class, for example, might affect consumption choices and effects. In contrast to Bandura and Gerbner's fascination with media violence effects, later research also sought to diagnose the potential positive impacts of media consumption. Dorothy Hobson's 1980 research, for example, explored the use of radio by working class housewives, concluding that women often used music programming to help them cope with the isolating experiences of looking after young children while their husbands and partners were at work. David Morley's famous 1986 study *Family Television* also challenged the idea that audiences universally watch or consume products in the same way, his study concluding that male viewers were more likely to watch factual programming, absorbing content in near silence, while female viewers were more likely to use media as a secondary activity while completing household chores.

What unites most of these studies is the notion that contextual factors play a huge role in the reception of media products – that an audience's gender, class status or ethnicity ameliorated the effects of media messaging. Importantly, research also identified that audiences are active consumers of content, seeking out products that provided specific benefits, while also rejecting content that didn't meet their individual needs.

Three named theorists who might challenge Bandura's thinking

- **Stuart Hall:** would argue that media products do not produce a cause and effect learning response – audiences decode the media they engage with using contextual knowledge.
- **Henry Jenkins:** emphasises the positive effects of media consumption – suggesting that the media forges communities and allows audiences to express themselves in positive and creative ways through fan engagement.
- **George Gerbner:** would argue that the media should not be measured just in terms of its impact on individual learning behaviours but also on the cumulative effects of mass media consumption on wider social attitudes.

16 Cultivation theory

George Gerbner

Born in 1919, Gerbner experienced first hand the growth of mass media, from its early infancy in the 1920s to the television boom of the 1960s and 1970s. It is difficult for contemporary audiences to fully comprehend a world without mass media or to appreciate the impact that mass television ownership produced. For Gerbner, however, that transition was a lived experience and must have prompted his interest in the effects of mass media consumption on wider society.

Gerbner's research, much like that of his academic contemporary, Bandura, focused on screen depictions of violence and the attitudinal changes that might be produced by watching television conflict. The conclusions that Gerbner formed in response to that research were profound in their suggestion that television viewing could radically change the way that we perceive the real world.

Concept 1: fear cultivation

Gerbner argued that media communications, principally television-based media, replaced a set of pre-existing symbol systems that had dominated the cultural and social lives of individuals up until the early twentieth century. Society, Gerbner suggests, uses religious or cultural products to guide the attitudes and behaviours of its constituent members. Those systems, prior to television, were embedded via the church or educational practices. Mass media, Gerbner argues, replaced these 'common symbolic environments' (Gerbner and Morgan, 2016, 193) to become the dominant socialising force of our age.

DOI: 10.4324/9781003361220-16

'Television,' Gerbner tells us, 'is the first centralized cultural influence to permeate both the initial and final years of life – as well as the years in between' (Gerbner and Morgan, 2016, 230). The sheer number of people watching television in the 1960s led Gerbner to hypothesise that the mass media produced a broad enculturation effect, transmitting ideas and attitudes on a scale that had not been witnessed before. The power of television, Gerbner claims, is not narrowly defined as something that can affect the behaviours of a few solitary individuals in society (as Bandura suggests): television, he argues, influences broad sections of society, homogenising attitudes and ideals across society as a whole.

Gerbner isolates the following factors that invest television with a capacity to effect widescale social change:

- **Television is easily decodable.** You do not need to read or be literate to understand television. The meaning of programme content is readily consumed by everyone, from pre-school infants to the elderly.
- **Television access is largely cost free.** Unlike other cultural products – the theatre, cinema or literature – television consumption is relatively inexpensive, and, as a result, is readily consumed across all sections of society, by rich and poor alike.
- **Television consumption is intensified.** Time spent watching television far outweighs comparable cultural activities such as church going or reading, amplifying further the effect of televisual messages.
- **Television is a centralised and homogenous producer of cultural symbols.** The centralised nature of television production means that cultural messages are controlled by a handful of media makers.
- **Television products are encoded using realism.** Television drama, Gerbner suggests, is so reflective of the real world that it is difficult for us to understand that fictional products are not constructed versions of reality. 'How many of us have ever been in an operating room, a criminal courtroom, a police station or jail, or corporate boardroom, or a movie studio?' Gerbner asks, 'How much of our real world has been learned from fictional worlds?' (Gerbner and Morgan, 2016, 232).

Box 16.1   Discuss it: how does television impact our view of the world?

- How much time do you spend watching audio visual media? How much time do your parents or guardians spend watching television?
- How much of your understanding of the real world is constructed through television?
- What effects does television watching have on society?
- Do you think Gerbner's arguments regarding the impact of television on social attitudes is just as valid in today's digital world? Why or why not?

The Violence Index

Gerbner's realisation that television could be having a profound effect on the collective consciousness of society led him to set up the Cultural Indicators project in 1969 to measure the levels of screen violence in television programming. He was interested in confirming exactly how much television content was driven by sequences that depicted symbolic aggression. Violence, Gerbner hypothesised, was a cheap mechanism that producers used to capture audience interest or to elicit easy emotional responses. Violence, he argued, had become an endemic feature of both fictive and factual television output.

The project's findings, dubbed the 'Violence Index' by Gerbner, revealed that his suspicions were correct and that depictions of on-screen conflict within mainstream US television were indeed widespread. Key findings recorded at the end of the project's nine-year tracking period in 1975 included:

- A total of 8 out of every 10 programmes across all networks contained some element of violence.
- More alarmingly, 9 out of 10 children's programmes at weekends contained violent content.
- The average number of violent episodes across programming per hour was 8 – rising to 16 per hour for children's programming.

Gerbner also indexed the following trends regarding character involvement in violence:

- Females were consistently depicted as more vulnerable than men, with 1.32 female victims recorded for each episode of violence as opposed to an average rate of 1.19 male victims.
- Elderly women, single and non-white females were especially prone to victimisation with white males found to be the least likely victims of violent acts.
- The victimisation of powerless female characters was a staple starter in a significant number of television dramas.

The issue of violent content was not just confined to television drama. Gerbner suggested that news-based media was equally problematic, in part, because of the high volume of time news shows occupy in broadcasters' schedules. Gerbner, too, highlighted the role of news ordering processes that push violent events to the forefront of coverage, rendering moments of extreme conflict more visible to audiences.

The effect of factual programming offers further significance in that viewers inherently understand drama-based violence to be fictitious at some level. Representations of real-world violence, however, have the capacity to convey a more profound attitudinal audience-based response. If we watch lots of media content that paints the real world as violent or aggressive, then, perhaps, we are more likely to believe that it is, Gerbner argued.

Box 16.2 Apply it: how violent are your set texts?

- Which of your set texts contain moments of violence? Look especially at TV and video game set texts.
- Which set texts contain the most numerous or significant moments of violence?
- Who are the victims and perpetrators of violence in your set texts? Are there any problematic trends? Are more women, non-white ethnicities or older people constructed as victims?

- What evidence could you present to suggest that news-oriented set texts are just as problematic as drama-based media forms in terms of the amount of violent content they report?
- Gerbner's Violence Index researchers included comic violence, accidents and natural disasters in their tallies. Is this problematic?

Examples of analysis that applies Gerbner's ideas to set texts from a range of exam boards are available at www.essentialmediatheory.com

Cultivating fear and danger

The Cultural Indicators project was designed to place pressure on American television networks to reduce violent content, and it succeeded, for a while at least, with a number of US networks pulling graphic depictions from prime-time output. Gerbner, though, was also interested in measuring the way television violence shifted the attitudes and outlooks of American audiences and devised a series of follow-up studies that compared the real-world perspectives of 'heavy viewers' with those who were less exposed to violent television content.

Gerbner's research conclusively established what he called a 'cultivation differential' – that those audiences who were exposed to more television content had a heightened perception of real-world violence. Heavy viewing not only made people less trustful of others, but also significantly increased their fear of becoming a real-world crime victim. Gerbner identified the following overarching viewing effects:

- **Resonance.** He found that people who lived in high crime areas and who were heavy television viewers were subject to a double-dose effect – that for those who had experience of crime, television viewing significantly amplified their fear of real-world crime.
- **Mainstreaming.** He also concluded that heavy viewers who were significantly less informed about real-life crime – perhaps because they lived in safer neighbourhoods – also reported significantly increased perceptions of violence in the real world. He

thus concluded that watching television could lead to attitudinal change irrespective of whether viewers had any real-world evidence to corroborate what they were seeing on screen.

Both mainstreaming and resonance suggest that heavy mass media consumption – no matter the extent of real-world experiences – made viewers susceptible to the messages of media products. Long-term exposure to media violence, Gerbner further suggested, resulted in viewers adopting 'mean world syndrome'. Television, he concluded, convinces its audiences that society is far more dangerous and violent than it actually is.

Box 16.3   Discuss it: how violent do you think the real world is?

- What effects does news reportage have on the public's perception of crime? Can you evidence media content that has potentially cultivated public fear?
- Do any of your friends or family members have an over-exaggerated fear of crime because of media consumption?
- Can audience fear of particular crimes be exaggerated by news reporting? For example, knife crime or burglary? What crimes is the media creating a moral panic about at this moment?
- In what ways does the public's perception of crime affect the way we treat criminals?

Concept 2: media consumption leads audiences to accept mainstream ideologies

Violence on television represents symbolic power

Television news and drama shows don't just present viewers with portrayals of violence, media narratives tell us who the victims and perpetrators are in those products. Television creates winners and losers, Gerbner infers. It organises social groups hierarchically by telling us who is most likely to die or be shot. Media violence, moreover, suggests who we ought to control and who we should trust to do the controlling. Gerbner draws our attention to the following symbolic effects that are created by on-screen violence:

- **Media violence defines powerless characters.** The over-representation of key groups in victim counts – women, non-whites, the elderly – is a symbolic demonstration, Gerbner argues, of their ideologically inferior status in the real world.
- **Media violence defines powerful characters.** The dominance of white males as heroic lawmakers or law enforcers reinforces their superior social position in the real world.
- **Narrative conventions reinforce authority.** The lack of tragic narratives and the dominance of happy endings in television drama construct a clear-cut ideological message. There may be bad people in the world, but the law and social authority will always win through. The good guys never die, of course.
- **News reportage stigmatises key groups.** Media narratives help to justify the use of violence against key groups – terrorists, protestors, criminals – and play a symbolic role in reinforcing existing sources of authority.
- **Audience protest is subjugated.** Because viewers interpret the world as mean or crime ridden, Gerbner suggested, they come to overly rely on established authority sources for protection. Thus, audiences are passive when confronted with real-world authorities or, likewise, their view of authority as all powerful (as represented by the media) makes them too afraid to take a stand against any perceived injustice.

Constructing content for the mainstream

Gerbner also takes aim at the financial imperatives that drive commercial television. Much like Curran and Seaton, he critiques the media's reliance on advertising revenue, arguing that commercial media forms need to develop mass audiences to sustain advertising income and, as a result, the media frames political debates and current affairs in ways that neutralise controversy.

'Competition for the largest possible audience,' Gerbner argues, 'means striving for the broadest and most conventional appeals, blurring sharp conflicts, blending and balancing competing perspectives' (Gerbner and Morgan, 2016, 308). Thus, mainstream media broadcasters sanitise alternative viewpoints by purposefully adopting a bland middle-of-the road perspective. This position means that they avoid offending or alienating mainstream audiences and advertising clientele on whom they are financially dependent.

Cultivation theory: magazines and the internet

Gerbner's interest in television violence was prompted by the radical expansion of television ownership during the post-war years. And although his research focused on the widespread effects of violence, he hypothesised that television could also be responsible for the enculturation of a range of other attitudinal changes and acknowledged that other mass media forms were capable of similar widespread effects.

The academic Jonathan Bignell, for example, took up Gerbner's cue, applying a cultivation theory perspective to analyse the effects of magazines on readers, concluding that lifestyle-oriented publications construct a fictional version of gender that readers apply to their real-world selves. 'By constructing a mythic community for men or women,' Bignell writes, 'magazines delineate the social meaning of gender' (Bignell, 2002, 77). Magazines, he concludes, enculture far-reaching beauty ideals that profoundly shape the way that men and women think about themselves and each other.

Box 16.4   Discuss it: does contemporary commercial media reinforce mainstream beliefs?

Mainstreaming effects in newspapers

- In what ways do the newspapers you have studied present ideas in a middle-of-the-road manner?
- What evidence could you present to suggest that the mainstream media deliberately avoids radical discussion so that both mainstream audiences and advertising revenues are maintained?

Mainstreaming effects of the internet

- In what ways has the introduction of advertising effected YouTube content? Has advertising sanitised vlogging?

- Free-to-view expectations of online newspapers means that a majority of news titles are dependent on advertising and sponsorship as income sources. How has this affected news content?
- Is Gerbner right that the media sanitises content? Are some online media products successful because they deliberately provoke controversy?

Mainstreaming effects of television

- Do advertising free streaming providers (Netflix/Amazon) take more risks than commercial broadcasters? What are those risks? Where are they evidenced?
- In what ways could we challenge Gerbner's idea that television constructs middle-of-the-road programming? Are modern audiences more tolerant of radical content?

Likewise, much commentary has been expended on the real-world effects of social media and the capacity for our increasingly divisive digital conversations to translate into real-world aggression. Max Fisher's *The Chaos Machine*, for example, carefully narrates the role of social media in fanning extremism and right-wing populism across the globe, implicating, for example, Facebook and YouTube content as essential ingredients in the 'Stop the Steal' campaign and the Capital riots insurrection of January 2021.

In the aftermath of Trump's defeat, Fisher tells us, 'An entire universe of Facebook groups rising as one, promoted Trump's rally as the great battle they had been preparing for' (Fisher, 2023, 320). Those groups, Fisher explains, helped sow the seeds of the widely held and misinformed belief that Trump had lost the presidential election because of voter fraud and criminal interference on the part of the Democratic Party, a view that resulted in an armed insurrection that saw thousands of right-wing supporters storm the US Congress.

Fisher points to social media algorithms that have the power to amplify extremist messaging for reposted content, likes or retweets to induce viral panics that have real-world consequences. Fisher also identifies the unwillingness and inability of social media executives to act when misinformation takes root on their platforms, arguing that social media 'machines are, in the ways that matter, essentially ungoverned' (Fisher, 2023, 340).

Box 16.5   Apply it: use cultivation theory to create exam responses for audience-based questions

Gerbner's cultivation theory can provide a useful starting point for exam questions that ask you to consider how audiences might respond to set texts or unseen products. Think about these questions to help construct exam relevant analysis:

- What kinds of fears does the media product produce?
- In what ways could the text amplify an audience's existing fears?
- How might the text produce new attitudes through mainstreaming effects?
- In what ways does the product convey symbolic power?
- Does the product present middle-of-the-road reportage to preserve its commercial integrity?

Exemplar: *Huck* (Eduqas). *Huck* magazine at first glance might stimulate the needs of an active audience, providing readers with thought-provoking think-pieces that ask them to explore their identity or to find courage in pursuing 'outlier' stances that defy the mainstream, yet we might also locate several narrative strategies in the set text that provoke more passive reader responses. Gerbner, for example, tells us that violence is used as a mainstream media ingredient – a shorthand narrative strategy that can garner instant audience interest, and, more interestingly, that can lead readers to adopt mean world syndrome. *Huck* supports that outlook, with binary conflicts used throughout the selected pages as a means of aligning the reader with the magazine's liberal perspective. Those presentations could be viewed as problematic, for example, Jacob Tobia's pronouncement that, 'Being perceived as "a man in a dress" is a death sentence' works against the

'Beyond Binary' article's call for gender fluidity, exaggerating levels of violence against the trans community. Similarly, the reportage of Muslim fanaticism in the Ocalan's Angels article produces a conflict-soaked think-piece that reflects a distorted perception of the Middle East as wholly violent.

Further exemplars for set texts from all exam boards are available online at www.essentialmediatheory.com

Table 16.1 Speak George Gerbner

Enculturation	The process of learning social norms or behaviours through watching others or by engaging with culture. The media contributes to the enculturation of individuals by making them adopt specific attitudes or outlooks.
Homogenised cultural effects	Television has a homogeneous cultural effect in that its reach and lack of content diversity makes us think the same things or adopt the same attitudes.
Mainstreaming	Gerbner suggests that some groups are less likely to be affected by television (more educated audiences or those who have not experienced violence in real life, for instance). Although the attitudes of these groups are affected to a lesser extent by the media, they are still prone to some attitudinal shift as a result of consumption. Television can, therefore, cultivate problematic attitudes and beliefs within mainstream society where they had not existed before.
Mean world syndrome	An outlook that considers the world to be far more violent or selfish than it really is.
Middle-of-the-road reportage	The use of balanced reporting to foster large-scale audiences and boost advertising revenue. Middle-of-the-road reportage positions new or radical ideas as dangerous, subtly enforcing existing power structures.
Resonance	The process of amplifying an idea, attitude or belief already held by audiences through media consumption.
Stigmatisation	The process of demonising groups, individuals or ideas through media representations.
Symbolic power	Those who have power in media narratives (in terms of gender, class, ethnicity) are legitimised as real-world power sources.

Table 16.2 Gerbner: ten-minute revision

Concept 1: *media products shape attitudes and perceptions of the world at large*

- Storytelling performs an enculturation role helping to shape our attitudes and social values.
- Mass media has replaced other institutions, most notably religion and education, as the principal constructor of symbolic storytelling.
- Television has had a homogenising effect on society – we all watch or engage in the same symbolic stories as a result of mass media.
- Television schedules are saturated with violent content that cultivates a widespread fear in society – mean world syndrome.
- The media can produce resonance or mainstreaming effects on audiences.

Concept 2: *media consumption leads audiences to accept established power structures and mainstream ideologies*

- Mass media narratives create symbolic representations of power that affect our real-world view.
- Mass media products over-exaggerate the power and scope of real-world authorities.
- Mass media products marginalise alternative viewpoints as a result of middle-of-the-road reportage.

Challenging Gerbner's thinking

Stuart Hall's reception theory model can be used to provide a counter perspective to Gerbner's cultivation theory. While Gerbner's analysis suggests that audiences have no choice in submitting to media effects, Hall, in contrast, argues that we can construct oppositional readings of texts – that we can use our individual knowledge or beliefs to question the media. Where Gerbner infers that audiences are passive receptacles of media messaging, Hall argues that readers and viewers have the potential to be active.

Uses and gratifications theory

Another theoretical model that challenges Gerbner's arguments that audiences are passive recipients of media messaging is uses and gratifications theory. Elihu Katz in the 1970s, for example, sought to identify the potential pleasures that underpinned the media consumption choices made by audiences, arguing that media consumers played an active role in seeking out media that satisfies specific social or psychological wants.

Katz was influenced by Abraham Maslow's humanistic approaches in psychology that argued that humans continuously try to satisfy a fixed range of motivations – his pyramid of needs identifying basic physical wants (food, shelter, security and so on) as having to be met before higher-order desires like love, kinship, self-esteem or status can be sought.

Katz identified that some of those higher-order needs might be met by the media and set about researching which cultural forms – novels, television, film or radio, for example – provided what kinds of gratifications. To guide his investigation, Katz devised the following list of uses and gratifications that might be realised by cultural products:

- **Cognitive gratifications:** where audiences use the media to provide information, knowledge or understanding. Consumption of news-based media, for example, provides audiences with knowledge and understanding of real-world issues.
- **Affective uses:** where audiences consume media content because they provide a specific set of emotional satisfactions or pleasures. Watching horror-driven products, for example, produces fear, whereas romances might elicit joy or sadness, action-based content excitement.
- **Integrative uses:** where audiences consume media products to enhance their status or social credibility. Lifestyle magazines might be read, for example, to learn how to achieve a specific fashion look that will enhance a reader's social status.
- **Social needs:** relates to media consumption that helps to strengthen real-world relationships. Media texts might be used, for example, as discussion talking points at family get togethers or in work-based situations, providing audiences with shared experiences that enable social connection.
- **Escape:** media consumption that removes audiences from their everyday lives. Consumption of otherworldly media – science fiction, historical drama and so on – might take place so that audiences can temporarily forget about the stresses and strains of work or school.

Bourdieu: media use as cultural capital

Another useful theory that can help us understand how audiences might use rather than be used by the media is Pierre Bourdieu's arguments concerning Cultural Capital. Bourdieu, importantly, argued that the kinds of cultural activities deemed acceptable by different social classes varies enormously – that visiting art galleries or listening to opera, for example, are respectable activities for the upper middle class, whereas tabloid newspaper consumption, football spectatorship or reality TV watching are more stereotypically viewed as working-class activities.

Bourdieu further argued that the expectations surrounding class-based cultural consumption operate as an invisible set of rules or a set of practices that can grant belonging to a particular class. Bourdieu, importantly, used the term 'habitus' to describe the internalised behaviours that outwardly demonstrate a class-based status. Having the wrong kinds of habitus, he argued, can also prevent class migration. Not understanding, for example, the kinds of language or behaviours we ought to use in an art gallery can prevent individuals from demonstrating middle-class sensibilities. Lacking a particular habitus might further translate into real-world barriers – candidates in job interviews, for example, might not be selected if their attitudes or dispositions don't tally with those of their prospective employer.

(Continued)

Table 16.2 (Continued)

Media products might be consumed, Bourdieu also argues, because they provide audiences with the sorts of knowledge and attitudes needed to belong to a particular class. Tabloid newspapers, for example, furnish working-class readers with extensive football knowledge via extended sports sections – a form of knowledge that helps grant those readers a working-class status. Broadsheet titles, conversely, provide knowledge of literary trends, theatre and the arts in lifestyle supplements that readers can use to showcase middle-class belonging. Bourdieu argues that audiences apply the 'logic of association and difference' when consuming cultural material, and that they choose to buy or not buy media products because of their preconceived class-based status. Bourdieu further suggests that cultural purchases can act as objectified cultural capital, that our book, DVD or magazine collections are physical displays of class-based identity, and that, for example, a display of niche coffee table magazines like *Huck* or *Adbusters* can be used to signal a middle-class status.

Two other named theorists who might challenge Gerbner's thinking

- **Henry Jenkins:** emphasises the positive effects of media consumption – suggesting that the media forges communities and allows audiences to express themselves in positive and creative ways through fan engagement.
- **Albert Bandura:** would argue that the media directly impacts an individual's behaviour and induces consumers to be violent. Gerbner, in contrast, suggests that media consumption prompts an attitudinal rather than a behavioural response.

17 Reception theory
Stuart Hall

Stuart Hall's 1973 essay, 'Encoding/Decoding', was groundbreaking. Prior to Hall's work, communications models defined the process of media consumption in a relatively straightforward manner, suggesting that the media constructed messages that audiences readily consumed without question. The media was thought to inject ideas into audiences, who in return offered minimum resistance to what they saw, read or heard. Hall suggested otherwise, asserting that media consumers were alert and critical readers, listeners and viewers.

Hall's writing perhaps captures the spirit of the era and the numerous possibilities that were unfolding for audiences during the 1970s – to explore alternative viewpoints and to challenge the mainstream ideologies of the post-war years. Certainly, Hall, as a Jamaican immigrant, understood what it meant to stand outside of the mainstream, critically aware of the way culture could be used to establish and maintain social inequalities. The revolutionary impact of his media writing, however, cannot be understated. Hall reframed the cause-and-effect consumption models of the 1950s and 1960s, acknowledging for the first time the theoretical possibility that audiences do not engage with media products as passive recipients but as critically engaged readers of media texts.

Concept 1: encoding and decoding

Encoding produces a mediated view of the world

In Hall's encoding/decoding circuit formula, media products are encoded using established production processes. A newspaper does not simply record events as they happen. Stories are harvested by

DOI: 10.4324/9781003361220-17

experienced reporters. Events are framed using established story structures. Editorial biases shape stories to construct versions of the truth that are entertaining, marketable or persuasive.

Encoding processes, therefore, construct a mediated worldview. Journalists do not just report the raw facts; they also present a carefully orchestrated version of those events. They curate interviewees who are chosen to convey a specific outlook. Accompanying footage is sequenced, with key imagery chosen to underline, question or justify those viewpoints.

Hall further suggests that media encoding processes are framed using a variety of formal codes, both visual and aural. These codes might not necessarily be connected to the stories reported, but they enhance the messages that are relayed. The visual look and colour coding of the television news studio, for example, gives weight and authority to the broadcaster's messages. The formal attire of newsreaders similarly conveys their professionalism, while the drum-laden intros of news bulletins are designed to imply gravity and impending seriousness. It is no accident that the BBC allows us to look beyond the presenter and see its vast newsroom with its army of journalists working in the background. The formal codes of news are thus weighted to convince us that news narratives have been carefully researched by a team of diligent and experienced professionals.

Encoding and the production process

Hall draws our attention to the following production factors that funnel media encoding:

- **Routines of production:** the way that products are made, and the routines follow channel-encoding effects. The 24-hour news cycle, for example, prompts newspapers to favour breaking news at the expense of older stories, while the use of courtroom reportage as a routine journalistic activity inevitably means that criminal cases feature heavily in news coverage. In other words, the processes used to manufacture media products play a crucial role in determining meaning. Understanding how media artefacts are made, therefore, helps us detect the hidden biases that products relay to their audiences.
- **Genre-driven mediation:** genre-driven rules often frame the visual or narrative structures of media products. In news

reportage, for example, stories are often constructed in a highly formulaic way, recycling familiar themes, events and characters in genre-driven rituals. Hall was particularly interested, for instance, in the way that newspapers demonised Black masculinity in the 1970s and 1980s, and the almost endemic use of the Black male mugger stereotype within reportage. We might argue that those same stereotypes have resurfaced in the contemporary media's coverage of the UK knife crime epidemic. In fictional products, too, the narrative structure and character expectations of genres routinely encode specific representations within products. In crime drama, writers continue to manufacture female victims and lone wolf masculine villains with genre-encoding rules presiding over any wider gender-based concerns.

- **Institutional context:** the media, Hall reminds us, is constructed by fixed networks of people who collectively create a selective perspective. The views of those networks might lead to political bias – indeed, media producers might deliberately choose to employ people who share the same political bias.
- **Predictions regarding audience taste:** media producers encode products in ways they think will appeal to their audience. Assumptions regarding audience tastes are used to make sure that products are commercially viable, yet the extent to which products predict or, indeed, infer audience thinking is highly debatable. Media producers may, in fact, be constructing rather than reflecting audience attitudes because of these practices.

Decoding

Hall suggests that media encoding provides us with an entry point to understanding the effects that products have on their audiences. An understanding that explores encoding effects alone, however, does not fully detail the process through which the media creates meaning. Products may encode meanings, Hall argues, but that does not necessarily suggest that all audiences understand or decode those ideas in the same way.

Media decoding, Hall argues, is not straightforward. Media products, he suggests, produce a variety of audience-based readings because the media is predominantly constructed using visual signs. These signs, he further suggests, create an iconic/

connotative effect rather than an explicit/denotative exposition. When we see an image of a cow, for example, we can all recognise and name the animal appropriately, but we do not arrive at the same conclusions regarding the image's connotative meaning. Some readers might associate cows with nature or regard them as a symbol that represents the English countryside. Conversely, vegans or vegetarians might construct a reading that considers how cows are exploited through farming, while dairy farmers or vets might produce an analytical assessment of the animal's physique or monetary worth.

In short, connotative readings are manufactured as a result of our individual experiences and knowledge. This leads Hall to conclude that the individual signs that encode media products are multi-accentual and that media texts are polysemic (poly = many/semic = signs). In plain English, Hall argues that audience members read products in different ways, and that those differences are the result of their contextual experiences. Some audience members might form readings that fall in line with the original intentions of a product's makers, while others will read against the grain of those intentions.

Box 17.1 Think about it: what is more important – encoding or decoding?

- Do you think that media encoding or decoding is more important in terms of the overriding effect of a media product?
- Are media products polysemic? What arguments might you present to suggest that they create stable messages?

Media misreadings

Hall is careful to highlight the difference between misreading a media product and producing a reading that is knowingly oppositional. Misreading occurs, he suggests, when audiences do not have the capacity to fully understand a product's intended message. Misreadings can be formed because of the following:

- **Overly complex narratives.** Misunderstandings can be prompted when stories use overly complicated structures or where narratives are too experimental. Surrealist narratives or postmodern expositions might, if too difficult to follow, prevent an audience from decoding a product successfully.
- **Ideas are too alien.** Hall also suggests that misreading can occur if the nature of content falls beyond the audience's everyday experience. A news story, for example, that narrates the attempted migration of refugees from a war-torn country might be so far removed from the everyday experiences of readers that they are unable to fully comprehend the intended encoding effects the story is trying to convey.
- **Language elements cannot be decoded.** Products can be undecipherable if they have been encoded using a foreign language or if they deploy vocabulary that is too complex for the intended reader.

Box 17.2   Apply it: do any of the set texts you have studied invite misreadings?

- Do any of your set texts construct narratives that are overly complex? What elements or moments of the narrative are particularly problematic?
- Because of their lack of dialogue and short length, music videos are particularly problematic in terms of generating misreadings. Are your set text music videos likely to produce misreadings? If not, how do they compensate for their lack of diegetic sound?
- Do any of the set texts you have studied use language that is too complicated for their intended target audience? What elements or moments of the narrative are particularly problematic?
- Do any of the products you have studied produce deliberately ambiguous messages? Does this make them impossible to decode?

Exemplar: *Riptide* (Eduqas). Vance Joy's *Riptide* music video delivers a non-traditional narrative, replacing linear storytelling with a postmodern exposition that is open to what Hall would call 'audience misreading'. Intertextual references, for example, made to the 1970s cult film *The Wicker Man* are used to construct an ironic female victim stereotype, while later scenes allude to the voyeuristic eroticisation of femininity we see in Bond movies. Joy's video deconstructs gender whilst also offering a critique of pop culture's portrayal of femininity. Yet that postmodern complexity creates, in Hall's terms, the potential for audiences to misread the video. The lack of dialogue, moreover, within music videos generally makes them much harder to decode than those media forms that use diegesis and scripted speech to help anchor meaning. *Riptide*'s deliberate attempt to disconnect the song's lyrics from accompanying imagery presents a further frustration, perhaps rendering the video as unintelligible for most casual viewers.

Further set text help is available for a range of products for all exam boards at www.essentialmediatheory.com

Concept 2: dominant, negotiated and oppositional decoding

Cultural hegemonies

Hall applies Antonio Gramsci's concept of hegemony to suggest that an invisible set of rules governs and directs our behaviours and beliefs. Hegemonies, Hall argues, define what we think is '"natural", "inevitable", "taken for granted" about the social order' (Hall, 1999, 516). More importantly, the mainstream media, he suggests, plays a crucial role in maintaining and reinforcing those dominant ideologies.

It could be argued, for instance, that newspapers endorse and reinforce the legitimacy of our parliamentary system through reportage. Political stories often feature as front-page leads, helping to reinforce the authority of our political leaders. Deferential interviews might convince us that politicians work to affect our best interests. News media might also persuade us that a private school education or a professional background makes for the best political leaders, and, as such, that it is natural that the upper middle classes dominate our political system.

These ideas, of course, are not 'natural' or 'common sense'. They are, in Hall's terms, social constructs – shared and distributed in ways that help to maintain the power of the social elites who dominate and control social structures. Hall, moreover, argues that those who wield social power maintain authority *because* they control the media, or are able, at the very least, to forge close relationships with media makers so that their vision of the world is communicated as 'natural' or 'inevitable'.

Box 17.3   Think about it: what evidence is there to suggest that your set texts reinforce dominant ideologies?

- What messages do the set texts encode regarding social power? Who do they suggest ought to be in control? Who are our 'natural' leaders?
- What messages do the set texts encode regarding gender and power? What roles do those products suggest are natural for males and females?
- What messages do your set texts encode regarding race and power?
- Can we really conclude that the contemporary media industry solely reflects dominant ideologies? In what ways do your set texts encode subversive messages?

Hall argues, however, that hegemonies and dominant ideologies aren't fixed. The hegemonic ideas that come to dominate must be applied and reapplied via the continuous stream of material that is authored by the media. The authors of that media, moreover, change continuously: audiences seek out new voices, while marginalised social groups find ways to make themselves heard within mainstream discourse. And much like high street fashion or the ephemeral nature of a music trend, we find that hegemonic ideas become outworn and are discarded while a continuous stream of new ideas bubble to the surface as replacements.

Cultural resistance and hegemonic agreement

Media producers might encode messages that reinforce dominant ideologies, but it is not necessarily true that all audience members will submit to those ideas in a passive or submissive manner. On the contrary, Hall suggests that audiences engage in a continuous assessment of consumed media, and, as a result, can resist the hegemonic encodings they are routinely subjected to.

Audiences, Hall tells us, create readings using 'situated logics' (Hall, 1999, 516) – filtering the world according to their individual knowledge and experience. A benefits claimant, for example, who has experienced poverty and hardship because of a benefits sanction will be less likely to accept a media message that promotes austerity politics. A life-long Labour Party supporter might similarly decode the right-leaning *Daily Mail* with a degree of scepticism while, conversely, the same 'situated logics' might lead Conservative Party voters to dismiss a *Guardian* editorial as equally misleading.

Hall argues that the following groups of media decoding are possible if we consider the potential effects of contextual factors and 'situated logics':

- **Dominant readings:** audiences decode media products, accepting the dominant cultural messages produced. Here, audiences knowingly agree with any hegemonic messages constructed.
- **Negotiated readings:** audiences might produce a negotiated reading if the encoder's message is acknowledged in general terms, but individual experiences lead an audience member to question or resist some aspects of the text.
- **Oppositional readings:** audiences understand the message but refuse to believe it, using their personal experience/ideological viewpoint to challenge the messages produced. Audiences knowingly produce contrary readings of the hegemonic statements produced by the media.

Box 17.4 Apply it: what multiple readings of your set texts might audiences produce?

Use these questions to help you identify how dominant, oppositional or negotiated readings of your set texts might be constructed by different audience groups:

- How might the political beliefs of the audience lead them to construct negotiated or oppositional decodings? What might these oppositional decodings be?
- How might the social class of readers lead them to produce an alternative reading of your set texts?
- How might males and females react differently to the set texts you are studying?
- In what ways might a contemporary audience react differently to the historical set texts you have studied? In what ways does their contemporary experience enable them to construct oppositional readings?

Exemplar: *Daily Mail* front page, Tuesday 13 June 2023 (OCR and AQA). The *Daily Mail*'s reputation for supporting right-wing perspectives is such that left-leaning readers routinely approach its reporting with huge scepticism. The front page on Tuesday 13 June 2023, for example, might trigger several oppositional readings. The anti-Labour bias of the front-page feature, for example, implores us to question the party's decision to vote against illegal migrant detention rules – a decision the *Mail* suggests doesn't support 'law-abiding citizens'. The paper simultaneously questions Labour's questioning of new laws that will give police forces bolstered powers to deal with public protests – a decision, the *Mail* argues, that aligns Labour MPs with the 'eco-zealots' of the Just Stop Oil movement. Persuasive language choice is at play throughout the copy, pushing readers to think of environmental activists as 'zealots' or fanatical extremists, while Labour's negatively connoted abandonment of new laws suggests sympathies for criminality.

Hall, however, would argue that readers' interpretations of hegemonic messaging are likely to be informed by their contextual knowledge. Labour-voting audiences or those sympathetic to the Just Stop Oil movement, for example, might perceive the article's binary presentation as overly reductive. Indeed, readers might dismiss the paper's output out of hand after recognising the paper as the author, rejecting all content as untrustworthy invective.

Further exemplar paragraphs for set texts from all exam boards are available at www.essentialmediatheory.com

Table 17.1 Speak Stuart Hall

Decoding	Media audiences read the messages that producers construct.
Dominant readings	Dominant readings occur when audiences knowingly decode texts in the way they were intended by media makers. Audiences agree with any hegemonic encodings.
Encoding	Media institutions encode media products – using honed processes and strategies to produce media products that communicate messages to their audiences.
Hegemony	The set of ideas that dominate within society – these ideas are usually formed by those groups who have power. Hegemonies often legitimise the power of elite social groups. The media plays a key role in distributing hegemonic messages to all sections of society.
Misreading	An audience reading that fails to correctly decode the intended meaning of a media product as a result of its complexity or illegibility.
Negotiated readings	Negotiated readings occur when audiences both resist and accept the messages constructed by a media product.
Oppositional readings	Oppositional readings occur when audiences use their individual knowledge, beliefs or experiences to construct a contrary reading of a media text.
Situated logics	Refers to the experience, knowledge and beliefs that an individual audience member uses when decoding a product. This might also refer to the physical environment in which decoding occurs.

Table 17.2 Hall: ten-minute revision

Concept 1: *Encoding and decoding*

- The media encodes messages using visual and aural cues.
- Media encoding is affected by institutional context, media production processes and genre-driven routines.
- Audiences do not decode the meanings that media producers affect in a straightforward way.
- Audiences can misread products if they are too complex or are untranslatable.

Concept 2: *Dominant, negotiated and oppositional readings*

- Media products tend to reinforce dominant ideologies and cultural hegemonies.
- Dominant ideologies are subject to change – again, the media plays a crucial role in effecting those changes.
- Audiences use 'situated logics' to decode media messages.
- Audiences can produce readings of products that accept the dominant ideologies they construct.
- Audiences can also use their contextual knowledge to read against the grain of a media product, thus producing negotiated or oppositional decodings.

Challenging Stuart Hall's thinking

Hall acknowledged that his encoding/decoding model was a theoretical concept only, a model that lacked any scientific data to prove that audiences read media products in the ways outlined. Some critics, for example, point to the idea that for most consumers the physical process of reading media output produces a temporal experience, and that most media texts are consumed too quickly for audiences to interpret and evaluate messaging in the ways that Hall outlined. Other theorists like Dayan and Katz point to the ritualistic nature of media engagement, arguing that nightly television viewing, for example, connects audiences to wider society, and in so doing produces an overriding sense of community or belonging, rather than one of oppositional difference.

Other theorists argue that Hall's encoding/decoding model is too blunt an instrument to assess the impact of real-life media consumption – that different media forms and contexts effect different sorts of engagement, and that what we watch and where we watch it has a mediating effect. Sonia Livingstone's research, for example, points to the increasingly fragmented nature of media consumption in the home, telling us that young audiences in particular are engaging in individualised media consumption. Screens, gadgets and internet-based streaming services, she argues, have constructed a fragmented 'bedroom culture', the effects of which are yet to be fully understood (Lievrouw and Livingstone, 2009).

(*Continued*)

Table 17.2 (Continued)

We might also critique Hall's assertion that media output tends to reinforce a hegemonic or dominant set of ideas. Media texts often assert a confused or complex set of messages, often authoring views or conclusions that are self-contradictory or subtly complex. We might further suggest that contemporary media products are less likely to reinforce the worldviews of a dominant social elite – that, for example, the digital revolution has had a democratising effect, providing audiences of different hues and outlooks with the necessary tools to author diverse output.

Three named theorists who might challenge Hall's thinking

- **George Gerbner:** would suggest that audiences find it difficult to resist the effects of media products. Gerbner's mainstreaming theory would suggest that even the least susceptible audience members experience attitudinal change as a result of media exposure.
- **Albert Bandura:** his Bobo doll experiments would suggest that the media has a causal effect on audience behaviours and prompts audiences to copy behaviours they have seen in the media.
- **David Gauntlett:** would argue that media products do not necessarily reinforce cultural hegemonies. Contemporary media products offer a wide range of identities and subversions that often work in opposition to dominant ideologies.

18 Fandom

Henry Jenkins

Jenkins' research represents, in many senses, an extension of Stuart Hall's audience reception model in that fan readings of professional media, according to Jenkins, often produce oppositional responses to the meanings intended by their creators. Indeed, fandoms, for Jenkins, are visible markers of an audience's capacity to produce aberrant readings of professional media, providing substantial evidence that audiences are active media consumers.

Jenkins' later academic research is similarly interested in the way that audiences consume the media, examining the impact that digital technologies have had on audience–producer relationships. Jenkins traces two major effects of the digital revolution: first, that media producers and their audiences have converged as a result of digital networking effects – that audiences and creators have forged a closer relationship as a result of digital networking; and, second, that audiences are increasingly engaging in participatory culture practises. Participatory culture, in Jenkins' view, covers a wide range of DIY media practices, but it is principally affected when audiences use technologies to form online communities that have a positive benefit. For Jenkins, the exponential growth of participatory culture is a potent force in the contemporary media landscape, empowering audiences to effect wider social change.

Concept 1: fan appropriation

In his groundbreaking 1992 book, *Textual Poachers*, Jenkins engages in what he calls an 'ethnographic' study of fandoms – an insider's account of how fans build communities. Jenkins was particularly interested in the print-based fanzines of the pre-internet

DOI: 10.4324/9781003361220-18

era whose lo-fi products were distributed by old-fashioned mail and authored by amateur writers who were keen to share the stories they had written in response to shows such as *Blake 7*, *Doctor Who* and *Star Trek*.

Jenkins' analysis suggested that those early fan communities were far more complex than they first appeared or were given credit for. 'Fan culture,' he tells us 'reflects both the audience's fascination with programs and [the] fans' frustration over the refusal/inability of producers to tell the kinds of stories viewers want to see' (Jenkins, 2013, 162).

Jenkins argues that fanfiction plugs the gap that exists between the needs of audiences and the commercially safe output of the shows they watch. Jenkins groups fanfiction output using the following categories:

- **Recontextualisations** are fan-produced stories that fill in missing scenes or provide backstory to explain character actions from a particular moment in a product narrative.
- **Expanded series timelines** provide imagined sequels for a particular show. The short-lived 1980s cult hit *Blake 7*, for example, was a particular frustration for fans who wanted the BBC to recommission it. Fans invented their own sequels when it became clear that the BBC was not going to green light new episodes.
- **Refocalisations** construct stories that reposition minor or secondary characters as central protagonists.
- **Moral realignments** supply antagonists and villains with backstories that explain their dark motives and morally dubious character traits.
- **Crossovers** are stories in which characters from one show might be placed within the context/timeline of another product. *Doctor Who*'s TARDIS, for instance, might appear in the middle of a *Star Wars* sequence.
- **Personalisations** are stories that place the amateur author at the centre of a professional narrative. The writer might play a heroic role or develop a romantic engagement with a product's protagonist.
- **Eroticisation:** Jenkins suggests that 'fan writers, freed of the restraints of network censors, often want to explore the erotic

dimensions of characters' lives' (Jenkins, 2013, 175). In the liberated world of fanfiction, eroticisation gives free reign to audiences who want to move beyond the secret nods and winks that are made within TV shows to create reworked (and subversive) adult reimagining's of character interaction.

Reconstructing hypermasculinity/realigning heteronormativity

Erotic fanfiction, perhaps, contributes most to the lay perception of fan activity as a marginal, slightly seedy exercise carried out by obsessive nerds; but it is this category of fan activity that attracted the most significant analysis by Jenkins. His early research focused on the subgenre of slash ('/') fanfiction in which heterosexual lead characters are repositioned within gay storylines. Slash fiction might engineer, for instance, a sexual liaison between two lead males or create stories that resolve in a romantic union between a product's masculine hero and their erstwhile male nemesis.

Jenkins' asserts, importantly, that slash fiction is often written by heterosexual female audiences who are writing to express their frustration at the dominance of hypermasculine tropes within mainstream television. Female audiences, Jenkins suggests, yearn for male characters who are less aggressive, and, in their absence, write fanfiction to reconstruct their on-screen heroes so they represent a sensitive or more feminised ideal.

Jenkins, too, alerts us to the marginalisation of gay characters within mainstream television, suggesting that the widescale absence of lesbian, gay, bisexual and transgender representations is negotiated by fans through imaginative reworkings in their fanfiction. Jenkins also suggests that source texts often provide the starting points for these appropriations – a male character might nod in a suggestive manner to a secondary male; dialogue might offer a hint of forbidden love. The writers of slash fiction merely pursue the subtle cues laid down by a show's professional writers, who, Jenkins tells us, are restrained from producing overt gay storylines by the commercial imperative to maintain heteronormativity to satisfy mainstream audience demands.

Box 18.1 Think about it: fanfiction and textual poaching

- Is today's media landscape dominated by a narrow range of character representations? Think about the stock characters used in TV drama in terms of gender, class, age or ethnicity.
- Examine the fanfiction that surrounds your TV set texts. In what ways does fan activity evidence the idea that audiences are active consumers?
- Does fan activity fill in any representation gaps present in the set text?

Exemplar: *Peaky Blinders* **(Eduqas).** Behind most television products lies a profusion of unofficial fan activity, with audiences of all kinds using digital media to share audience-generated creations unsanctioned by show producers. Jenkins tells us that these moments of textual poaching often vent audience frustrations regarding the limited gender-based representations of programming, with slash fanfiction used, for example, to imaginatively insert LGBTQ+ identities into content that is overwhelmingly heteronormative. A cursory look at the plethora of *Peaky Blinders* fanfiction output provides substantial evidence to corroborate Jenkins' research, with amateur writers manufacturing gay siblings for Tommy Shelby or narrating homoerotic relationships for the heterosexual lead of the official show. Such content, of course, also provides substantial evidence that audiences are active interpolators of content, using digital tools to fill in the gaps that commercial output deems too risky for mainstream consumption.

Concept 2: audience–producer convergence in the digital age

Fan communities

By sharing fanfiction with like-minded others, individual audience members can also forge connections with a wider community.

Importantly, Jenkins tells us, the development of the internet has facilitated an exponential explosion of textual poaching practices while also prompting a convergence of audience–producer relations. While fans were once reliant on the physical distribution of their fan output via handmade print-based products, digital media, with its peer-to-peer networking capabilities, has sped up the process of fan communication, enabling a wider range of fan networks to develop.

The digital revolution has impacted on fandom in the following ways:

- **Digital technologies have given fans a new range of tools to express their voice.** While traditional fandoms relied heavily on fanzines, contemporary fan culture works within a wider scope of formats, including video remixes, YouTube parodies and recreations, mashups and fan-based artwork.
- **Digital networking has enabled an ever-widening diversity of professional media to have fan followings.** While fan communities were once restricted to products that had a cult status, fandoms are now attached to nearly all film and TV media. From *Songs of Praise* to *Star Wars*, from *My Little Pony* to *Lego*, most media products have a fan community connected to them.
- **Fan engagement can be realised in real time.** Through contemporary digital networks, fans can share, interact and communicate with one another both during and immediately after broadcast transmissions.

Audience power, digital media and instant feedback

Fandom has also enabled what Jenkins calls 'consumer activism' (Jenkins, 2013, 175), whereby the instantaneous reactions of audience members adhere to form an informal focus group that speaks back to media producers. In this sense, fan engagement acts as a real-time assessment of a product's appeal. Media producers, moreover, are ever alert to the collective voice of these fan groups – soliciting and channelling fan interaction via social media hashtags to help shape the direction and content of their products.

Fans, however, can deliberately channel their collective voice into campaigns that are designed to change or boycott products. Online petitions and hashtag memes can be quickly orchestrated on social media to vent fan anger when a character is killed off or, potentially, to 'call out' more serious concerns regarding representation issues.

Nourishing fan bases to exploit the digital labour of audiences

Jenkins, too, outlines the extent to which contemporary media producers court and nourish fan bases to construct brand awareness and to maintain product loyalty. Audiences, he suggests, play an integral role in distributing and circulating modern media products through social media platforms. By inducing audiences to share or 'like' content online, media makers can market or advertise media for minimal cost.

In the traditional media landscape, fans and producers occupied distinctly separate territories. Fans consumed, while producers laboured in isolation to make the products that so occupied their audiences' interests. Both sides of this traditional consumption equation rarely interacted. The digital media landscape, however, enables a much closer producer/consumption relationship. Audiences and producers have converged, with audiences now playing an integral part in content development, while producers are ever more reliant on the free digital labour of their audiences to market and distribute their products within the fragmented broadcast networks that make up the modern media landscape.

Social media tactics used to drive audience engagement

The following audience–producer convergence strategies are deployed by contemporary media products:

- **Transmedia storytelling.** Products are 'transmedia' if they are relayed across multiple platforms. Web-based content might outline character backstories. Fake social media accounts might be used to give fictional characters a real-life presence. Transmedia storytelling of this kind builds the fictional universe of a brand, rewarding loyal fans with additional content while also expanding the storytelling possibilities of a product. A mobile-friendly transmedia story format also gifts producers the ability to market their products through smartphone ownership.

- **Promotional preview material release.** Producers exploit fan power by releasing promotional material through fan networks. Using fan labour to market and advertise products in highly cost-effective ways.
- **Social media hashtags.** Fan debate can be successfully channelled using hashtags – this also allows producers to track fan opinion.
- **Product maker interactions.** Interviews, post-show web chats and 'behind the scenes' footage are incredibly easy ways to bring fans and producers together. These moments promote a personal engagement with products.
- **Fan reposts.** Audience engagement is further facilitated by re-posting content or comments made by fans. In this way, media producers can construct a sense that they are engaging with fans at a personal level.
- **Textual poaching invites.** Products deliberately include material that is designed to prompt a fan response. For instance, when James Bond hints at his bisexual past in *Skyfall*, fans were invited to manufacture material that recontextualised 007's heterosexuality – directing Bond audiences to engage in textual poaching practices for the purpose of brand cultivation.
- **Competitions, giveaways and other loyalty rewards.** Products maintain the visibility of their brands by providing a steady stream of digital rewards. Giving away downloadable extras, fan kits, wallpapers and regular updates are all designed to keep products alive, and their audiences primed for sequels or further releases.
- **Crossover events.** Products often team up with other brands to take part in joint events. Crossovers enable brands to gain exposure to other product's fan bases.

Box 18.2   Research it: diagnose the level of audience–producer convergence in your set texts

Use the following questions to help structure your research into the effects and scope of audience–producer convergence regarding your set texts.

Diagnosing audience effects on products

- In what ways do the media set texts you are studying construct audience feedback mechanisms? What social media hashtags do they use?
- What do the fans tell their producers on social media platforms?
- Have the set texts been subject to an online campaign to change any aspects?
- Has audience power shaped the set texts you are producing?

Diagnosing producer use of fan labour

- How do products take advantage of the free digital labour of their fans to help market and distribute their products?
- Have trailers or other promotional material been released on YouTube? How many hits, reposts or 'likes' has this material gained?
- Do set text products deliberately nourish fan groups or fan activity? Do they make fan kits available for download? Have they constructed a fan wiki or an official fan website?

Further audience–producer convergence help sheets are available for set texts from all exam boards at www.essentialmedia theory.com

---

Box 18.3   Revise it: diagnose the use of social media to promote/distribute set texts

This activity is particularly useful for exam questions that ask you to identify digital marketing strategies used by media producers. It can also be useful when discussing how set texts engage with their audiences through digital technology. Analyse relevant set texts using the following prompts:

- How has social media been used to market or advertise the product? Diagnose 'likes' or 'share' stats to help build a picture of the effectiveness of this strategy.
- In what ways do set texts used transmedia storytelling to enhance brand visibility?
- Research the social media tactics deployed by set text marketers. What notable strategies did they employ? How effective were they? What is innovative about their use of social media?

Exemplar 1: *Killing Eve* (Eduqas and OCR) – use of fan power as a marketing device. Contemporary television dramas routinely construct official fan outlets to propagate audience interest, using what might be called the free digital labour of fans to produce publicity. Jenkins argues that such activity has been dialled-up by the digital revolution, whereby producers effect product visibility when fans share material across their personnel networks. The BBC's *Killing Eve* ancillary webpage evidences some of the tactics that producers have used to nurture a *Killing Eve* fandom, curating videos and accompanying embed codes of clips that have viral potential, as well as a link to the *Obsessed with…Killing Eve* podcast series that gives voice to fan discussion topics and plot analysis. The official website also contains limited downloadable freebies in the form of a *Killing Eve* alarm clock audio clip and links to BBC interviews with the cast, the latter activity nurturing a behind the scenes engagement that rewards viewer interest.

Exemplar 2: *Assassins' Creed Franchise* (Eduqas) – using transmedia storytelling to build brand engagement online. Fan activity, Jenkins tells us, provides a vital function for contemporary producers – helping to satisfy audience interaction needs while simultaneously providing the means to circulate a brand's identity and credentials. Fandoms are particularly important to franchised game product, where the maintenance of audience loyalty from one iteration of a gaming title to the next is needed to sustain brand longevity. Fandoms, too, provide game makers with an informal feedback mechanism to assess brand impact. One way that fan engagement can be nurtured is via the use of transmedia storytelling – using as many different platforms as possible to tell the story of the brand, and exploiting the advantages of different media forms to create maximum visibility. *Assassin's Creed*, for example, has been translated into mobile games, a Hollywood blockbuster and book series, all helping the gaming title to build an imaginary *Assassin's Creed* universe that fans can spend time in. The official Discord server also provides fans with opportunities to share user-generated art, fanfiction and gameplay tips, as well as encouraging fans to submit ideas for future iterations of the franchise. Such material not only keeps the brand warm but also provides an informal focus group that helps Ubisoft track game play features that work and don't work.

Further set text help is available for a range of products for all exam boards at www.essentialmediatheory.com

Concept 3: fans use participatory culture to effect wider social change

Cyber utopianism and Nicholas Negroponte

In many senses, Jenkins is a torch bearer for a largely optimistic view of the internet's potential. Nicholas Negroponte was one of the first commentators to recognise the earth-shattering potential of the web during its infancy in the 1990s. 'The information superhighway,' Negroponte wrote in 1995, 'may be mostly hype today, but it is an understatement about tomorrow. It will exist beyond people's wildest predictions' (Negroponte, 1995, 231). Negroponte, like Jenkins, embraced the digital revolution with open arms. Digital technology, he argued, will be 'a natural force drawing people into greater world harmony' (Negroponte, 1995, 230). 'We will socialise in digital neighbourhoods in which physical space will be irrelevant,' he prophesied, 'The digital planet will look and feel like the head of a pin' (Negroponte, 1995, 6).

Negroponte's optimism regarding digital technology can be grouped into the following arguments – arguments that are equally applicable to Jenkins' view:

- **The internet provides personalisation benefits:** the internet will enable us to consume media/information that is tailored to our needs and desires.
- **The web will be a democratising force:** because no one oversees the internet, it is immune from the abuses of large-scale organisations, governments or powerful multinational companies. An open access internet is a democratised space where every voice can be heard.
- **Miniaturisation advantages:** the internet will make the world a smaller place where ideas can be shared regardless of geographical proximity. This feature, cyber utopians argued, will result in the collapse of cultural differences and the erosion of social divisions.

Jenkins – the cyber utopian

Jenkins' thinking mirrors much of Negroponte's early cyber optimism. 'Audiences,' Jenkins argues, 'empowered by these new technologies ... are demanding the right to participate' (Jenkins, 2006a, 24). New technologies, he suggests, both democratise and miniaturise the world in that they provide ordinary audiences with the means to participate in wider social discussions. Participatory culture gives us all a voice, Jenkins argues, with communities forming around these digital discussions in ways that clearly mimic Negroponte's 'digital neighbourhoods'.

Jenkins is careful, however, to distinguish the practices that constitute participatory culture from the wider term 'Web 2.0'. For Jenkins, Web 2.0 defines a wide range of *commercial* activities that major media corporations use across the web – product distribution, sales/marketing functions and so forth. Stripped to its essential core, Web 2.0 is a business model driven by profit.

Participatory culture, Jenkins argues, is distinctly different in that its motives are community and knowledge oriented. Participatory culture exists not to make money, but to allow its members to exchange information and to express themselves creatively while providing a space in which fan creations can be shared with others.

From cultures to online participation

The roots of participatory culture, Jenkins claims, can be found in the folk traditions that preceded the mass media era – in the songs and music that working-class musicians shared with one another before mass radio broadcasting. Participatory culture today can be found in amateur arts groups and drama clubs – places where ordinary people can create, share and experiment. Jenkins further suggests that these communities have migrated to become digital networks – existing alongside, yet distinctly different from, the commercial activities of Web 2.0.

What excites Jenkins most about participatory culture is its value as an identity enabler. The online fanfictions written in response to traditional media products give voice to an audience's desires and needs. Peer-to-peer videos fill the gaps that professionally produced media products cannot or will not occupy. And, in making and sharing DIY media, fans are engaging in community-based discussion.

Jenkins, moreover, perceives that the internet has the capacity to translate that discussion into political engagement. We can see that process in action when we look at the #MeToo campaign that formed in response to the Harvey Weinstein allegations. What started out as a Hollywood scandal concerning the alleged abuse of women by media mogul Harvey Weinstein quickly mushroomed into an online global campaign that protested misogyny and male abuse more generally. Jenkins, too, draws our attention to groups like the Harry Potter Alliance – an organisation that has channelled fan power into global political activism through its campaigns to promote worldwide gender equality, among other things.

Box 18.4   Discuss it: in what ways is the internet a force for social good?

- Is the internet a force for social good? What concrete evidence can you present to support arguments that it exerts a positive influence on society?
- Can you think of any online campaigns that have tried to create social change? Have they been effective?
- In what ways does the internet create purposeful communities?

Box 18.5   Discuss it: in what ways is the internet problematic?

- How has social media affected political debate in the UK?
- Look carefully at the user comments on the online versions of your newspaper set texts – how would you describe the tone of the debate? Is the commentary problematic?
- Do people really use YouTube to create peer-to-peer connections or has it been hijacked for more commercial purposes?
- In what ways is the internet controlled by a handful of global companies? In what ways is their dominance problematic?

Table 18.1 Speak Henry Jenkins

Audience–producer convergence	The coming together of media producers and audiences, principally through digital communications.
Cyber dystopianism	The belief that digital technologies have an adverse effect on society.
Cyber utopianism	The belief that digital media can and is creating positive social change.

(Continued)

Table 18.1 (Continued)

Media democratisation	Placing media power in the hands of ordinary audience members.
Fan labour	The work, often free of charge, executed by fans and audiences to distribute or construct media for larger companies.
Participatory culture	The use of DIY media by audiences – usually to effect change or to share information. Participatory culture is not devised for commercial purposes.
Textual poaching	Appropriating media products for purposes that were not originally intended.
Transmedia storytelling	Using multiple media platforms to tell stories.
Web 2.0	The commercial activities of the web.

Table 18.2 Jenkins: ten-minute revision

Concept 1: *fans appropriate media texts, producing readings that are not fully authorised by media producers*

- Jenkins suggests that audiences are able to use professional texts as 'creative scaffolding' on which they craft their own readings of products.
- Textual poaching can be used by marginalised fans to explore alternative readings to mainstream culture.
- Textual poaching in the digital age can take many forms, including fanfiction, remix culture, fan art or video parodies.

Concept 2: *fans and media makers have converged as a result of digital technology*

- Digital technologies have brought audiences and producers together.
- The digital revolution has expanded the scope of fandoms.
- Producers use their fans' digital labour to promote and market media.
- Contemporary media producers deliberately construct material to engage fan interest.

Concept 3: *fans use participatory culture to effect wider social change*

- Participatory culture is distinctly different from the commercial activities of Web 2.0.
- Participatory culture allows individuals to share and develop ideas with a like-minded community.
- Participatory culture can create social change.

(*Continued*)

Table 18.2 (Continued)

Challenging Jenkins' thinking

Jenkins can be criticised for the one-sided nature of his discussion – for presenting, perhaps, an over-inflated optimism regarding the potential benefits of our digital networks. In his 2008 book, *The Cult of the Amateur*, Andrew Keen, for example, draws attention to the effect that user-generated content has had in terms of shifting the quality of our media experiences. Keen mourns the loss of traditional media production, arguing that professionally produced content is made by highly trained media specialists who work, for the most part, with ethical integrity. For Keen, traditional media production is important because it fulfils a gatekeeping function. Traditional media producers, for example, filter news output so that only the most reliable information becomes public. Professional media outlets further filter cultural production so that only the best music, the best film and the best TV are made public.

Conversely, participatory culture allows amateur journalists to unwittingly mislead or radicalise our viewpoints with one-sided debate. Participatory culture might have democratised the media, but it has also allowed fake news to garner as much attention as authentic journalism. Participatory culture might have given us a remix culture, but even the most cursory look at YouTube will reveal an endless stream of second-rate products – endless reaction videos, for example, or banal comment pieces that have been quickly produced by product-sponsored influencers.

Jenkins neatly divides professional and amateur production into two, suggesting that audiences can disentangle these distinct strands. But, for Keen, the divide between those two worlds has blurred – and that is problematic. YouTube vlogging gives us authentic content, he suggests, yet others work as nothing more than extended advertorials that are designed to coerce us subtly and unknowingly into buying sponsored content.

Other theorists are hugely critical of Jenkins' assessment regarding the importance of participatory culture, pointing to the fact that user activism plays a very minor role in the cyber landscape. Christian Fuchs, for example, concludes that the 'internet is predominantly capitalist in character. Social media are not exclusively an expression of commercial culture but companies … that all share the feature of wanting to sell commodities in order to accumulate profits' (Fuchs, 2021, 81). Fuchs highlights the following features of cyber space that question Jenkins' view that participatory culture has a significant role:

- **Free digital labour exploits audiences.** Fuchs concludes that large companies dominate user experiences, using audience attention as a commodity that it can sell to advertisers.
- **Influencer capitalism.** Fuchs, too, points to the dominance of a select few influencers on social media who both model capitalistic practice as a lifestyle ideal to vulnerable audiences (commodifying themselves and their art for commerce) while also exploiting audience attention for the purposes of product placement and other advertising/merchandising synergies.

(*Continued*)

Table 18.2 (Continued)

- **Private ownership of open networks.** Fuchs also highlights the fact that most of the platforms monopolising our time on the internet are privately owned, turning the community-owned resources and user-authored content of open networks into private profit. YouTube, for example, translates public content into private profit. Airbnb turns the homes of ordinary people into rented lets that it skims profits from. Uber profits from the time and expense taxi drivers expend on their fares.

Five named theorists who might challenge Jenkins' thinking

- **James Curran and Jean Seaton:** argue that the internet is dominated by an oligopoly of commercial companies thus minimising the potential effects of participatory culture.
- **David Hesmondhalgh:** might agree that the internet has resulted in audience–producer convergence but also would argue that the media industry is still heavily reliant upon traditional marketing activities to reduce product risk. Media makers might engage in fan-based listening activities to construct or adapt products, but formulaic product design (using stars/genre codes) remains a consistent focus of product content.
- **Sonia Livingstone and Peter Lunt:** suggest that the global nature of the net and the volume of material uploaded make effective regulation very difficult. New technology might open up the media to democratising forces and the development of new communities, but it is also open to potential abuse.

19 The end of audience

Clay Shirky

'We are living,' Shirky tells us, 'in the middle of the largest in-crease in expressive capability in the history of the human race' (Shirky, 2008, 106). The economic and social impact presented by the digital revolution, he suggests, can be compared to that of Gutenberg's printing press in the fifteenth century. Gutenberg's invention makes him the great-grandfather of mass communica-tion whose invention of the printed page placed English transla-tions of the Bible in the hands of ordinary citizens and assisted in the overthrow of religious state power in the late medieval period. Shirky argues that the internet roll-out has had an equally revolu-tionary impact, placing mass communication tools in the hands of audiences, democratising media production so that ordinary peo-ple can organise and communicate widescale social change.

Concept 1: everybody makes the media

Communications and broadcast media technologies

Shirky argues that the emergence of new communications tech-nologies in the late nineteenth and early twentieth centuries – the telephone, fax machines, pagers and so forth – allowed mass *one-to-one communications* to take place over distances that had previously presented senders and receivers with enormous obsta-cles. The twentieth century, Shirky continues, also bore witness to the parallel development of a range of *broadcast media technologies* that kindled a one-to-many communications revolution.

Shirky argues that the broadcast media of the twentieth century – cinema, radio and television – are a historical anomaly and that the dominance of these forms within our leisure time

DOI: 10.4324/9781003361220-19

created and nurtured a state of audience passivity that hadn't previously been experienced. Broadcast media consumption, Shirky claims, means that 'at work we're office drones, at home we're couch potatoes' (Shirky, 2010, 11). At no other point in history, he infers, were audiences as subdued as they were in the latter half of the twentieth century.

Shirky also points to the respective public and private characters of those newly emergent twentieth-century communications technologies. Telephone-based conversations, Shirky explains, take place between just two participants and are typically private in nature. Conversely, broadcast media is designed for public consumption. The scale and expense, moreover, of the equipment needed to make broadcast-quality content limited the production of television, film or radio products to a small number of organisations that had the financial clout to buy and maintain broadcast equipment. Television communication might create content that is publicly distributed, but the limited number of creators engaged in manufacturing content, Shirky argues, effected a one-to-many communications dynamic. That, dynamic, Shirky concludes, means that twentieth-century media power lay in the hands of the few rather than the many.

The digital revolution: the convergence of personal and broadcast media forms

Shirky argues that the advances made to computer-processing power during the early 1990s enabled communications and broadcast media technologies to converge. The miniaturisation of technology enabled, in short, the invention of devices that could be used for both private and public communication. Email, for example, can be directed to a single recipient (one-to-one communication) or can be broadcast as a marketing mailshot (one-to-many communications). A similar blurring of broadcast and personal communication technologies is enabled through social media in that users can direct messages to single followers within their networks, or post updates to larger groups.

Digital innovations, Shirky further argues, substantially reduced the production barriers that had previously prevented audiences from making their own broadcast media. YouTube users, for example, can make their own content and distribute it to mass audiences without the need to own prohibitively expensive production studios or editing suites. Likewise, social media users can garner followings that rival the audience reach of established lifestyle magazines or traditional media broadcasters using nothing more than smartphone technology.

The simultaneous merging of public/private technologies, coupled with the reduction of broadcast entry barriers, leads Shirky to conclude that contemporary digital media exists as a spectrum of personal and broadcast media effects. At the communications end of that spectrum, we find small-scale, close-knit groups who share content within the confines of a secure messaging group. Think here of an extended family unit using WhatsApp to share personal photographs or of a group of classmates using a messaging network to collaborate on a homework project. Social media of this kind shares the same hallmarks as the communications-based technologies of old: conversations are constructed for a private audience and are two-way in nature.

Digital media and mass amateurisation

Shirky also highlights the potential for contemporary audiences to use peer-to-peer digital networking to cultivate mass broadcast followings. Indeed, the power of the digital revolution is such that everyday users can procure the same kind of celebrity status that was once the sole preserve of cinema, television and radio. Shirky tells us that mass amateurisation in the contemporary age is effective because:

- **Amateur products can be distributed quickly and on a global scale.** While traditional mass broadcasting relies on television and radio transmitters or on chains of cinemas, digital media can be globally distributed without any substantial financial outlay. Similarly, the production processes of traditional television broadcasters are incredibly slow when compared with those of YouTubers who make and distribute content at the touch of a button.
- **Digital distribution enables audience feedback.** The one-way communications dynamic of traditional mass broadcasting means that audiences are not able to provide feedback to producers. Digital producers, conversely, react quickly to audience

feedback, using 'likes', 'shares' and user-generated commentary to diagnose impact – often using that data to develop and refine further content.

As a result, peer-to-peer digital networks now compete with, and in some instances have usurped, the reach of traditional mass broadcasting providers. But, Shirky suggests, any expansion of these amateur networks comes at a cost. The larger one's audience, he argues, the more difficult it is to engage in meaningful one-to-one conversations with any single recipient. What might begin as a one-to-one communication-oriented conversation turns into the impersonal one-way dynamic of a broadcast media relationship once a mass viewership is engaged. The unusually short lifespans of some celebrity vloggers can perhaps be explained because of this dynamic, in that YouTubers often construct initial audience appeal through a personalised engagement with a small fan base. That initial intimacy, and potentially the authenticity of the vlog, becomes much harder to sustain as those fan bases expand.

Box 19.1   Think about it: the convergence of communications and broadcast media

- In what ways do your online set texts engage a 'communications'-oriented relationship with their audience?
- Do any of your online set texts exemplify mass amateurisation media making?
- In what ways do these online mass amateurisation set texts exemplify Shirky's idea that online media quickly adopts a broadcast relationship when mass audiences are achieved?

Filter first, publish later

To ensure that the huge sums of money needed to make and distribute products are well spent, traditional media broadcasting, Shirky tells us, effects a robust filtering process. Quality controlling the content of traditional broadcast media, he explains, helps producers cultivate the mass audiences needed to justify or sustain production.

The pre-vetting of content by traditional broadcasters is a necessity, Shirky argues, ensuring that the cash reserves of traditional broadcasters are only spent on products that have the most potential to be popular and profitable. As a result, established editorial processes dominate traditional production. Quality control processes, Shirky further argues, can be readily applied to mass media because of the relatively small number of products that are made.

In the digital world, conversely, Shirky suggests that a 'publish first, filter later' mentality dominates. The ease with which digital media can be assimilated and published significantly reduces publication barriers, while the lack of traditional commercial overheads – salary expenses, personnel costs or more general running costs – means that amateur producers can publish higher-risk content because the potential impact of failure is financially low. Indeed, Shirky claims that failure is an endemic feature of the internet and that the web is a space that invites constant experimentation: 'by reducing the cost of failure,' he writes, the web, 'enable[s] ... participants to fail like crazy' (Shirky, 2008, 246).

The impossibility of pre-filtering

The 'publish first, filter later' model of the internet might invite experimentation, but the lack of editorial control enacted by digital content makers also presents some significant problems. Traditional broadcasters might be inclined to play it safe, but the editorial processes they use to control production perform a vital gatekeeping role. Those controls protect audiences from fake news or politically extreme content. They shield vulnerable audiences from excessively graphic material or explicit narratives. 'Mass amateurization,' Shirky thus argues, 'has created a filtering problem vastly larger than we had with traditional media, so much larger, in fact, that many of the old solutions are simply broken' (Shirky, 2008, 246). The sheer volume of media uploaded to the internet today makes it almost impossible to check or corroborate content before it is published.

The future is digital

Traditional mass media might construct quality products with reliable and accurate content, but, Shirky concludes, their long-term chances of survival in today's digital world are slim. Digital networks and mass amateurisation, he argues, will inevitably come to dominate the media landscape. Shirky cites the following fatal flaws in the structure and scope of traditional mass media activity:

- **The high overhead costs of traditional media** (salaries, costs of premises, taxation) make them uncompetitive. In comparison, mass amateurisation-authored content can be made with much smaller budgets.
- **The slow decision-making processes** used to manage traditional media institutions make it harder for them to adapt to changing market conditions. Amateur digital media, in comparison, can adopt quickly to changing audience tastes.
- Traditional media companies are **risk averse** because of the editorial processes used to ensure that programming achieves quality. Mass amateurisation-oriented media operate a 'publish first, filter later' model that does not readily identify risk as a significant barrier.

Box 19.2   Discuss it: is Shirky right to suggest that traditional media is outmoded?

- Is Shirky right to suggest that the web has brought about a mass amateurisation revolution? Are traditional broadcasters going to die out? Why do you agree or disagree?
- How has the loss of professional media gatekeeping disadvantaged audiences?

Exemplar: JJ Olatunji (Eduqas). The initial success of JJ Olatunji – better known as KSI – in commanding the attention of his fans lay in his FIFA gaming vlogs, in which he invited audiences to share in the highs and lows of his less than glamorous FIFA gaming antics. His everyday persona, like many other pre-2010 YouTubers, created a connection with a young male gaming-obsessed audience who had largely been neglected by traditional media broadcasters. YouTube's peer-to-peer video-sharing service gave

---

amateur producers like KSI the means to cheaply produce and distribute content – to effect the kind of one-to-many broadcasting relationships that had only been available to large-scale producers. The ability for audiences to join in with KSI's conversations, to speak back to him and to fellow fans, has further affected what Shirky would call one-to-one communications benefits – helping KSI to cement a sense of connection with his growing army of fans.

Shirky also tells us that mass amateur content will inevitably surpass the reach of more traditional broadcast forms, that their lo-fi approach and use of YouTube-driven metrics enables them to readily adapt to changing audience tastes in ways that a *filter first, publish later* media can't compete with. KSI, certainly exemplifies that dynamic, his reinventions as a rap music artist, failed Hollywood star, boxer and inventor of the Prime drink helping him to achieve an elite level YouTuber status, his channel commanding over 16 million subscribers with uploads regularly achieving views of 3 million or more. KSI exemplifies an elite class of entrepreneur influencers who have managed to translate audience connectivity into huge financial rewards.

Consumers speak back to media makers

Digital innovation and mass amateurisation have placed significant pressures on traditional media makers, forcing them to radically rethink their production and distribution models or face extinction. And, in the same way that their audiences have used digital technology to mimic broadcasting, Shirky argues that traditional broadcasters have reciprocated by integrating one-to-one communication within their production practices.

Newspapers now invite readers to comment on stories using online feedback tools. Video games connect and encourage player feedback via fan-oriented connectivity, and television makers encourage viewer conversations by deploying social media hashtags. Indeed, Shirky argues, those traditional media makers who resolutely fail to realise the importance of effecting a two-way conversation with their audiences will not survive the digital revolution. Contemporary consumers, he tells us, have come to expect that they can make contributions to the public conversations engaged by the broadcast media, and if mass broadcasters do not facilitate that need, they will find that their services are no longer relevant. (See Table 19.1 for further details regarding the specific effects of the digital revolution in key areas of the media industry.)

Table 19.1 Effects of the digital revolution in key industries

Newspapers	• The explosion in blogs, online celebrity gossip, news sites and social media has contributed to declining readerships for newspapers.
	• Some news brands have embraced mass amateurisation by incorporating citizen journalism into their products, inviting everyday readers to share their experiences with other readers.
	• The 'filter first, publish later' model adopted by newspapers means that their products often look and feel very safe when compared to their online competitors. Some newspapers have tried to combat this perceived safeness by recruiting provocative contributors (dubbed 'contrarians'). The *Daily Mail*'s use of Boris Johnson as a column writer serves as an interesting example of this process.
	• Online newspapers have embraced the use of reader commentary to promote audience engagement. The degree to which comments features are used varies, with some papers (*The Times* and *The Guardian*, for example) restricting their use to less contentious news stories. Moderation of comments also varies enormously, with some titles applying much stricter rules than others.
	• Newspapers now operate a 'digital first' policy – breaking stories online as soon as they appear. News viability, some would argue, is based upon the ability to publish news before competitors. News brands, in this sense, utilise Shirky's *publish first, filter later* model, with some critics arguing that the race to break news first diminishes quality reporting.
Television	• Television broadcasters have fought back, using YouTube as a marketing tool and as a means to cultivate fan engagement through additional footage (behind the scenes clips, artist interviews, alternative edits).
	• Television and cable networks now sign successful YouTubers to make mass media content – capturing online experimental content that has found success.
	• Producers engage in web chats and other forums to effect personal connections with their audiences.
	• Television makers use social media hashtags to facilitate audience feedback or to promote audience conversations during broadcasts. Producers refer to this as 'second screening'.

(*Continued*)

Table 19.1 (Continued)

	• Mainstream television's embrace of high-quality, multi-season, long-form storytelling offers products that YouTube cannot copy. This has helped traditional broadcasters maintain audience share.
Film marketing	• Services such as YouTube have helped level the playing field for independent filmmakers giving them access to lucrative marketing and distribution channels.
	• Major production companies use YouTube analytics to help them predict the potential viability of a film release. Film companies determine where they ought to book cinemas and for how long using data gathered from marketing released on social media.
	• Much like television, producers use YouTube to garner publicity and interest through the release of additional material.
	• Persona marketing on social media platforms is used to mimic one-to-one connectivity between filmmakers and their audiences. Fictional characters are often given a web presence to cultivate fan power.

Box 19.3   Apply it: diagnose the effects of the digital revolution on your set texts

- In what ways do your set texts deliver the benefits of digital technology?
- In what ways do your online set texts evidence a more experimental approach to content than their traditional media rivals?
- In what ways do your set texts invite audience feedback?
- In what ways have your broadcast media set texts been adversely affected by the digital revolution? Think here in terms of increased competition, diminishing advertising revenues or the potential reduction in quality that has occurred as a result of a general weakening of gatekeeping across all media sectors.
- In what ways have broadcast media set texts adapted to the digital revolution? How do they engage two-way conversations with their audiences?

Exemplar paragraphs that apply Shirky's ideas to set texts from all exam boards are available at www.essentialmediatheory.com

Concept 2: everyday communities of practice

Shirky argues that groups with shared interests, values or identities have always wanted to make contact with one another. In
the pre-digital world, however, both physical and financial barriers
prevented those groups from forming. In contrast, Shirky tells us,
the internet roll-out has enabled the widespread construction of
what he calls 'communities of practice'. The internet, he argues,
enables groups of individuals to overcome the physical barriers of
the pre-digital world, and 'groups, once assembled, can be quite
robust in the face of indifference or even direct opposition from
larger society' (Shirky, 2008, 210).

Communities of practice are notable, Shirky suggests, for the
following reasons:

- They are capable of creating social change. The flash mobs that
  propelled the Arab Spring, for instance, were enabled by social
  media activism, helping to topple a series of repressive regimes
  in the Middle East.
- They are incredibly resilient when threatened – online communities can disband and regroup very easily when threatened
  or censored.
- They are self-policing and driven by non-profit motives.
- They can also coalesce around socially undesirable subjects.
  Shirky highlights, for example, the challenge that pro-anorexia
  groups have presented in promoting dangerous lifestyle choices
  to vulnerable young women. Online political or religious extremism, too, fans real-world violence.

**Box 19.4   Think about it: communities
of practice – good or bad?**

- What examples of online activism have you encountered
  that have prompted positive social change or allowed
  marginalised groups to have a more powerful voice?
- What recent examples of negative online behaviour can you identify that have had adverse real world
  consequences?

The 'bargain' of audience engagement

Shirky suggests that audiences and producers are engaged in a transactional exchange when media products are consumed and that audience–producer relationships are defined through an unofficial 'bargain' that is brokered between both parties. In traditional media consumption, that transactional bargain is relatively straightforward in that hard cash is usually exchanged to view a product. Money is traded for a cinema ticket or a cable television subscription: media purchases, in other words, produce the promise of a viewing pleasure.

The bargains made online, however, are complicated by the fact that we expect to receive content, for the most part, without spending any real money. This does not mean that online consumption is transaction free. On the contrary, YouTube viewers can only consume the uploads posted if they watch the commercial advertising that precedes them. The bargain made by audiences when reading online news is that you allow internet cookies to be installed so that personalised advertising can be displayed alongside story content.

Shirky's 'bargain', interestingly, also governs the kinds of conduct that audiences unofficially agree among themselves as acceptable for the online communities in which they participate. The rules governing online comment etiquette are not necessarily written down – they exist as an unofficial agreement that has been negotiated by users about the way they ought to behave when conversing with one another online. In online fandoms, for instance, it is universally accepted that stories are not shared for commercial gain or that you do not steal a fellow author's work.

The most interesting feature of the bargain, for Shirky at least, is that digital audiences can exercise a form of collective power that can shape or even determine the rules that govern their media engagement. If, collectively, we all decide that YouTube advertising is so obtrusive that we stop watching it, then the service would have no choice but to revise its commercial strategy. In short, audiences have the power to shape online media content and, furthermore, have the communication tools to effect collective action against services if the need arises.

Shirky argues, too, that while the rules that govern small-scale communities of practice are easily and clearly defined, those same bargains tend to break down when products achieve mass audiences. An online fan group with less than 100 members will communicate within a clear set of expectations that are shared by all members. Posts that infringe those rules will be speedily censored or removed. Those rules breakdown, however, when online communities become larger and produce competing subgroups that will inevitably shape their own rules of engagement. Thus, the large-scale nature of digital giants like Facebook will inevitably lead, in Shirky's view, to a conflict of user interests. Such platforms promise interconnectivity and provide the necessary tools to enable those promises, but the scope and scale of the subgroups that operate within their networks will inevitably employ the site for purposes that are contradictory.

Box 19.5   Apply it: big services do not always produce beautiful effects

- Identify the 'bargain' that allows audiences to use your online set texts for free. What do users unofficially agree to in order to access free content?
- In what ways do producers create benefits for themselves as a result of making online content free?
- In what ways does internet advertising compromise the experience of online browsing?
- In what ways does online advertising compromise the integrity of set text content?

Challenge question

- In what ways do the large-scale audiences of your set texts inevitably lead to audience conflict? How, for instance, do reader comments on online news sites demonstrate a clash of expectations?

Exemplar paragraphs that apply Shirky's ideas to set texts from all exam boards are available at www.essentialmediatheory.com

Table 19.2 Speak Clay Shirky

Broadcast media	Broadcast media (television, radio, newspapers) act like a megaphone enabling one-to-many communications. Information, in a broadcast relationship, will usually flow in one direction, from the sender to the receiver.
Communications media	Communications media (telephones and faxes) effect a two-way relationship in which senders and receivers are engaged in private conversations.
Digital communications convergence	Digital technologies have merged broadcast and communications media effects. Emails, for instance, can be both private and public – they can also have single or multiple recipients.
Gatekeeping	Limiting access to information – usually affected by traditional media broadcasters to maintain the quality of their products.
Mass amateurisation	The use of digital media by everyday audiences to produce broadcast media.
Second screening	Viewing traditional media while engaging with accompanying content on another device. For example, using a mobile phone to join in a social media conversation while watching a television show.

Table 19.3 Shirky: ten-minute revision

Concept 1: *everybody makes the media*

- Shirky highlights the revolutionary impact of digital technology in speeding up media production processes.
- Media consumption patterns have changed from a broadcast model that involves one sender and many recipients to a many-to-many model.
- Traditional media, Shirky argues, uses a 'filter then publish' model to provide quality content.
- Shirky suggests that the internet has resulted in a 'publish now, filter later' model due to lower production costs and reduced entry barriers to media production.

Concept 2: *everyday communities of practice*

- Audiences actively shape their own rules of engagement with professional media products.
- Digital technologies have resulted in an explosion of what Shirky calls 'communities of practice'.

(*Continued*)

Table 19.3 (Continued)

Challenging Shirky's thinking

Undoubtedly, Shirky's writing is imbued with a celebratory optimism regarding the web's potential. His outlining of digital media as an engine for social change, effected by everyday citizens, is for many overplayed. Critics point, for example, to the role that big tech platforms like YouTube or Google play in directing our attention to a relatively small number of services or sources. Top 10 Google searches, for example, monopolise audience attention, while YouTube algorithms reward channels that don't necessarily give us the best information, but do have the biggest viewer hits. Big tech companies, too, are accused of datafication practices, using our engagement with free platforms to collect information on our likes, dislikes, shopping habits and so on, so that data can be sold to advertisers or other commercial partners.

Others centre more firmly on the problematic nature of YouTube commodification, arguing that covert advertising – channel sponsorship and product placements deals – sanitise content or unwittingly exploit audience engagement. Commodification tends to ensure that only young YouTubers gain sponsorship deals, skewing mainstream content to reinforce narrow beauty standards or heteronormative ideals. Other writers like Sophie Bishop suggest that YouTuber search algorithms tend to reinforce gender-based stereotypes, directing female audiences to beauty and fashion vloggers, while males are pointed to gaming or sports-related topics.

The commodification of services like YouTube also leads Marxist theorists like Christian Fuchs to question the way that major digital platforms exploit the digital output of amateur producers, describing the work of mass amateur producers as providing free digital labour for money rich social media brands like TikTok or YouTube. Crafting a successful social media channel, Fuchs further argues, requires huge reservoirs of patience, luck and hard work, work that produces huge financial rewards for a minority of elite-level vloggers and influencers, but, for the most, produces little financial reward. Those digital labourers, Fuchs argues, work to enrich platform owners who monetise their unpaid-for content via advertising.

Three named theorists who might challenge Shirky's thinking

- **James Curran and Jean Seaton:** argue that the internet continues to be dominated by an oligopoly of commercial companies.
- **David Hesmondhalgh:** might agree that the internet has resulted in audience–producer convergence but would argue that the media industry is still heavily reliant upon traditional marketing activities to reduce product risk.

Bibliography

Arguedas, A. R., Mukherjee, M. and Nielsen, R.K. (2023). *Women and leadership in the news media 2023: evidence from 12 markets*, Reuters Institute. Available at: https://reutersinstitute.politics.ox.ac.uk/women-and-leadership-news-media-2023-evidence-12-markets (accessed 15 September 2023).

Bandura, A. (1973). *Aggression: A Social Learning Analysis.* Englewood Cliffs, NJ: Prentice-Hall.

Barthes, R. (2006). *S/Z.* Malden: Blackwell.

Barthes, R. (2007). *Image, Music, Text.* New York: Hill and Wang.

Barthes, R. (2009). *Mythologies.* London: Vintage Books.

Baudrillard, J. (1987). *The Ecstasy of Communication.* New York: Semiotext(e).

Baudrillard, J. (1995). *The Gulf War Did Not Take Place.* Bloomington, IN: Indiana University Press.

Baudrillard, J. (2018). *Simulacra and Simulation.* Ann Arbor, MA: University of Michigan Press.

BFI (2018). *Statistical Yearbook 2018.* Available at: https://www.bfi.org.uk/sites/bfi.org.uk/files/downloads/bfi-statistical-yearbook-2018.pdf (accessed 9 April 2019).

BFI (2023). *Official 2022 statistics reveal a record £6.27 billion film and high-end television production spend in the UK*, BFI. Available at: https://www.bfi.org.uk/news/official-2022-statistics (accessed 15 September 2023).

Bignell, J. (2002). *Media Semiotics.* Manchester: Manchester University Press.

Black Lives Matter (2019). *What We Believe.* Available at: https://blacklivesmatter.com/about/what-we-believe/ (accessed 15 April 2019).

Bush, G. W. (2002). State of the Union Address, 29 January, The Senate, Washington. Available at: www.washingtonpost.com/wp-srv/onpolitics/transcripts/sou012902.htm (accessed 10 June 2019).

Butler, J. (2007). *Gender Trouble.* New York: Routledge.

Curran, J. and Seaton, J. (2010). *Power without Responsibility: Press, Broadcasting and the Internet in Britain.* 7th edn. London: Routledge.

Evans, J. and Hesmondhalgh, D. (2005). *Understanding Media: Inside Celebrity.* Maidenhead: Open University Press.

Fisher, M. (2023). *Chaos Machine: The Inside Story of How Social Media Rewired Our Minds and Our World.* London: Quercus Publishing.

Fuchs, C. (2021). *Social Media: A Critical Introduction.* 3rd edn. London: Sage.

Gauntlett, D. (2002). *Media, Gender and Identity.* London: Routledge.

Gauntlett, D. (2008). *Media, Gender and Identity.* 2nd edn. London: Routledge.

Gauntlett, D. (2011). *Making is Connecting.* Cambridge: Polity Press.

Gerbner, G. and Morgan, M. (2016). *Against the Mainstream.* New York: Peter Lang.

Giddens, A. (1991). *Modernity and Self-Identity.* Cambridge: Polity Press.

Gilroy, P. (2004). *After Empire.* Abingdon: Routledge.

Gilroy, P. (2008). *There Ain't No Black in the Union Jack.* London: Routledge.

GLAAD (2023). *Where we are on TV report – 2021–2022,* GLAAD. Available at: https://glaad.org/whereweareontv21 (accessed 15 September 2023).

Gleeson, J. (2021). *Judith Butler: 'we need to rethink the category of woman',* The Guardian. Available at: https://www.theguardian.com/lifeandstyle/2021/sep/07/judith-butler-interview-gender (accessed 15 September 2023).

Greenhill, S. (2022). *Why a free press is a vital part of our democracy,* Daily Mail Online. Available at: https://www.dailymail.co.uk/news/article-10814849/Why-free-Press-vital-democracy-owner-Daily-Mail-Lord-Rothermere.html (accessed 15 September 2023).

Hall, S. (1999). Encoding/Decoding. In: S. During, ed., *The Cultural Studies Reader,* 2nd ed. New York: Routledge.

Hall, S., Evans, J. and Nixon, S. (2013). *Representation.* 2nd edn. London: Sage.

Hesmondhalgh, D. (2019). *The Cultural Industries.* 4th edn. London: Sage.

Hollywood Diversity Report (2022). Social Sciences UCLA. Available at: https://socialsciences.ucla.edu/hollywood-diversity-report-2022/ (accessed: 15 September 2023).

hooks, b. (1982). *Ain't I a Woman.* London: Pluto Press.

IPSO (2021). *Editors' code of practice,* IPSO. Available at: https://www.ipso.co.uk/editors-code-of-practice/ (accessed: 15 September 2023).

Jenkins, H. (2006a). *Convergence Culture.* New York: New York University Press.

Jenkins, H. (2006b). *Fans, Bloggers and Gamers*. New York: New York University Press.

Jenkins, H. (2013). *Textual Poachers*. 2nd edn. New York: Routledge.

Jenkins, H. (2019). *Video Games myths revisited: new Pew study tells us about games and youth*, Henry Jenkins. Available at: http://henryjenkins.org/blog/2008/10/video_games_myths_revisited_ne.html (accessed 8 April 2019).

Keen, A. (2008). *The Cult of the Amateur*. London: Nicholas Brealey.

Keen, A. (2012). *Digital Vertigo*. New York: Constable & Robinson.

Lévi-Strauss, C. (2004). *The Savage Mind*. Oxford: Oxford University Press.

Lievrouw, L. and Livingstone, S. (2009). *Handbook of New Media*. London: Sage.

Livingstone, S. and Lunt, P. (2012). *Media Regulation*. London: Sage.

Merrin, W. (2005). *Baudrillard and the Media*. Cambridge: Polity.

Neale, S. (2001). *Genre and Hollywood*. London: Routledge.

Negroponte, N. (1995). *Being Digital*. New York: Vintage Books.

O'Carroll, L. (2012). *Leveson Report: Key points,* The Guardian. Available at: https://www.theguardian.com/media/2012/nov/29/leveson-report-key-points (accessed 15 September 2023).

Ponsford, D. (2022) *What next for Lord Rothermere – the most powerful person in British News Media*, Press Gazette. Available at: https://pressgazette.co.uk/news/lord-rothermere-daily-mail-dmgt/ (accessed 15 September 2023).

Procter, J. (2004). *Stuart Hall*. London: Routledge.

Propp, V. (2009). *Morphology of the Folktale*. Austin, TX: University of Texas Press.

Romero, M. (2018). *Introducing Intersectionality*. Cambridge: Polity.

Shirky, C. (2008). *Here Comes Everybody*. London: Allen Lane.

Shirky, C. (2010). *Cognitive Surplus*. London: Allen Lane.

Stokel-Walker, C. (2019). *YouTubers: How YouTube Shook Up TV and Created a New Generation of Stars*. Kingston-upon-Thames, Surrey: Canbury Press.

Sullivan, J. L. (2013). *Media Audiences: Effects, Users, Institutions, and Power*. London: Sage.

Sweney, M. (2019). *Out of print: NME's demise shows pressure on consumer magazines*, The Guardian. Available at: https://www.theguardian.com/media/2018/mar/12/nme-vogue-death-print-magazines (accessed 8 April 2019).

Sweney, M. (2022). *Twitter 'to lose 32M users in two years after Elon Musk takeover'*, The Guardian. Available at: https://www.theguardian.com/technology/2022/dec/13/twitter-lose-users-elon-musk-takeover-hate-speech#:~:text=The%20number%20of%20global%20monthly, social%20media%20platform%20in%202008 (accessed 15 September 2023).

Tanatarova, E. (2023). *Jealous' transgender woman murdered three sex workers because they were 'more attractive than she could ever plan to be', criminologist suggests,* Daily Mail Online. Available at: https://www.dailymail.co.uk/femail/article-12361037/Jealous-transgender-woman-murdered-three-sex-workers-attractive-plan-criminologist-suggests.html?ico=topics_pagination_desktop (accessed 15 September 2023).

Todorov, T. (1977). *The Poetics of Prose.* Oxford: B. Blackwell.

Townsend, M. (2019). *Rise in UK use of far-right online forums as anti-Muslim hate increases,* The Guardian. Available at: https://www.theguardian.com/world/2019/mar/16/rise-far-right-online-forums-anti-muslim-hate-wave (accessed 7 April 2019).

Twenge, J. M. (2023). *Generations.* New York: Atria Books.

UCLA (2018). *Hollywood diversity report,* UCLA. Available at: https://socialsciences.ucla.edu/wp-content/uploads/2018/02/UCLA-Hollywood-Diversity-Report-2018-2-27-18.pdf (accessed 15 April 2019).

Williams, P. (2013). *Paul Gilroy.* London: Routledge.

Zoonen, L. van (1994). *Feminist Media Studies.* London: Sage.

Index

Note: **Bold** page numbers refer to tables and boxes

abjection 136–7, **140**
absent representations 121–2,
   123, 125, **137–8**
Adbusters **232**
advertising 12–13, **28**, 66–8,
   226–7; effects on the internet
   168–9, 201, 271, **272**, **274**;
   effects on newspaper content
   156–8, **160**, **167**, 202;
   effects on television content
   225–6; and identity 147;
   regulation of **184**, 189; and
   self-regulation 183
Advertising Standards Authority
   (ASA) 182, **184**, 189
albionic representations 100–2, **104**
Amazon Prime 38, 136, 184, 188
Anderson, C. **205**
Apple TV+ 38, 136
artificial scarcity 197
Assassin's Creed 187, 202, 254
Attitude magazine 67, **74**
Atypical **26**
audience-producer
   convergence 248–9,
   250–1, **257**
auteur effects **55–6**

Bandura, A.: and media modelling
   208–11; and video games
   214–16
Barthes, R.: anchorage 5, 7; and
   connotation/denotation 1–3,
   7; five code symphony 7–11;
   and ideology 12–15

Baudrillard, J.: and advertising
   66–9; and the ecstasy of
   communication 62–3; and
   meaning implosion 66; the
   procession of the simulacra
   61–2
The BBC 173–4, 234, 246, **253**;
   difference from commercial
   media 55, 171–2; radio **174–5**;
   regulation of 181, 183, **184**
Beyoncé, *Formation* **124**,
   128, **152**
Bignell, J. 226
binary oppositions **228–9**, **242**
Black Beauty is Beauty, Sephora
   68–9
Black female stereotypes
   119, 122
Black Lives Matter **126–7**
Black Panther **199–200**
Black representation 82, 93–4
Bourdieu, P. **231–2**
brand acquisition 195–7
branding 68, 147, 156, **200**
British Board of Film Classification
   (BBFC) 181, **185**
Butler, J. **30**, **118**; and gendered
   hierarchies 134; and gender
   subversion 134–7

Channel 4 171–2, 181, 183
character archetypes 21, 31–2, **34**,
   36, 47
citizen-focused regulation
   179–81, **192**

Communications Act 2003 181,
  189, **190, 192**
communities of practise 270
conglomerate ownership
  160–3, **169**
consumer-based regulation 178–9,
  186, 187, 190, 191, 192
countertypes **89**
cultural codes 10
cultural homogenisation 220, **230**
Cultural Indicators Project 221–4
Curran, J. and Seaton, J. **60**,
  196, 225, **260, 274**; and the
  BBC 171–5; diverse ownership
  patterns 173–4; and the internet
  168–70; media ownership
  and creativity effects 156–8;
  proprietor ownership effects
  164; television formats 170–1

Daily Mail 94, **167–8**, 240, **241**
Daily Mirror 1–3, **80–1, 159,
  203–4**
Daily Telegraph 55, **58**, 161
Deutschland 83 23, **71–2, 151**
Disney 160–3, 195, 197, 202
Disney+ 38, 136, 162, 188,
  197, 202

editorial codes of conduct 183
encoding 212, 234–6, 237, 240,
  242–3
enculturation effects 220, 226,
  229–30

Facebook **148**, 192, 227, 272
fandoms 245–7, 249, **253–4**,
  258, 271
fanfiction 246–8, **254**, 256
fan labour 251, **252**
fan power **269**, 251, **253**, 256
feminism 51, **52**, 112–13, **118**,
  121, 124–5
Fender, S. 89
Fisher, M. 227–8
Fleabag 56
free market government policy
  168, 170
free radical press 156–7

Freud, S. 130–2, **133,** 207
Fuchs, C. **259–60**

Games Rating Authority 181, **185,
  187,** 214
Gauntlett, D. **105, 118, 142,
  192, 244;** and advertising
  147; comparison to Butler, J.
  and Zoonen, L. van 152–4;
  and DIY media 148; and
  self-help books 145–6; and
  transformational narratives 146
gender: hierarchies of 134; as
  performance 130–1; and
  subversion of 135–6, **137, 145**
genre: and binary oppositions
  19, **20**, 25, **27–8**; formatting
  strategies of **199**; hybridisation
  of 52–3; marketing function
  of 56–7; and narrative 35;
  repetition and difference in
  46–50; subversion of 50–1; and
  verisimilitude 47
Gerbner, G. **218**; and the Cultural
  Indicators Project 221–3;
  and fear cultivation 219–20;
  mainstreaming and resonance
  effects on audiences 223–4;
  middle-of-the-road reportage
  225–6
Giddens, A. 143–4, **145**
Gilroy, P. **30, 92, 129, 155**;
  civilisationism and 94;
  postcolonial melancholia 100–1
globalisation 144, **154**, 157, **167**;
  impact on regulation of **192**
The Guardian 55, 183, **184**,
  240, **268**

Hall, S. **30, 60, 218, 230**;
  audience misreadings 236–7;
  compared to Gerbner, G.
  230; cultural hegemonies and
  238–40; encoding/decoding
  233–6; otherness 83, **87**;
  representation, theories of 76;
  stereotypes 82–7; transcoding
  effects 88
Harry Potter Alliance 256

Have You Heard George's Podcast?
174–5, 177
Hesmondhalgh, D.: artificial
scarcity 197; expansion strategies
used by the media 195–7;
independent labelling 198;
internet effects on the media
industry 200–2; managing media
risk 193; product formatting as
risk reduction 197–8
heteronormativity 134–6, **140**,
141–2, **153**, 247
Homeland **49**, 53, 171
hooks, bell **69**; absent
representations 121–2; Black
female stereotypes 120, 122;
and intersectionality 124–6; the
legacy of slavery 119–20; and
white feminism 121
horizontal integration 160–1,
163–4, **175**, 195
hyperreal inertia 66, **67**, **68–9**
hysterical news values 165–6,
167, **175**

incest taboos 24, 130
The Independent 183
Independent Press Standards
Organisation (IPSO) 182–3,
184, **190**
internationalisation **196**, **204**
internet: commercialisation of 201,
259–60; and cultivation theory
226–7; cyber dystopian readings
of 201, **257**, **274**; cyber
utopianism and 255–6, **257**;
DIY culture and **148**, 256–7;
effects on audience 261–4,
270–1; and fandoms 249–51;
gatekeeping and 265; impact
of 168–70, 200–1, 202, **205**;
regulation of **184–5**, 188–9
intersectionality 124–6, **127–8**
intertextuality 10, 53, **65–6**
intertextual relay 57, **58**, **59**

James Bond 24, **56**, **114**, **238**, 251
Jenkins, H. **74**, **105**, **129**, 177,
192, 201, **206**, **218**, **232**,

245–60; audience-producer
convergence 248–51; and fan
fiction 246–8; and participatory
culture 254–6; and textual
poaching **248**, 249, 251; and
video games 212, 216

Katz, E. 230–1
Keen, A. 259
The Killing **113**, 171
Killing Eve **22**, **43–4**, **56**, 113,
114, **139**, **253**
Kristeva, J. 136, **136–7**

Lacan, J. 130, 131, 132, **133**
Levi-Strauss, C. **16**, **45**, 130;
binary oppositions as ideology
24–5; function of binary
oppositions 21; types of
oppositions in the media 18–19
Livingstone, S. and Lunt, P.:
citizen and consumer-based
regulation 179–80; and
globalisation 188–9
long tail distribution 205

mainstreaming effect 223–4,
226–7, **228**, **229–30**, **244**
male gaze 107–8, **109**, 113, 116,
117, **142**
Marxism 165–6
mass amateurisation 263–4, 266,
267, **268**, 273
mean world syndrome 224–5,
228, **229**, 230
meaning implosion 66, **67**, **73**
media: expansion strategies
of 160–3; gatekeeping of
188, **259**, 265–6, **273**;
objectification in 107–8,
112, **114**, 115–16, **117–18**,
123, **153**; pluralism 166,
176; proliferation of 66, 143,
145, **154**, 171; selection
processes in 76, **77–8**, **78–80**;
violence 209, 210–11,
213–16, 219, 221–4
message reduction 13, **14**, **15**
moral panics 216

Mulvey, L. 106
myths: binary oppositions in 17–18; social function of 12–13, 24

narrative: ideological effects of 12–13, 41–2; non-traditional forms of 36–9; oppositions in 19; and the three act structure 32–6; transformative effects in **42–3**
narrative image 57, **59**
naturalisation 12, **14, 90**
Neale, S. **45, 177**; audience pleasures and genre 50; auteur effects 54; and genre conventions 46–8; and genre hybridity 52–3; genre subversion 50–1, **51–2**; marketing function of genre 56–7
Negroponte, N. 254–5
Netflix 38, **58**, 136, **137, 159**, 171, **173**, 197, **213**; mainstreaming effects in **227**; regulation of **184**, 188
News Corporation **159–60**, 160–1, 165
newspapers: binary oppositions in 25; commercial effects on 157–8, 165, 166, **166–7**; cultivation theory and **226–7**; and cultural capital 232; and cultural hegemonies 238; impact of digital revolution on 202, 267, **268**; institutional mediation and 55; production process effects 234–5; proprietor control of 164–5; regulation of 178, 182–3, **184, 190**; representation effects of **78–80**, 82, 94, 101–2
No Offense **40–1**, 146

Oedipus Complex 24, **132**
OFCOM 181–2, **184**, 188, 189, **190, 192**
online influencers 189, **191, 259**, **267, 274**

otherness 83, **87**, 93, **96, 104**, 123, 126, **128**

participatory culture **74, 105, 129, 177**, 201, **203, 205**, 245–54, 255–6, **257, 259–60**
Peaky Blinders **20**, 69, **87, 248**, 288
power circularity **87, 90**
pre-filtering 265
proairetic codes 8, **10, 15**
Propp, V.: character archetypes 31–2, **29**; narrative structure 33
public service broadcasting 55, **56**, 170, 171–2, 174–5, **176, 186, 190**, 193

quest hero 31, **33**

Radio 4 **174**
realism 64, 70, **149**, 220
reception theory **16, 92, 230**, 233–40
regulation *see* Livingstone, S. and Lunt, P.
representation: absent representations 121–2, 123, 125, **129**, 135, **137, 138, 141**; ethnicity and race **30**, 83, **85, 129, 149, 151**, 153, **248**; and exclusion 83, **87, 90**, 132; femininity **14, 40, 52, 56, 89**, 106–8, **109, 113**, 119–22, **123, 127–8, 238**; sexuality **30, 118**, 135–6, **138**
representational modelling effects **217**
resonance effect 223–4, **229–30**
The Returned 40–1, 146
River Island's 'Labels are for Clothes' campaign 7
role models **149–50**, 208–9, **210, 217**

scheduling 54, **56, 159**, 174, **213**
self-regulation 183, **190, 191**
semantic codes 8, 10

serialisation 198, **199**, **205**
Shirky, C. **177**, 201, **206**; the bargain 271; broadcast and personal media differences 261–2; communities of practice 270; digital media advantages 265–6; effects of the digital revolution **268–9**; mass amatuerisation effects 263–4; publish first/filter later 264–5
social media 52, 64, 73, **91**, 161, 169, 204, **253**, **257**, 267, **269**; convergence effects and 250–1, **251–2**, 262–3; cultivation theory and 227–8; digital labour and 250, **274**; and fourth wave feminism 112–13; Gauntlett commentary on 148; and political activism 126, 129, 249, 256, **259**, 270; regulation of **184**, 188–9, **190–1**
star power 55, **57**, 198, **199**, 202, **205**, **212**
stereotypes 63–9, 95–6, **101**; and power 63–4; transcoding of 68–9
Stranger Things 53
stylistic oppositions 19, **22**, **25**, **27**, **29–30**
symbolic codes 10
symbolic violence 83, **90**

Tehran **49–50**, **98–9**, 171
television: and advertising 121, 157, 225; Black female representation in 121–2; and cultivation theory 219–20, 223; and fan fiction 245–7; and heteronormativity 135–6; homogenising effects of 220, **230**; impact of digital revolution on 202, **268**; male dominance of 111; modelling effects of 220, 224–5; and multi-protagonist formats 146; narrative structure of 19, 34, **35**, 36–9; one-to-many effects

of 261; proliferation of 170–1; public service broadcasting and 171–2; as realised fiction 69–70, **71**; regulation of 181–2, **184**, **190**; representations of Englishness in 100–1; textual poaching **248**
Tide advert 8–10
The Times 55, **102**, 103, **159**, 161, 202, 268
Todorov, T. **16**; and ideological effects of narrative 41–2; Propp's influence on 31–4, 36; subversion of the three-act formula 37–9; the three-act narrative ideal 34–6
transcoding 88
Trump, D. 192, 227
Twentieth Century Fox Film and Television 162
Twitter (now known as 'X') 177, 251–2

uses and gratifications theory 230–1

Vance Joy, *Riptide* **238**
verisimilitude 47, **48**, **71**
vertical integration 160, 161–3, **176**, 195
video games 187, 216, 267; regulation of 214; and violence 210–11, 214, **214–15**

web 2.0 **177**, 255–6, **257**
white feminism 121

Zoonen, L. van 106–18, **142**; comparisons with the theoretical ideas of Gauntlett, D. and Butler, J. 152–3; effects of male domination of the media 111; female objectification by the media 106–7; female spectatorship 107–8; representations of masculinity 115–16

Printed in the United States
by Baker & Taylor Publisher Services